D0214509

MANAGING DISCIPLINE IN SCHOOLS

The management of discipline is an essential element in educational practice, and at a time when teachers and managers are anxious about reported increases in violence and other forms of anti-social behaviour there's a need for practical guidance and a review of current thinking.

Based on the author's experience and research in a range of primary and secondary schools, this book presents accessible summaries of relevant legislation and guides the reader through management theories towards improved practice. The book features case-studies and refers to the most recent research and legislation.

The author places the teacher at the centre of the management of discipline in schools, and by focusing on teacher and pupil esteem, the classroom and the whole-school context, the author demonstrates that a disciplined environment is not only essential but achievable.

The author describes the support networks within education as well as providing a multi-agency approach. Written in an accessible style, the book highlights the real problems that teachers in all schools can encounter and offers real solutions.

Sonia Blandford has taught in both primary and secondary schools and has held a variety of middle-management posts. She is currently a senior lecturer in education at the Oxford Centre for Education and Management Services.

EDUCATIONAL MANAGEMENT SERIES

Series editor: Cyril Poster

Recent titles in this series include:

CONTINUING PROFESSIONAL DEVELOPMENT
Anna Craft

SUCCESS AGAINST THE ODDS
The National Commission on Education

MANAGING SPECIAL NEEDS IN THE PRIMARY SCHOOL
Joan Dean

MANAGING THE PRIMARY SCHOOL (2ND EDN)
Joan Dean

THE SKILLS OF PRIMARY SCHOOL MANAGEMENT
Les Bell and Chris Rhodes

LIBERATING THE LEARNER
Edited by Guy Claxton, Terry Atkinson, Marilyn Osborn and Mike Wallace

MANAGING PARTNERSHIP IN TEACHER TRAINING AND DEVELOPMENT
Edited by Hazel Bines and John M. Welton

CREATING AN EXCELLENT SCHOOL: SOME NEW MANAGEMENT TECHNIQUES
Hedley Beare, Brian Caldwell and Ross Millikan

TEACHER APPRAISAL
Cyril and Doreen Poster

MANAGING TEAMS IN SECONDARY SCHOOLS
Les Bell

EDUCATION FOR THE TWENTY-FIRST CENTURY
Hedley Beare and Richard Slaughter

PARENTS AND SCHOOLS: CUSTOMERS, MANAGERS OR PARTNERS?
Edited by Pamela Munn

SCHOOL-BASED MANAGEMENT AND SCHOOL EFFECTIVENESS
Edited by Clive Dimmock

EFFECTIVE SCHOOLING FOR THE COMMUNITY
Tony Townsend

MAKING GOOD SCHOOLS: LINKING SCHOOL EFFECTIVENESS AND SCHOOL IMPROVEMENT
Edited by Robert Bollen, Bert Creemers, David Hopkins, Louise Stoll and Nijs Lagerweij

INNOVATIVE SCHOOL PRINCIPLES AND RESTRUCTURING
Clive Dimmock and Tom O'Donoghue

THE SELF MONITORING PRIMARY SCHOOL
Edited by Pearl White and Cyril Poster

MANAGING RESOURCES FOR SCHOOL IMPROVEMENT: CREATING A COST EFFECTIVE SCHOOL
Hywel Thomas and Jane Martin

SCHOOLS AT THE CENTRE: A STUDY OF DECENTRALISATION
Alison Bullock and Hywel Thomas

DEVELOPING EFFECTIVE SCHOOL MANAGEMENT
Jack Dunham

MEETING THE CHALLENGES OF PRIMARY SCHOOLING
Edited by Lloyd Logan and Judyth Sachs

RESTRUCTURING AND QUALITY IN TOMORROW'S SCHOOLS
Edited by Tony Townsend

THE ETHICAL SCHOOL
Felicity Haynes

MANAGING DISCIPLINE IN SCHOOLS

Sonia Blandford

London and New York

First published 1998
by Routledge
11 New Fetter Lane, London EC4P 4EE

Simultaneously published in the USA and Canada
by Routledge
29 West 35th Street, New York, NY 10001

Typeset in Baskerville by Routledge
Printed and bound in Great Britain by Page Brothers (Norwich) Ltd

British Library Cataloguing in Publication Data
A catalogue record for this book is available from the British Library

Library of Congress Cataloguing in Publication Data
Blandford, Sonia.
Managing discipline in schools/Sonia Blandford.
p. cm.
Includes bibliographical references.
ISBN 0-415-17491-0
1. School discipline – Great Britain.
2. Classroom management – Great Britain. I. Title.
LB3012.4.G7B63 1998
371.3'0941–dc21 97-43206
CIP

ISBN 0–415–17491–0

TO CHARLIE

CONTENTS

List of illustrations viii
Foreword ix
Preface x
Acknowledgements xii
A note on the text xiii

1 Discipline: principles and practice 1

2 Government policy and legislation 9

3 Community 24

4 Management 37

5 Senior and middle managers 50

6 Classroom management 60

7 Support agencies 78

8 Alternative models 93

9 Good practice 105

10 Policy 125

11 Professional development 144

12 Self-evaluation 157

Appendices 167
Bibliography 177
Index 183

ILLUSTRATIONS

FIGURES

3.1	Think Community plan	35
4.1	School management – external agencies	41
4.2	School management structure – large primary or secondary school	42
4.3	The planning process	46
5.1	Disruptive pupil – sequence of events	59
6.1	Stress levels	63
6.2	A model of stress levels	64
6.3	Classroom seating plan	75
7.1	Mission statement	81
9.1	The learning community – behaviour management	107
9.2	Behaviour management plan	109
9.3	Student council structure	120
11.1	Staff development model	147
11.2	A model of mentoring	151

TABLES

5.1	The effects of the Education Reform Act (ERA) on school management	51
6.1	Classroom disruption	62

FOREWORD

There has long been a need in the Routledge education management series for a book on the management of discipline. The general public believes, often reacting to incidents that make the headlines in the tabloid press, that there is a widespread breakdown in school discipline. Teachers respond by blaming the decline in family and societal values that makes their task in schools difficult, sometimes impossible.

This book, written by a highly experienced teacher, now a valued member of a university School of Education, has as a basic tenet that it is counterproductive to spend time assigning blame. Schools need to devise strategies for the improvement of discipline and, essentially, involve all staff, governors, parents and the community in their implementation.

The book has four outstanding merits. First, it 'sees things as they are', concerning itself with the issues faced by teachers and managers in schools and how they can be addressed. This does not mean that the author has ignored relevant research findings; indeed, their inclusion is a significant merit of the book, but not its central purpose.

Second, the book abounds in tried and tested case studies and in details of a wide range of national and local schemes that promote practical responses to indiscipline in schools.

Third, it covers complex matters, such as the procedures for statementing special educational needs or for the exclusion of pupils who can no longer be contained within the school, with precision, but also with concern for the pupil and the family as well as the teachers in the school.

Fourth, the reader, whether primary or secondary, newly qualified or long experienced, will find a great deal of practical help, skilfully and clearly presented. Indeed, the readership should extend well beyond the practising teacher. Governors, LEA officers, student teachers and their university and college staff will be among the many who will benefit from the book.

Cyril Poster
Series editor

PREFACE

At a time when teachers and other professionals are increasingly worried about reported increases in violence in schools and other forms of anti-social behaviour there is a need to publish a book that addresses real needs and provides real solutions. The purpose of this book is, therefore, to provide a framework for the management of discipline in schools.

Teaching and learning are challenges which should be rewarded. By focusing on pupil and teacher needs, and the development of self-esteem the emphasis is on support and collegiality in schools. Teachers 'need to know' if they are to meet the demands of their pupils.

Chapter 1 defines discipline within the context of theory and practice. The chapter encompasses established literature enabling the reader to develop an understanding of the key issues. The chapter also engages in a discussion of key issues in this field – in particular school/community factors emanating from field research.

Chapter 2 introduces the reader to central government recommendations and statutory regulations for the management of discipline in schools. It details the findings and recommendations of the Elton Committee Report *Discipline in Schools* (DES 1989). The statutory requirements for pupils with special educational needs are also presented. These provide the reader with an insight into the provision for pupils who are identified as having emotional and behavioural needs. The Code of Practice (DfE 1994a) is also a source of guidance for teachers on how to manage pupils who are disruptive in their classrooms. This multi-agency approach is advocated in the 1997 White Paper *Excellence in Schools* (DfEE 1997a), details of which conclude the chapter.

Chapter 3 defines the school as a community. There is a critical discussion on school ethos and suggestions to managers on how to relate a school vision to practice. The reader is also advised on how to create and maintain teams within the school community and how the school can enhance its standing in the local community.

Chapter 4 focuses on the key principles of education management that relate to the management of discipline in schools. Planning and communication strategies are provided following a discussion on the function of management in schools.

Chapter 5 defines the roles and responsibilities of middle and senior managers in relation to the management of discipline in schools. The structures and mechanisms of effective school management are described, as are strategies for meeting pupil, parent and teacher needs.

Chapter 6 concentrates on the needs and responsibilities of class teachers. The issues of stress, behaviour management, communication and support are addressed.

Chapter 7 places local education authority agencies in the context of mainstream schools. Comprehensive information on the support and guidance that is available from experts within the education service is presented for managers and teachers to consider in relation to their own practice.

Chapter 8 introduces the reader to alternative models for the management of discipline that are currently practised in schools in England and Wales. Assertive discipline, Schools Outreach, Family Support Centres, Primary Exclusion Project, peer mediation and the 'no-blame' approach are described and evaluated.

Chapter 9 examines good practice in schools. The emphasis is on success and solutions, and includes peer counselling, home-school contracts and partnerships with education welfare officers. This provides the reader with positive strategies in the management of discipline in schools.

Chapter 10 describes policy, procedures and practices as contained in a school discipline policy. Examples of good practice are used to illustrate how to create a policy that encompasses aims, rules, rewards and sanctions, and how to monitor and evaluate its effectiveness.

Chapter 11 discusses teacher training, induction and continuing professional development. The status of in-service programmes is evaluated and guidance is given on how schools can adopt a multi-agency approach to training and professional development.

Chapter 12 focuses on self-evaluation, the process by which schools and teachers can reflect on their practice. Theoretical principles are examined in relation to practice. The key elements of effective discipline in schools – shared beliefs and values and self-esteem – are discussed as a conclusion to the chapter and book.

The behaviour of pupils in schools is influenced by its management, its relationship with support agencies and the community. Teachers need to know that they are not alone in the classroom and that there is a network of support that exists to guide practitioners in the management of discipline. As recognised by the government, an effective multi-agency approach to support good discipline and behaviour at a local level is vital.

This book is based on my own experience in a range of schools and interviews with leading professionals. Each chapter addresses a fundamental element of teaching practice that encompasses all levels of the profession. Much of the research focused on an existing network in the Unitary Authority of Bristol where good practice is evident. Research found that professionals, from a range of services, work together to meet the needs of pupils and teachers in what is recognised as a demographically diverse area.

ACKNOWLEDGEMENTS

The approach to the writing of this book was to gather a team of interested and valued practitioners; it would not have been written without their expertise, encouragement and time. I acknowledge the use of material from and wish to express my thanks to Anne Gurner, Bristol South Special Educational Needs Support Team; Sue Jackson, Bristol North Special Educational Needs Support Team; Tonia Robinson, Bristol City Educational Psychology Service; Ray Priest, Headteacher, St George's Community School, Bristol; Gordon Bailey, Schools Outreach; Christine Stockwell, Bristol Mediation; Christopher Wardle, Behaviour Coordinator and Tina Moon, Deputy Headteacher, Pen Park School, Bristol; Louise Smith, Bristol City Special Educational Needs Support Team; Kate Schnelling, Family Services, Education Department, Oxfordshire County Council; Marian Shaw, Oxford Centre for Education Management and Services; Denise Dew-Hughes and Hakan Sari, Doctor of Education students, Oxford Brookes University; and Cyril Poster, Series Editor.

Special thanks go to Jaqui Price, Education Welfare Officer, Bristol City Education Department and Gill Tippet, Children's Officer, Bristol City Education Department. I would also like to thank Jean McPhee, Gill Fox, John Wood, Paul Trembling and Linet Arthur for their contributions to the production of this book.

Finally, I would like to pay tribute to the patience and support of my husband, Charlie Eldridge.

A NOTE ON THE TEXT

The material in Appendix D may be reproduced free of charge for use in your school.

1

DISCIPLINE: PRINCIPLES AND PRACTICE

Discipline and management are central to effective schools. All teachers are responsible, as professionals, for managing discipline in schools. Self-esteem and self-confidence are central to the management of discipline. Teachers need to have a sense of self-worth in order to recognise and meet pupil needs. Critical to practice is the relationship between teachers, pupils, parents (and families), senior management, governors, local education authority support agencies, educationalists and central government. The purpose of this book is to provide a framework for the management of discipline in schools that recognises both pupils' and teachers' needs.

As this book addresses a fundamental element of educational practice its intended readership encompasses all levels of the profession. At a time when teachers and other professionals are increasingly worried about reported increases in violence and other forms of anti-social behaviour in schools, there is a need to identify pupil and practitioner needs and relate these to management. Essentially, this book provides practical support for teachers, managers and other professionals involved in the management of discipline in schools. This chapter defines discipline in the context of educational theory and practice.

DEFINITION

Defining discipline sounds easy. It is a term frequently used by practitioners, members of the school community and society in general. Whether there is a shared meaning is doubtful, as the range of behaviours and attitudes regarded as disruptive and requiring discipline is vast. In practice, any definition, and subsequent interpretation of discipline, will reflect the beliefs and values of all members of the school community. Where there is no shared understanding, tensions will exist and possibly crises will occur. There is a need for all members of the school community to identify pupil needs and have a shared understanding of discipline policy, procedures and practices.

Consistency is a fundamental problem in educational practice, as there are so many variables that influence teaching and learning. The wholly incorrect assumption that discipline implies 'doing something to someone' reflects the needs of those who like to control members of the school community. Effective, and lasting, discipline focuses on the ability of individuals to control themselves – self-discipline. If all members of the school community were self-disciplined individuals there would be very few, if any, problems.

So, if it is accepted that discipline is concerned with the development of internal mechanisms that enable individuals to control themselves, there will need to be agreed boundaries for attitudes and behaviour. The management of discipline in schools is the responsibility of all members of the school community. Individuals will therefore need to know and understand what is acceptable to other members of the school community. A discipline policy that clearly states the needs and expectations of pupils and teachers will provide the necessary framework for procedures and practices. As Chapter 10 explains, in order for there to be a shared understanding, all members of the school community need to participate in the decision-making process leading to the publication of a discipline policy.

The outward manifestation of the ability of individuals to either discipline themselves (self-control) or have discipline thrust upon them (control) is displayed in their attitude and behaviour towards others and their environment. The boundaries of acceptable behaviour should allow schools to function as harmonious and humane communities in order to create an environment conducive to serious learning (Docking 1980: 12). Where boundaries are accepted pupils will have the self-control to manage their behaviour and attitudes without authority figures.

PUPILS

Central to the management of discipline in schools is the ability of educational practitioners to identify pupil needs. The aim of schooling is to develop autonomous human beings who can fulfil their potential in the culture and society in which they live. Teachers therefore need to recognise individual strengths and weaknesses of their pupils. If pupils have low self-esteem this will impact on their ability to relate to members of the school community in a confident manner. Self-esteem and self-confidence engender respect. If pupils can respect themselves, they can respect others and their environment. The development of self-esteem in pupils will reflect their relationship with their peers, parents, family, teachers and other members of the school community. Teachers with low self-esteem will have difficulties developing the self-esteem of their pupils.

Pupils with low self-esteem may behave in an uncooperative manner. Their frustration and anger will cause them to behave irrationally, disrupting those around them. A wide range of behaviour may be considered to be disruptive. In practice, it will be problematic, inappropriate and disturbing to pupils, parents, teachers and other members of the school community. While it is the minority of pupils whose behaviour leads to exclusion (temporary or permanent) these children represent the tip of the iceberg. Pupils' behaviour does not fall into precise categories of 'normal' and 'disruptive'; it is on a continuum from cooperative to totally unacceptable. Very few pupils consistently occupy the same point on the continuum.

Inevitably, any definition of discipline is context-based, relating directly to each educational practitioner's perception of pupil behaviour (Watkins and Wagner 1987). Pupils' behaviour and practitioner expectations will vary depending on:

- time, according to the day of the week, subject, teacher and other pressures
- place, in the classroom, corridor, outside of the school gates, or at home
- audience, depending on informal and formal settings, for example, assembly or meal-times
- individual characteristics and labelling, pupils with reputations for disrupting lessons may be treated differently from their peers or an Afro-Caribbean pupil compared with a white middle-class pupil.

Whether a pupil's action is perceived as disruptive will depend on who does it, where, when, why, to whom, in front of whom, and so on. The labelling of pupils whose behaviour is disruptive is wholly inappropriate and will damage their self-esteem. The ascribing of a label can be the cause of disruptive behaviour as the pupil attempts to maintain his/her status or title. A loud pupil will know how to behave in order to be recognised. Negative labelling will have negative results.

Pupils should be encouraged to take responsibility for their behaviour. Ultimately, pupils must learn to control themselves so that they can behave and work quietly even when a teacher is not watching them, this is what they must be able to do as autonomous adults. Teachers must provide opportunities for pupils to take responsibility for themselves and others through classroom and extra-curricular activities.

TEACHERS

Teachers are often criticised for their inability to teach. Maintaining a pattern of behaviour that enables all pupils to learn and all teachers to teach will be defined, in practice, by a teacher's ability to prevent disruptive behaviour in their classrooms. The majority of teachers have a fairly well-defined idea of the boundaries between acceptable and unacceptable behaviour as agreed in their school's discipline policy. However, there are a minority of teachers who are unable to either define or maintain these boundaries. The management of discipline in schools should not, as Walker (1989: 174) describes, be a matter of 'survival, the stuff of nightmares'. Teachers need the mechanisms and tools to manage discipline and, critically, they need support.

Management of discipline is central to effective teaching and should be central to teacher training. A teacher's inability to control a pupil or class prevents the process of education and learning from happening. While higher education institutions have addressed the issue of classroom management in schools, there is still much to be done in defining the support systems that are available to practitioners, students and teachers.

Teachers should not feel isolated, and further training beyond qualification is required to provide the support necessary for teachers to be effective in the classroom. A teacher should be able to teach. While discipline is an integral element in teaching it should not dominate classroom practice. When teachers are unable to maintain discipline they should feel confident that support is available and will be provided. In-service training (INSET) that enables teachers to develop their knowledge and understanding of the nature of discipline and the management systems/support agencies available is critical to good practice in schools.

Teachers need to feel confident in their role as educators and be able to access and utilise the many agencies that exist to provide them with support. In the minority of schools, teachers are reluctant to admit that an individual or class is creating a problem that prevents them from teaching. In doing so the teacher is not meeting their own needs and, more critically, the needs of their pupils. Any admission should not be perceived as a confession of weakness; in practice, the identification of such problems reflects personal strength. The management of discipline in schools requires teachers to have knowledge and understanding of local education authority (LEA) support agencies and management teams whose job it is to deal with difficulties that arise. Practitioners need to have a shared understanding of their roles and responsibilities according to the school discipline policy, procedures and practices.

Teachers should be assured that support will be given if they are unable to deal with disruptive behaviour, for example:

- resistance to teacher direction
- argumentativeness or procrastination
- defiance, insolence and disregard for the teacher's role
- frequent 'low-level' behaviours such as calling out, not listening to instructions or just talking.

Teachers who are successful at keeping order in their classrooms and meeting pupils' needs are those who are skilled in preventing disruptive behaviour. This will be dependent on a number of factors, including:

- personality
- appearance
- communication skills
- teaching skills
- curriculum knowledge.

Inevitably, teachers will need support from others; they cannot be expected to work in isolation. Practitioners are mutually dependent on each other. Managing discipline in schools is a shared responsibility for which teachers need to develop a shared understanding.

Managing discipline in schools is critical to reducing teacher stress (Rogers 1996). Disruptive behaviour, poor working conditions, time pressures, poor school ethos, health and emotional problems all contribute to a teacher's diminishing self-esteem, lack of confidence, and will impact on their ability to teach. Teachers and managers should aim to reduce stress levels wherever possible by creating a supportive and caring environment.

MANAGEMENT

School managers should aim to create an atmosphere whereby teachers are able to run organised and effective classrooms in which the abilities of individual pupils are given due opportunity for development, in which teachers can fulfil their proper functions as facilitators of learning, and in which children can acquire the techniques for monitoring and guiding their own behaviour (Docking 1980).

The general atmosphere and practices of schools can, and do, make a substantial difference to pupil behaviour and attitudes. Research (Rutter *et al.* 1979; Mortimore *et al.* 1988) has shown that a range of factors influence pupil behaviour:

- academic balance, appropriateness of the curriculum
- reward and punishment systems
- environment
- pupil responsibilities
- teacher modelling
- classroom management
- whole-school management
- support systems
- communication systems
- home-school relationship.

School managers will need to consider each of the above in relation to their own school. Good leadership and effective management are fundamental to effective schools. The need to provide a structure as a point of reference for both pupils and teachers is recognised by practitioners and researchers (Jones 1989). 'Knowing that they are there' enables teachers to concentrate on teaching and learning rather than discipline. Headteachers who know their staff and pupils are essential in the management of discipline in schools. However, the headteacher should not be seen as the 'panacea for all ills'. A headteacher leads a senior management team, which, in turn, is responsible for middle managers and teachers.

In practice, effective headteachers are democratic, sharing in the decision-making of developing and implementing discipline policy, procedures and practices. They support, assist and coordinate the work of teachers, parents and education professionals to discover and meet pupils' needs. Headteachers know that a great deal could go on in their school of which they would never be aware unless teachers and pupils felt confident to call on them to address problems and to make suggestions for changes.

Ultimately, headteachers are responsible for ensuring that all members of the community establish appropriate standards of behaviour in the school to which they belong. Managing discipline is at the root of managing the school as a community. Appropriate policies and structures need to be in place to facilitate this process.

LEA SUPPORT

The role of LEA support staff in relation to schools changed significantly with the 1988 Education Reform Act (ERA). Practice within LEAs is varied and experience has shown that several have complex support structures that remain unknown to practitioners in schools. Central to the effectiveness of LEA support teams is their ability to communicate their role to classroom teachers.

Often the point of contact in schools is the special educational needs coordinator (SENCO). SENCOs are expected to identify and manage a variety of special educational needs. Special educational needs are defined by the 1993 Education Act as significant learning difficulties or impediments that prevent a pupil from accessing the same educational facilities and opportunities as others. A procedure is to be followed (see Chapter 2) if teachers are to receive support from other agents in the education of these children. Severe emotional and behavioural difficulties (EBD) are identified in the Code of Practice for special educational needs (DfE 1994a).

In practice, all teachers should have knowledge and understanding of the Code of Practice as this provides a framework for recognising and managing pupils with behavioural problems. Rather than leaving the SENCO to deal with all pupils with behavioural and learning difficulties, teachers should consider their responsibilities to pupils in their classrooms. The Code of Practice also provides a framework for managing pupil behaviour prior to the pupil reaching special needs status. If teachers are to prevent pupils from being excluded they should work with support agencies in the management of discipline in their schools.

Headteachers and LEA agencies consider why, when the services of education welfare officers and educational psychologists exist, the number of children identified as being disruptive has increased? A key factor is that there are teachers who are unaware of the availability of such services until such time as their pupils' behaviour is beyond their control. A greater understanding of the good practice that exists is required by both teachers and LEA support agencies. Knowledge of support agencies' roles and responsibilities is needed if teachers are to develop the skills needed to manage discipline in schools. Prevention is better than cure.

THE SCHOOL COMMUNITY

> The behaviour of pupils in a school is influenced by almost every aspect of the way in which it is run and how it relates to the community it serves. It is the combination of all these factors which give a school its character and identity. Together they can produce an orderly and successful school.
> (DES 1989: 8)

A school should be central to its local community. In order to be so, schools have to become a community within a community. A school needs to develop an identity, one that reflects the values and beliefs of its members. The school environment is critical to the management of discipline. Schools need organisational structures, rules and aims if they are to be effective. All members of the school, as a community, should have shared participation in the creation of the ethos of the school. As active players in the daily life of the school, pupils, teachers, parents and support agencies need to relate to each other.

The more isolated teachers feel within their community the more difficult the management of discipline becomes. The organisational structure of the school should reflect the psychological and sociological make-up of its community. All schools are different. All pupils have different emotional, behavioural, social and educational needs.

A comprehensive plan may not provide a cure-all for discipline problems that happen in the classroom, corridor, playground or beyond the school gates; but in the process of identifying the needs of the school as a community, teachers, support agencies and managers can develop an approach to the management of discipline appropriate to their school. All members of the school community should take responsibility for their environment and others within the community.

SOCIETY

Since Callaghan, in his Ruskin College speech (1976), commented on the developing climate of scepticism about the aims and achievements of schools, there has been belief by the majority of politicians that educational practice needs to change in some way. This has left teachers feeling demoralised and deprofessionalised. The prevailing view appears to be that teachers are expected to keep order in the classroom, to the extent that a teacher's personal integrity depends on success in keeping order.

Many explanations of undisciplined behaviour in schools suggest that the cause lives within the pupil, or their family and background. Schools have to cope with the consequences of social dysfunction and with peer group attitudes to anti-social behaviour. More specifically, teachers may be on the receiving end of incidents of violence and anti-social behaviour that exist in certain elements of society. In essence, teachers are considered, by some, to be responsible for society's ills.

The proliferation of labels for dysfunctional families and the effects on children distort the reality experienced by children in schools. Schools do make a difference, although it is unclear how the differences and the nature of the influence are generated. As an example, the urban crisis and associated disruptive behaviour have compounded the view that indiscipline in schools is responsible for urban decline. This simplistic, and wholly incorrect, assumption can only serve to isolate pupils attending inner-city schools from those who live and are educated in suburbia and the countryside. Disruptive behaviour is irrational, and can occur in any context in any school.

Casting aspersions on a pupil's adjustment or the stability of his/her family should not be an easy alternative to providing an appropriate and stimulating educational programme. Such critical incidents should not reflect on pupils. Children cannot be held responsible for the parents' actions. In cases of family difficulties, the school community and support agencies should provide support for both the pupils and their families. Teachers are responsible for the impact they have, educationally, on their pupils. Teachers need to understand the process of education in order to be able to function in an effective way. Schools should provide a stable, caring environment for all pupils, irrespective of whether they are working with the support or indifference of families. The role of school in relation to a pupil's cultural and social differences should be supportive.

2

GOVERNMENT POLICY AND LEGISLATION

The management of discipline in schools is central to effective teaching and learning. If teachers are unable to manage a class, they will be unable to teach. Central government, past and present, has recognised the need for schools to maintain a disciplined environment that is safe and secure for all pupils and teachers, yet discipline is rarely mentioned in the context of education reform. In practice, legislation has been created to deal with problem pupils (1993 Education Act), and guidance for teachers is provided in *Discipline in Schools, Report of the Committee of Enquiry* chaired by Lord Elton (DES 1989) and in Circular 8/94 (DfE 1994b).

The Elton Committee of Enquiry into discipline in schools was established by the Secretary of State for Education and Science in March 1988. The Elton Report provided guidance to senior management teams and classroom teachers through recommendations that the committee believed would secure a real improvement in all schools. The committee found that there were no simple or complete remedies as discipline is a complex issue. Critically, they recognised the importance of clearly stated boundaries of acceptable behaviour, and of teachers responding promptly and firmly to pupils who test those boundaries.

The report concluded that the central problem of disruption could be reduced by helping teachers to become effective classroom managers. The importance of initial and in-service training courses was highlighted, particularly the need for initial teacher training courses to include specific practical training related to motivating and managing pupils, and dealing with those who challenge authority. The committee suggested that in-service courses should aim to refine classroom management skills and to develop patterns of mutual support among colleagues.

Further recommendations included headteachers and senior management teams taking a lead in developing school plans for promoting good behaviour. The committee considered that the headteacher's management style was a critical factor in encouraging a sense of collective responsibility among staff and a sense of commitment to the school among pupils and their parents.

The quality of the school environment was also deemed to be important, as was the atmosphere or ethos of the school. The report suggested that the most effective schools were those with the best relationships with parents. The school's discipline policy should be communicated fully and clearly to parents. The committee also advised that parents have a responsibility to provide their children with firm guidance and positive models through their own behaviour. The importance of parent-teacher associations was highlighted as a means of creating both formal and informal channels of communication about behaviour. The report concluded that there was a need to increase parental accountability for children's behaviour. The report suggested that pupils were also to be encouraged to take more responsibility for their own and their peers' behaviour.

The committee recommended that LEAs should make provision for cost-effective support services for schools and individual pupils. It suggested that the most effective provision would be based on support teams of specialist teachers working in mainstream schools, with access to places in on-site and (as appropriate) off-site units. The committee stressed the need for rapid assessment of the special educational needs of pupils with emotional and behavioural difficulties by all LEAs.

The report indicated that attendance rates were relatively stable and that any significant differences in the rates for individual schools could not always be explained by the differences in catchment areas. The committee urged headteachers and teachers to act in order to minimise unauthorised absence and truancy.

The committee considered that relationships with local police forces should be encouraged in order to reflect the contribution that police could make to education for responsible citizenship. The committee also highlighted the importance of the school governing body in the development and monitoring of the school discipline policy and appointment of staff, especially that of the headteacher.

The report urged LEAs to develop management information systems to target consultancy and support services for schools in difficulty. The committee believed that behaviour problems were sometimes associated with the use of supply teachers and recommended that steps should be taken to minimise their use. Interestingly, the report did not identify a relationship between class size and pupils' behaviour.

The Elton Report did much to illustrate the need for clear management of discipline in schools. The fundamental flaw in the process was the status of the report and its relationship to educational reform. Although the report was commissioned by the government following the Education Reform Act (DES 1988), it was an advisory document only. LEAs, governing bodies, headteachers and teachers were at this time dealing with the introduction of Local Management of Schools (LMS) and the implementation of the national curriculum. Discipline was not integral to education reform and therefore lacked status as an issue to be addressed by schools. The many problems identified by the Elton Committee remain unresolved.

1994 DFE CIRCULARS

Having identified the need to tackle discipline in schools, the government focused on providing advice on a range of issues relating to pupil behaviour and discipline, emotional and behavioural difficulties, and the education of sick children. The six Circulars were concerned with:

- pupil behaviour and discipline (8/94)
- education of children with emotional and behavioural difficulties (9/94)*
- exclusions from school (10/94)
- the education by LEAs of children otherwise than at school (11/94)
- the education of sick children (12/94)*
- the education of children being looked after by local authorities (13/94)

(* joint with the Department of Health)

The circulars were intended to help schools maintain good behaviour and discipline based on good practice described in the Elton Report. Much of what was included in the circulars reflected the government's emphasis on school leadership and the introduction of the national curriculum. The circulars also provided invaluable guidance on the complexities of the 1993 Education Act and subsequent legislation. The following summaries are an introduction to Circulars 8/94, 9/94 and 10/94 and, as such, provide a framework for practice relating to post-ERA policy and legislation.

Pupil Behaviour and Discipline, Circular 8/94 (DfE 1994b)

The specific aims of this circular were to:

- help schools to manage pupil behaviour effectively
- encourage a whole-school approach to behaviour and discipline
- help schools to promote respect for others among young people
- promote firm action against all forms of bullying
- reduce levels of truancy from school
- reduce the poor behaviour which can lead to pupils being excluded, either temporarily or permanently.

The DfE emphasised the need for the ethos of the school to include a clear vision of the values which matter within the school and in the surrounding community. The DfE stressed the importance of a whole-school behaviour policy that reflects the role of the school in ensuring that children grow into responsible adults, thus benefiting society as a whole. Such a policy should help schools manage pupil behaviour effectively, encourage a whole-school approach to behaviour and discipline, help promote respect for others, promote firm action against bullying and reduce levels of truancy. In addition to the creation of a whole-school policy, Circular 8/94 detailed the roles and responsibilities of schools, senior managers, teachers, governors, parents and pupils in relation to the management of pupil behaviour.

The organisation of policies, the school's environment and overall ethos can all have a strong influence on pupil behaviour. The DfE recommended that school behaviour policies should set the boundaries of acceptable behaviour and that these should be known and understood by all pupils. The policy should be developed by the school community and published in the school prospectus. Essentially, the policy should encourage respect for others and self. The DfE recommended a formal dress code for pupils in order to enhance the status of the school within the community and considered the role of the headteacher to be central to the school in determining measures to:

- promote self-discipline and proper regard for authority among pupils
- encourage good behaviour and respect for others among pupils
- ensure that the standard of behaviour of pupils is acceptable
- regulate the conduct of pupils.

The DfE stated that the headteacher should consult the LEA before determining the above. Importantly, the power to exclude a pupil from the school is exercisable only by the headteacher.

The DfE considered the role of teachers to be pivotal in the management of discipline in schools. Effective teachers operate under clearly understood rules, give clear presentations, have clear work requirements of pupils, give clear instructions, handle misbehaviour quickly and calmly, ensure that work is appropriate to pupils' abilities, set clear goals, start and end lessons on time and minimise interruptions. Critically, teachers should be able to feel that their work to maintain discipline in the class takes place within the framework of the school's overall behaviour policy. Schools should provide support for teachers, and teachers should not be blamed for failures in maintaining good order.

The DfE regarded the role of the governing body to be central in influencing the ethos of the school. Governors should lead in establishing principles for the school's policy on behaviour and discipline, and should consider exclusions in the context of agreed principles. In essence, governing bodies have a general responsibility for directing the conduct of the school; headteachers must have regard to any guidance they may offer in relation to particular issues.

The impact of parental influence in shaping pupil attitudes and behaviour was highlighted in the circular. Each pupil's home life has a direct and powerful effect on the way he/she interacts with other pupils and those in authority.

The circular advised that pupils were more likely to behave and learn if they felt responsible for their learning and were capable of success. Peer group pressure is a significant factor in this aspect of behaviour management. In addition to providing a framework of roles and responsibilities in schools, Circular 8/94 also provided guidance on rewards and punishments, home-school agreements, truancy, bullying, racial and sexual harassment, and external support services.

The DfE recommended that rules of behaviour be constructed to ensure that pupils learn to expect fair and consistently applied punishments and suggested that punishments should be fair, consistent and in proportion to the offence. Essentially, pupils and parents need to be aware that bad behaviour is unacceptable and will be punished.

Parent-school partnerships offer benefits in the management of pupil behaviour. The DfE suggested that home-school agreements should offer benefits as well as sanctions. The DfE also advised that in cases where a child's behaviour at school indicated serious problems at home, schools must be alert to the need to involve social services departments. The circular also emphasised the need for schools to be seen to act firmly against bullying.

The circular stated that the prevention of truancy should be an integral part of a school's behaviour policy. Governors and teachers are responsible for maintaining and monitoring attendance. Good practice in teaching and discipline was considered synonymous with good practice in preventing truancy.

LEAs are able to provide valuable support to schools through external support services. The DfE advised that it is helpful for LEAs to inform schools on how to involve support services and on the functions they perform. The *Code of Practice on the Identification and Assessment of Children with Special Educational Needs* (DfE 1994a) details the specific legislative functions of education welfare officers and educational psychology services.

The Education of Children with Emotional and Behavioural Difficulties, Circular 9/94 (DfE 1994c)

Circular 9/94 differs from Circular 8/94 in that it focuses on a specific group of children that exists within the education system. Intended for LEAs and schools, it was framed in the context of the Code of Practice (DfE 1994a). Published jointly with the Department of Health, it provided guidance on good practice in the education of children with emotional and behavioural difficulties in mainstream schools. The circular included recording, guidance on when further specialist advice is likely to be needed and advice on provision in special schools.

In Circular 9/94 the DfE stressed the crucial nature of early and effective liaison between LEA education and social services departments over placements and funding. Circular 9/94 also covered a number of other issues, including the involvement of health services with children needing psychiatric care, the particular needs of very young children and of girls and young women, the considerations which should guide schools in exercising controls, and sanctions over children with emotional and behavioural difficulties (EBD). DfE guidance on the identification of EBD children should be known and understood by all educational practitioners.

Children with EBD are on a continuum. Their problems are clearer and greater than sporadic naughtiness or moodiness and yet not so great as to be classed as mental illness. EBD may show through withdrawn, depressive, aggressive or self-injurious tendencies. There may be one or many causes; family environments or physical or sensory impairments may be associated.

Whether the child is judged to have EBD will depend on the nature, frequency, persistence, severity, abnormality and cumulative effect of the behaviour, compared with normal expectations for a child of the age concerned. There is no absolute definition.

Dealing with children with EBD may be seen as an intractable and frustrating task for teachers. The difficulties are genuine but EBD is often engendered or worsened by the environment, including the school's or teachers' responses. Schools have a significant effect on children's behaviour, and vary widely in the extent to which they help children overcome their difficulties. There are various definitions of emotional and behavioural difficulties. It may be argued, for example, that all children have an emotional and behavioural difficulty of some kind at some point in their development, and that this is normal.

Emotional and behavioural difficulties range from social maladaptation to abnormal emotional stresses. They are persistent (though necessarily permanent) and can often contribute to learning problems. They may be multiple, and may manifest themselves in many different forms and severities.

Children with emotional and behavioural difficulties cover the range of ability found in mainstream schools, but generally respond unusually or in an extreme fashion to a variety of social, personal, emotional or physical circumstances.

Their behaviour may be evident at the personal level (for example, through low self-image, anxiety, depression or withdrawal; or through resentment, vindictiveness or defiance), at the verbal level (for example, the child may be silent or may threaten, interrupt, argue or swear a great deal), at the non-verbal level (for example through clinginess, truancy, failure to observe rules, disruptiveness, destructiveness, aggression or violence), or at the work skills level (for example through an inability or unwillingness to work without direct supervision, to concentrate, to complete tasks or to follow instructions). Many such children are unable to trust or to form relationships with peers or adults.

Children with emotional and behavioural difficulties have special educational needs. In the terms of the legislation, they have 'learning difficulties' because they are facing barriers which cause them to have significantly greater difficulty in learning than most of their peers. These impediments affect their achievement and sometimes that of others. They also cannot pay attention to what they are taught and they lack motivation.

Dealing with children with emotional and behavioural difficulties can, at worst, be seen as an intractable and frustrating task for schools. There will be genuine concerns about the management of teacher time if other pupils are also to receive their fair share of attention, about the apparent wilfulness in the behaviour of some of the children concerned and about the many other associated pressures and problems that face teachers. However, schools have responsibilities towards all their pupils; the evidence suggests that the way they work with such pupils really

does make a difference, even where the problems are created or exacerbated outside the school.

Early identification of EBD is important. Signs may emerge very early, including in nursery groups and playgroups. Effective systems of communication are needed between social services, health and education, EBD teachers, educational psychologists and experienced teachers.

The 1994 Code of Practice (as referred to in Sections 157 and 158 of the 1993 Education Act) gives practical guidance on the discharge by LEAs and all maintained schools, including self-governing schools, of their functions towards all children with special educational needs with or without statements. Although the Code is not prescriptive, LEAs and schools (and health services and social services departments, in supporting the LEA in the exercise of their functions) must all have regard of the SEN Code of Practice as follows:

Stage 1

The Code of Practice advises that during Stage 1, responsibility for the child's educational programme should remain with the class teacher or year/form tutor, supported where necessary by the special educational needs coordinator (SENCO) in the context of the school's behaviour management policy. Stage 1 essentially concerns the gathering of information and registering a child's special educational needs. Provision is defined largely in terms of increased differentiation within normal classroom work. The class or subject teachers may wish to draw on a range of strategies under the following headings:

- Observation – teachers will need to observe the child's behaviour carefully to distinguish any patterns over different times of the day or during various activities, and when the child is working with different children or adults. It will be particularly important to draw together the observations of all the staff who work with the child for the first Stage 1 review.
- Definition of priorities for action – teachers will need to build up a clear picture of the aspects of the child's behaviour which cause most concern, and this should inform provision to be made in the classroom.
- Action – in the case of disruptive behaviour, teachers will wish to give the child clear guidance on what is expected of him or her, to give focused praise and encouragement for acceptable behaviour and achievement, to consider adjustments to classroom arrangements where necessary, to organise better for success (including seating arrangements, pupil groupings and the location of equipment) and to consult the child and consider how he or she can reflect on the behaviour, developments, achievements and areas for attention. The SEN coordinator may need to advise on action if the child is showing signs of an emotional difficulty.

- Review – the information to be marshalled for the first Stage 1 review is set out in the Code of Practice. At this point teachers should report on the effectiveness of action taken.

At Stage 1, as envisaged by the Code of Practice, it is particularly important that the information marshalled by the school is examined carefully with a view to eliminating a number of possible explanations for the child's emotional behavioural difficulties (for example, any hearing or visual impairment, undetected poor health which may be causing anxiety, language delay, home or social factors or general or specific learning difficulty). Each of these would naturally require a quite different response from the school. It is important to incorporate in the school's analysis any views from the parents, and any opinions which may have already been expressed by support services or agencies.

If, at the first consideration of the child's needs and behaviour, no clear indications of the causes emerge from the information marshalled by the school, the school should consider further what it is doing to solve the child's difficulties and whether its own practices or those of the teacher concerned are in some way contributing to the difficulty.

If this is the case, the school or teacher should consider carefully whether, by adjusting their practices, they can reduce or resolve the difficulty.

Stage 2

The Code of Practice sets out the arrangements for review that are envisaged for strategies to resolve children's difficulties. If, after two review periods at Stage 1, the provision made has not resulted in the child making satisfactory progress, the class teachers and SEN coordinator may decide to move the child to Stage 2. In such cases, observation and the exploration of possible solutions then need to be progressively refined, for example:

- observation – at Stage 2 teachers may find it helpful to analyse the timing and frequency of the most difficult behaviour and to focus more precisely on one particular behaviour.
- review – the school will need to keep its approach under review in line with the factors set out in the Code of Practice.

At this stage, teachers will be seeking information from health and social services and any other agencies closely involved with the child, and will be developing an individual education plan. They may advise on the handling of any emotional disturbance or the structuring of a behaviour management programme specifically designed to reduce the incidence of undesirable actions. Approaches will need to be modified in the light of any new information from within or outside the school that has been marshalled at Stage 2. The plan should normally be implemented, at least in part, in the standard classroom setting.

Support for the child in the class may take a variety of forms, and may be offered to the teacher (indirect support) or directly to the child. In either case, the precise arrangements for in-school support should be specified in the child's plan. Indirect support may involve time from a colleague to conduct detailed observations, or specialist help in developing strategies for working with the child. The plan should include the conditions under which the child should receive help, in terms of learning activities, or the child's behaviour, or both. At any of the school-based stages of assessment and provision, the school may recognise the need to supplement its own skills and expertise with those of support agencies from outside the school (see Chapters 7, 8 and 9).

Any withdrawal from the classroom should be contemplated only for short periods of time and where this arrangement best promotes the learning of the child and that of the other children in the class. Withdrawal should be used wherever possible to help the child concentrate on his or her work, which should remain under the close direction of the class teacher. The precise conditions that apply to the child's withdrawal from the classroom should be specified in the individual education plan, and should be understood by all those who teach him or her. The conditions should include the circumstances under which the child is to be withdrawn, the purpose and duration of any period of withdrawal, the arrangements for the child's immediate supervision and the manner of the child's return to the classroom.

Stage 3

If, after up to two review periods at Stage 2, the child's progress is not satisfactory, additional expertise should be sought and the child should move to Stage 3.

The Code of Practice advises that at Stage 3 schools supplement their own skills with those of support services from outside the school. These may include teachers in a learning or behavioural support service, peripatetic teachers, the educational psychology or welfare services, occupational, speech or physio therapists or, if appropriate, child health, mental health or social services to identify the problem behaviour and to implement any strategy to solve the problem. Support services may be able to help the school reconsider the range of responses to the child's behaviour that have been attempted so far.

The specialists concerned may be able to suggest a further range of strategies and assist the school in exploring their effectiveness. The educational psychology service offers assessment and support, including advice on the range, availability and appropriateness of other support services. The educational psychology service can also refer the parents to, or consult relevant colleagues in, the mental health services.

Recording at Stages 1–3

Accurate records need to be kept throughout the school-based stages of assessment and provision. Records should be written in such a way that they can be shared with parents as necessary. As suggested in the Code of Practice, records should be begun by the child's teacher, with the guidance of the SEN coordinator as appropriate, as soon as concern is first registered (at Stage 1). Detailed accounts of the school's analysis of the child's difficulties and records of the range of strategies used by the school will be needed for a number of purposes, including the following:

- to inform the school's own work with the child. A record of strategies that have worked well or less well at one stage will inform the approaches of the school at the next
- to inform discussions with the child's parents and with the child
- to inform teachers at a new school, should the child move during the school-based stages
- to provide factually-based information to any outside service that may be approached for support at Stage 3.

This will enable the school to make the best possible use of advisory and support services and, should the efforts of the school ultimately result in insufficient progress for the child, will provide the basis for the school asking the LEA to carry out a statutory assessment. In such cases the school will need to draw upon detailed records over a period of time, in order to compile their evidence in support of such a request.

The child's school file should include details of the parents' views and their involvement, the child's views, and the involvement of health and social services and any other agencies. During Stages 1–3 the record should include accounts of observations of the child, the individual education plans at Stages 2 and 3, and summaries of decisions taken at review meetings.

At Stage 3, the SEN coordinator or head of the learning support department should ensure that the record is maintained in greater detail to demonstrate patterns and trends over time. Dated copies of reports, notes of discussions and minutes of planning meetings, case conferences of interviews with parents should be kept together on file. Any particular changes at home mentioned by the parents and likely to cause difficulties for the child should be recorded (and the parents so informed). Notes should be kept on how links with other agencies or support services (such as education welfare or educational psychology services) have been maintained, including how the advice is currently being translated into practice. The effects on the child of any organisational changes should be noted (for example, those arising from working in a smaller group, withdrawal or timetabled counselling away from the class), along with how any changes have been linked to educational progress, relationship-building or developing the child's self-esteem.

***Exclusions from School*, Circular 10/94 (DfE 1994d)**

Circular 10/94 advises that the use of exclusions as a sanction in schools should be kept to a minimum. There should be consistent practice in the use of exclusion

and, critically, prompt resolution of exclusions, so that pupils are out of school as little as possible.

The DfE advised that reasonable prior steps should include alternative sanctions, interviewing the pupil and parents, identifying special educational needs, negotiating agreements with the pupil and parent, issuing a formal warning, withdrawing from class or involving social services or the police.

Further, pupils who show signs of emotional and behavioural difficulties which are not resolved by the general arrangements embodied in the school's behaviour policy should move to the school-based stages of assessment and provision as advised in the Code of Practice (DfE 1994a) and in Circular 9/94 (DfE 1994c). The prompt recognition of children's difficulties, and the commencement where appropriate of the school-based stages, may alleviate the child's difficulties and avoid the need for a late exclusion. The DfE advised that when determining the appropriateness of exclusion as a sanction any punishment should be appropriate to the offence; each incidence of poor behaviour needs to be examined individually in the context of the established school behaviour policies with which staff, parents and pupils are familiar, and, if appropriate, in the light of the criminal law. The headteacher should, in all cases, first consider the following factors in relation to the behaviour:

- the age and state of health of the pupil
- the pupil's previous record at that school
- any particular circumstances unique to the pupil which might sensibly be taken into account in connection with the behaviour, for example, strained or traumatic domestic situations
- the extent to which parental, peer or other pressure may have contributed to the behaviour
- the degree of severity of the behaviour, the frequency of its occurrence and the likelihood of it recurring
- whether or not the behaviour impaired or will impair the normal functioning of other pupils in the school
- whether or not the behaviour occurred on school premises or when the pupil was otherwise in the charge of school staff, or when the pupil was on the way to or from school. An important consideration in cases of doubt is the extent to which behaviour away from the school had a serious impact on the life of the school
- the degree to which the behaviour was a violation of one or more rules contained in the school's policy on behaviour, and the relative importance of the rule(s)
- whether the incident was perpetrated by the pupil on his or her own, or as part of a group (using one pupil as a scapegoat should always be avoided)
- whether consideration has been given to seeking the support of other agencies, such as the education welfare service or educational psychology service.

Where a headteacher decides to exclude a child for a fixed period, the following procedures apply: the headteacher must without delay – if possible, on the day of the exclusion – inform the pupil's parent of the exclusion, the length of the exclusion and the specific reason for it. If the pupil is being looked after by a local authority in accordance with Section 22[1] of the Children Act 1989, the Local Authority should be so informed.

The formal notification, which will have to follow later if notice is first given verbally, should provide sufficient particulars to ensure that the reason for exclusion is fully understood and that all of the relevant circumstances are made known. The Secretary of State believes that notification should be in writing and in addition, if appropriate, oral notification should be given. The notification must inform parents that they have the right to make representations to the governing body and the LEA. It should also give them the names and addresses of the appropriate person to contact. Parents, or the pupils themselves if over 18, should be invited to inform the governing body and LEA in writing of their intention to make representations.

If the exclusion is for more than five days or involves the loss of opportunity to take a public examination, the headteacher must also, and at once, inform the governing body and the LEA. The governing body and the LEA must also be informed of each period of exclusion once an aggregate of more than five days has been reached in any term. The requirement to report exclusions to the governing body and LEA provides them with the opportunity to intervene if appropriate. There is of course no need to intervene if they are content with the headteacher's actions. Good practice within various LEAs ensures that all fixed term exclusions are reported by schools to the LEA and governors.

The governing body has the power to direct the headteacher to reinstate a pupil who has been excluded for a fixed period in excess of five days in the term or where the pupil may lose an opportunity to take a public examination. The LEA may also direct reinstatement, subject to the same restrictions mentioned above, but must consult the governing body first. If the governing body is convening a meeting to discuss an exclusion case, it will usually be appropriate to invite the LEA to send a representative. All parties will then have a ready opportunity to make their views clear.

The governing body will also need to decide, according to their own circumstances, how to proceed on receiving notice from the headteacher that the pupil has been excluded. If a public examination is involved, or the exclusion is for more than five days in aggregate, the decision might be endorsed or reinstatement directed by the chairperson's action (subject to the provisions of the Education (School Government) Regulations 1989 allowing the chairperson or vice-chairperson to act in cases of urgency). The governing body will in any case need to be able to act urgently either on their own account or in response to an approach from the LEA if the latter is minded to use its own power of reinstatement.

If the parents give notice to the LEA or governors that they wish to make representations, the governing body should arrange and convene a meeting to discuss

the exclusion as soon as is practicable. The meeting should be arranged at a time and place convenient for the parents, within reason. It is recognised that in the case of a short fixed period exclusion, the pupil will usually be back in school before the meeting is arranged; but the meeting may nevertheless serve the purpose of enabling the parents to be satisfied that their views have been heard and perhaps the record set straight.

Parents should be given the opportunity to make written and oral representation in an environment which avoids intimidation and excessive formality. Under Regulation 25 of the Education (School Government) Regulations 1989, governing bodies may delegate to a committee functions conferred by, or under, Sections 24 to 26 of the 1986 Education Act. Regulation 26(6) requires that at least three members of the governing body, none of whom should be the headteacher, should comprise the committee convened for the purpose of considering exclusion. The governing body should also advise parents and pupils that they may, if they wish, have someone of their choice to accompany and assist them at the meeting. The decision of the meeting and the reason for the decision should be clearly communicated to the parent without delay.

If the headteacher decides to extend the fixed period exclusion for a further period or, in a very exceptional circumstance, to replace the fixed period exclusion with one which is permanent, the parent or pupil should again and without delay be informed of the decision and of their rights of further representation. The headteacher must also immediately inform the LEA and governing body if the exclusion is extended or made permanent. The headteacher of the excluding school should, wherever practicable, make arrangements for the pupil who is excluded for a fixed period to receive school work to do at home and to have it marked until he or she returns to school. The governing body should keep these arrangements under review.

Circular 10/94 advises that permanent exclusion should only be used when:

- it is a last resort, and all reasonable steps have been taken to avoid exclusion
- allowing the child to remain in school would be seriously detrimental to the education or welfare of the pupil or to that of others
- proper consideration is given to the possibility that a pupil behaving unacceptably may have special educational needs which require attention in the context of SEN Code of Practice (DfE 1994a)

Following a permanent exclusion governing bodies, LEAs and independent appeal committees need to act swiftly according to a tight timetable to resolve the future of the pupil concerned.

1997 EDUCATION ACT

The measures contained in the 1997 Education Act aimed to strengthen the commitment between headteacher and governors to work together on school discipline. The Act introduced six new measures that strengthen previous discipline rules by:

- requiring governors of all maintained schools to ensure that every school has policies to promote good behaviour and discipline and to publish the discipline policy for parents, pupils and staff
- confirming that it is lawful for teachers and other authorised staff to use reasonable force to prevent a pupil committing an offence which might cause injury or damage, or disrupt good order and discipline
- giving schools powers to impose detentions without parental consent
- allowing more flexibility for exclusions so that a pupil may be excluded for a period of 45 consecutive days in one school year rather than the current 15 days a term
- requiring appeals committees to consider the interests of other pupils and staff at the school, as well as of the excluded pupil, in deciding if the pupil should be reinstated
- allowing schools to make home-school agreements a condition of admission.

EXCELLENCE IN SCHOOLS

Following the general election, the new government prepared the way for an Education Bill. As part of a consultation process, a White Paper *Excellence in Schools* was published describing how the government intended to raise standards in schools. The government proposed that by 2002: 'There will be . . . better support in schools for pupils with behaviour problems, less need to exclude pupils from school, and better education for those who do not attend school' (DfEE 1997a: 7).

The White Paper suggested that good discipline depends on partnership; improving home/school links and the quality of teaching will make a major contribution to reducing indiscipline. The government were to reflect on the effects of the provisions of the 1997 Education Act on school discipline policies and after-school detention and to offer advice on good practice.

Excellence in Schools also advocated 'assertive discipline' (see Chapter 8), a system involving the whole school in a concerted effort to improve and maintain discipline through a clearly understood behaviour framework, emphasising positive encouragement as well as sanctions. Bullying and truancy were also considered, the government suggested early intervention and the wider dissemination of good practice.

An important, and much needed review of exclusions was proposed, the government consulted on detailed new guidance for schools and LEAs over the appropriate circumstances for exclusion, appeals and arrangements for pupils' subsequent education, and about the merits of financial incentives for schools to admit pupils excluded by others.

The government also advocated an effective multi-agency approach to support good discipline and behaviour within LEAs. The government (DfEE 1997a: 57) advise that LEAs provide support for schools in improving the management of pupil behaviour. They also advise that LEAs should review the type and nature of provision available outside mainstream schools for pupils with behaviour problems. The government consider that LEAs are responsible for the arrangements for effective coordination between relevant local agencies, and for involving the youth service and voluntary sector.

3

COMMUNITY

A school should be central to its local community. To this end each school has to become a community within a community. Members of the school community will also be members of their local community; as such they will reflect the beliefs and values of their local community. These will be conveyed through the action, behaviour and attitudes of the pupils, staff (teaching and non-teaching), parents, governors and local education authority.

This chapter begins with a discussion of the meaning of the school as a community and how this impacts on the management of discipline. The following section focuses on developing a shared understanding of beliefs and values. Recognising the importance of staffing, the next section describes the development of teams and open decision-making through effective management and communication. The chapter concludes with the description and analysis of a case study 'Think Community'.

The ethos of a school which reflects the beliefs and values of its members is critical to the management of discipline. All members of the school, as participants in the school and local community, should have a shared commitment to the creation of the school ethos. It is axiomatic that schools need organisational structures, aims and guiding rules if they are to be effective. As active players in the daily life of the school, pupils, teachers, parents, governors and support agencies need to relate to each other, sharing an understanding of the goals and targets that are to be achieved in an effective school. The determination of these goals is reflective, individual and collective:

- reflective, in that the school mirrors the local community, sharing key players and their beliefs and values
- individual, as all members will have their own identity with their personal goals and objectives
- collective, shared understanding of common beliefs and values that create a sense of community bound together by a recognisable identity and geographical location.

The more isolated that pupils, teachers and non-teaching staff feel within their community the more difficult the management of discipline becomes. If the central issue in the management of discipline is the identification of common boundaries, then consistency is the key. Without shared beliefs and values, members of the school community will not be able to have a shared understanding of what is acceptable and what is not. Equally, a school may need to exert in an assertive manner, beliefs and values that do not reflect those of the local community. In such situations shared beliefs and values within the school are critical.

In order to access and participate in the school community, members need to know and understand the organisational structure of the school. By identifying the needs of the school as a community, pupils, parents, teachers, support agencies and managers can develop a structure that suits their school. Parents need to know the system that will enable them to discuss their child's education in an appropriate manner. Parents need to access managers and teachers within a structure that reflects a shared understanding of the boundaries that exist between the acceptable and unacceptable. There is a link between identifying pupil and teacher needs and creating a structure to meet those needs. Clear communication will lead to clear understanding and shared values.

The 1997 general election focused heavily on education, specifically each party's approach to the raising of standards in our schools. Key issues included literacy and numeracy, teacher training and career development, resources and pupil discipline. If schools are a reflection of society, then there appeared to be much to be concerned about. Or is there? The majority of schools appear to function at a reasonable level, providing compulsory education for all 5–16 year olds and a considerable number of 16–19 year olds. The central concern is the effectiveness of this process.

The underlying principles of the government's education policy are expressed in the White Paper, *Excellence in Schools* (DfEE 1997a: 66–8). These include:

- Schools are responsible for their own standards. They should continuously and actively seek to improve their performance so that every child can succeed.
- There is value in encouraging diversity by allowing schools to develop a particular identity, character and expertise.
- Schools should be free to make as many decisions as practical for themselves, in particular on internal management, resource allocation and day-to-day operation.
- But that freedom must be accompanied by accountability to parents, the local community, and the wider public for what they achieve.

Significantly, the government is to introduce a new framework for schools:

- community schools . . . similar to the existing county schools (which account for some 14,000 out of 22,000 primary and secondary schools in England)
- aided and foundation schools . . . employing their own staff and owning their own premises, broadly as voluntary aided and GM schools do now.

The emphasis on community reflects the caring, sharing ideology of the government; in practice it provides schools with a framework that focuses on people not structures. The application of the principle of community provision to pre-school, primary, secondary and special schools has been debated since the 1970s (Midwinter 1975). Key features of such provision include improved home-school relations and broader usage of the school for the whole population. The principles on which community provision is built, are based on certain assumptions alluded to throughout this book:

- education is part of social provision, strongly related to all other branches of social provision. Education does not exist just as an academic entity in its own social vacuum
- social provision is determined by the prevailing social and economic framework of society
- throughout civilised history, the level of social provision has sustained societies in an unequal manner, balancing those who 'have' with those who 'have not'
- both social and educational provision have become more centrally controlled
- there has been a move towards devolution of power at an operational level, reflecting the need to provide community-type activities led by the community
- there is a greater emphasis on participation that has contributed to the emancipation of the teacher.

Within the context of community, it is necessary to consider how education contributes to the total life-long experience of its members. The home, local area and neighbourhood all contribute to the education of the community. As a consequence there are varying degrees of good and bad influences on members of the school and local community. There is therefore a need for the education system to enter into dialogue with the local community, and to recognise its impact on the school community. The community as a whole influences and participates in the educational process. The management of discipline in schools should reflect the factors that determine the nature and culture of the community it serves. In sum:

- Special and cultural interaction – the school can exert its influence on the life and minds of the people. Equally the neighbourhood, home and culture of the people can influence the school. The totality of the experiences of all those concerned in the educational process have an effect one upon the other.

- Administration and control – the geographical and managerial system within the social and cultural framework. The structure gives shape and form to the beliefs and values of the community in its social and cultural being.

Community, therefore, can be defined as multidimensional in terms of location, structure and process:

- location – where it is, the influence of the environment and systems of control
- structure – the administrative elements and guidance that determine equality of provision
- process – the management of people and development of a shared understanding of beliefs and values.

Critically, education in schools should be concerned with education *within* and *for* communities, not *of* communities (Poster 1982). Community education, as with all education, begins with and for the individual. The role of the community educator is not dissimilar to the traditional role of the teacher: to educate individuals in order that they become autonomous and are able to participate in the community in which they choose to live. The element of choice is important; some members of the community may wish to remain in the same setting for much of their lives while others may choose to experience other communities. Education should provide individuals with the tools whereby they are able to make such choices.

Society

It is axiomatic that schools are, at all levels, inextricably linked with society. The school community is a reflection of society accommodating the beliefs, values and organisational systems that exist beyond the school grounds. Teachers cannot change the society in which their pupils live; they must engage with society in meeting pupils' needs. Society is not static; passive learning only operates in a stable culture (Walker 1989: 175). Teachers are often in the unenviable position of being expected to ensure cultural continuity and stability in a society which does not possess these attributes.

In the management of discipline, teachers need to know and understand the cultural differences that exist within society today. Polarisation of pupils is a reflection of polarisation in society. Schools need to avoid failing the majority of pupils in order that the few succeed. School management teams and teachers should examine the school as an informal social system reflecting differences which are real, and working to implement more fully the principle of equal value. Equal opportunity policies can only apply to those who have the opportunity to be equal. The National Children's Bureau study of socially disadvantaged children *Born to Fail?* (Wedge and Prosser 1973: 60) concluded that 'education as a "social distributor" of life chances often compounds rather than eases the difficulties of disadvantaged children'. Twenty years on this still prevails as substantiated in the more recent study by the National Commission on Education, *Success Against the Odds* (NCE 1996).

While middle-class values drive the education system, the needs of pupils from differing backgrounds are often neglected and misunderstood. As society changes, schools need to adapt. Discipline has a multiplicity of meanings among the many diverse cultures and classes represented in our schools. When considering discipline, describing a school community in formal terms can be counter-productive. The culture and background of all pupils should be considered in the development of a discipline policy appropriate to the school community.

SCHOOL CULTURE AND VISION

As schools function within a community there is a need to create an identity which acknowledges and reflects where the community is and where it would like to be; this is also applicable to pupils, parents, teachers and support agencies.

Schools, like other communities, have their own atmospheric characteristics and personalities. An understanding of the culture of schools is required before considering the management of discipline. The culture of each school is determined by individual and collective beliefs and values. Schools do not consist of homogenous groups of people with shared identities; schools are collections of individuals within a shared culture. The vision for the school is contained in the school development plan and policy statements that provide the rationale for practice. A school culture will manifest itself in many forms:

- practice – rites, rituals and ceremonies
- communications – stories, myths, sagas, legends, folk tales, symbols and slogans
- physical forms – location, style and condition of the school buildings, fixtures and fittings
- common language – phrases or jargon common to the school.

In the context of managing discipline in schools, the culture of the school (its sense of community) will influence the effectiveness of behaviour management. The culture of the school may also determine the need for behaviour management. The personality of the school is a reflection of the way in which the work is done. The effect of an organisation's structure goes well beyond the allocation of work and management, and will affect the perceived culture of the school. Every member of the school community will have his/her agenda; teachers will have to be aware of the inevitability of such differences.

Strategically, all schools should have a school development plan that determines where the school will be within a given period of school life. The school development plan will be driven by the school community, their beliefs and values, goals and aspirations. It should be based on a vision which will move the organisation forward from where it is now to where it would like to be. Vision statements and policy documents also provide an insight into the school ethos – that which is distinctive in character and often intangible.

A vision should be realistic and attractive to all members of the organisation. A precise goal is more credible than a vague dream. A specific definition of vision within the school context would be the school's aims. These are notably achievement orientated and, as such, should be shared by members of the school community.

ETHOS

Differences between schools may be explained in terms of organisational and social structure. Differences between schools also reflect the interpersonal relationships that create the ethos, the shared beliefs and values. The whole-school feeling exists to such an extent that it drives the school as a community towards achieving goals.

The relationship between discipline and ethos exists, yet is intangible and, therefore, difficult to define. Ethos and discipline are both multidimensional, as no single definition would apply to the many situations that occur in the life of the school community. Ethos will influence discipline, as discipline will influence ethos. Institution and social structure will, in practice, impact on school community members' judgement on behaviour and discipline.

Analysis of school management and pupil behaviour is often directed at the individual teacher, whose skills in managing young people are so consequential to the life of the classroom (Hargreaves 1984). It is also directed at the institution as a whole, as the general ethos, climate or philosophy of a school has its own powerful consequences. The teacher and the pupil are, of course, interdependent; what is unclear is precisely how this interaction works.

Organisation in terms of management structure will influence the ethos of the school. Management and organisation are discussed in more detail in Chapter 4. Aspects of organisation are also linked with pupil behaviour (Coulby and Harper 1985: 136), including:

- school rules or codes of behaviour
- the timetable, arrangements for lunchtimes and breaks and general movement around the school
- responsibilities that teachers have towards one another and to different groups of pupils
- the school communication system, the reliability and accuracy of the information about pupils that is passed from one to another
- the nature of teachers' contacts with parents
- the in-service training and support offered to teachers.

Writers (Jones 1989; Tattum 1989) suggest that the creation of good order, supported by a system of monitoring pupils, will lead to a positive ethos. In this context, ethos has both content and process. Content refers to policy, structure and curriculum; process refers to the school culture, quality of social relationships and channels of communication. The means of achieving good order and a positive ethos is by:

- a common staff policy on behaviour that will encourage consistency
- developing positive staff attitudes towards pupils' needs
- teachers presenting themselves as good models in the way they prepare and conduct their lessons
- the use of effective praise and rewards to develop teacher and pupil self-esteem and self-confidence
- encouragement of all members of the school community to take responsibility for and to encourage participation in school activities.

Teacher–pupil relationships are central to creating a positive and tolerant atmosphere as opposed to an authoritarian one: 'The most important characteristic of schools with a positive atmosphere is that pupils, teachers and other staff feel that they are known and valued members of the school community' (DES 1989: 90).

Teachers and pupils have a right to expect support from the senior management team of the school. They should feel free to ask for help and assistance when required. The ethos of the school will be influenced by the headteacher and senior management team. Good headteachers are warm, friendly, courteous people who know their job. Members of the school community should have confidence in the headteacher and senior management team.

Equally, a good headteacher will know the strengths and weaknesses of all teachers and will be able to help them develop their skills, experiences and knowledge. Senior managers are in a position of responsibility that will impact on all members of the school community. They assist and coordinate the work of teachers, parents and support agencies in order to develop the pupils in their care.

The importance of the headteacher's management style in relation to school ethos and the management of discipline can not be overestimated. Headteachers need to give a clear sense of direction and transmit high expectations to staff and pupils, while involving all members of the school community in the determination of a discipline policy. The general atmosphere and practices of schools make a substantial difference to pupil behaviour. Components of an effective discipline regime will include:

- clarity of expectations
- atmosphere conducive to effective learning, with members of the school community adhering to a sensible and fully understood code of behaviour

- a successful combination of firmness and kindness, together with the expectation of courtesy
- warmth and humour in relationships
- support which helps to combat the problems of a difficult environment
- a general demonstration of sensitivity.

There is a distinctive link between the atmosphere created in schools and their environment. A school building that is uncared for, regardless of age, will reflect an uncaring community; it will also incite misbehaviour. Crowded corridors and stairways, graffiti on the walls, basic uncleanliness and poor toilet facilities do not encourage respect. Working in an environment that is in need of repair (as most schools are) creates stress; working in an environment that is unhealthy is not conducive to effective teaching and learning. Members of the school community need encouragement too, in order to fulfil their potential. A stimulating environment will produce stimulating results. Members of the school community need to consider how to create a positive environment. This may include:

- a tidy, inviting reception area
- good, quality displays of pupils' work and achievements that reflect the full range of ability
- bright, open spaces
- carpeted floors
- clean buildings throughout
- no litter, adequate bins that are emptied
- working and clean toilet facilities
- plants, pictures and photographs
- tidy bookshelves
- easy access to computers and reference material
- supervised areas for study
- separate, clean dining area
- adequate facilities for every subject, for example, physical education and music store areas.

The management of the school environment is the responsibility of everyone in the school community. The development and maintenance of the environment can be a key activity within the school, directly relating to school discipline. Much can be made of any school building.

Community is an essential concern of schools; as such the development and maintenance of a sense of community is a primary function. The following describes and analyses a community-based project developed as a means to address the management of discipline in schools. As a case study the essential contribution to this book is the implementation, management, review and analysis of good practice.

COLLABORATION WITH THE COMMUNITY

Police

Schools should liaise with the local community police officers on matters concerning:

- juvenile crime
- domestic violence
- vandalism
- truancy
- drug-related crime
- race-related crime.

Teachers should be aware of the criminal status of their pupils and families, for example, those involved in drug abuse. Matters of extreme confidentiality should be dealt with by school management. Teachers and pupils should feel safe and secure in the school environment. Senior managers should have a rapid-response system for emergency situations. Many inner-city schools have an alarm button, similar to those found in banks, to alert police when needed. Pupils and parents can present a threat to teachers; police presence may provide the necessary level of authority required at difficult times. Police should be notified of all evening activities held on school premises in order that they may patrol school grounds effectively.

Parents

Parents should do everything they can to help their children relate cooperatively to adults and other children. Parents can have a powerful effect (according to the situation/age of the pupil) on children's behaviour, ensuring that pupils arrive at school on time, have suitable clothing, necessary books or equipment and ensuring that homework is completed on time. Some difficult pupil behaviour is brought about by adults who are unprepared for their role as parents. Teachers should be alert to the difficulties and pressures which arise from unstable family relationships and the impact of unemployment, homelessness, family bereavement and illness.

An active partnership between parents and schools offers great benefits. The interaction between home circumstances and school practices is complicated but important. Opportunities for teachers and parents to share their concerns about pupil behaviour can help guide the school as it develops and maintains its policy on behaviour and discipline.

Schools should provide welcoming environments for parents. Schools can use prospectuses and other communications to convey and reinforce the nature of parental responsibility and the notion of home-school partnership. Contact with parents should not be confined to parents' evenings; it should be an integral part of school life. It may be possible to bring together groups of parents to discuss problems in an atmosphere of mutual support.

Schools have found home-school contracts to be of significant benefit in involving parents constructively in considering pupil behaviour. Such contracts, which specify the expectations of pupils, parents and the school, have proved useful in setting out for parents their particular responsibilities in relation to their child, and in defining the school's role and policies. Contracts are likely to work best if they offer the prospect of benefits as well as sanctions. Schools can insist on their being part of the admissions process. An example of a home-school contract is shown in Appendix A.

Sometimes a child may be with a foster parent or residential social worker, or with another relative because of a court order. These carers also have a general responsibility to work with the school and pupil. They may have much to contribute in terms of understanding why a child is behaving poorly and what might be done to improve matters.

Good behaviour, as well as bad, should be drawn to parents' attention, and early notice given of particular difficulties with an individual pupil. Each school's behaviour policy should make clear the matters considered to be of sufficient importance to require notification of parents.

Sometimes family breakdown may result in children having very disrupted lives and moving between different homes, or moving out of areas where they had established friendships. For some pupils, the school may be the only secure, stable environment.

It has been shown that when children have relationships outside the family in which they feel valued and respected, this helps to protect them against adversity within the family. Pupils may nonetheless feel inhibited about discussing changes in their lives such as family breakdown. Some children take primary responsibility for caring for parents who are sick or disabled. This may have an adverse effect on children's emotional and educational development. The school's processes for recording and identifying pupils with problems should be sensitive to possible links between behaviour and other experiences in a child's life. This may lead to the need to involve other agencies or support services in order to assist the pupil's development.

In cases where a child's behaviour at school indicates serious problems at home, schools must be alert to the need to involve social service departments. The position of children being looked after by local authorities is considered in detail in Circular 13/94 (DfE 1994g). Advice is available from local social service departments on the procedures and steps to be taken to resolve a disciplinary problem involving children in care, teachers will need to know the range of options open to them.

In practice, parents need accurate information and regular feedback about what is happening in schools. The information should be clear, comprehensive and user-friendly. It should also be communicated in a style and language appropriate to its audience. Parents and carers should also have an influence on the way schools are managed. They have a vital role in fostering good behaviour. Many schools have very successful parent-teacher associations open to all members of the school community. These can provide a framework for effective partnerships between home and school.

CASE STUDY – THINK COMMUNITY

This study is based on an initiative that evolved as a consequence of increasing pressures relating to discipline on a school in a major city in England. The large, 11–16 comprehensive school located in the centre of a housing estate had encountered many challenges in its thirty-year history and recent local riots were to impact on the management of discipline in a significant way. Pupils were of mixed ability and lived within a five-mile radius of the school. Many of the seventy teachers had worked at the school for over twenty years. The members of the senior management team were all new to their posts, not new to the school.

The need to define a strategy for the management of discipline that reflected the impact of recent community events had been expressed by the majority of staff during an INSET day at the start of the academic year. Following the initial consultation with teachers, the deputy headteacher and two heads of year created a working group to tackle the problem. A questionnaire was then sent to all parents and pupils to determine their views on improving standards of discipline within the school.

Aims were agreed:

- to raise the education performance of all pupils
- to increase the morale of teaching and non-teaching staff
- to increase the involvement of parents in their children's education
- to increase a sense of responsibility within the school community.

Areas of concern/development were also identified:

- a need to share responsibility for the school building, classrooms, corridors and stairs
- a need to create a recognised code of practice within the school encompassing:
  - respect for the environment
  - respect for each other
  - respect for property
  - overall improvement of the site.

The staff members (teaching and non-teaching) were then consulted on how to achieve the above. Several practical suggestions made were to be implemented by designated teams within the school as shown in Figure 3.1.

Improving the school site

To do:	*Action:*
Litter	Tutor groups
Displays	Subject teams
Lockers	Tutor
Create picnic areas	Senior management team/caretaker
Graffiti	Year teams

Developing a sense of community

Create a school council	Tutors/ senior management team
Pupil reception	Head of Year 9
Tutor group peer support	Head of Year 11
Reading partner scheme	Special Educational Needs coordinator
School bulletin	Headteacher
Celebrate success (media)	Senior management team
Community drug centre	Parents

Code of Behaviour

INSET	LEA
Assemblies	Head of year/senior management team
Introduction of sanctions/ rewards	Tutors

Parental involvement

Increase publicity of parent consultation evenings	Senior management team
Open access	Senior management team
Develop Parent Teacher Association	Parent governors

Figure 3.1 Think Community plan

The general framework for the development and implementation of the Think Community project was 'bottom up'. All teachers and pupils were involved in consultation with senior managers and LEA advisory staff.

The effectiveness of the project was monitored over two years. The practical targets were all achieved but the success of the project in fulfilling its aims was more difficult to define. Staff members were not completely committed to collecting litter with their tutor groups. Previously assertive discipline (see Chapter 8) was considered by the local education authority to be a more appropriate system of rewards and sanctions than the existing system. The introduction of an alternative system had a negative impact on the confidence of the teaching staff. The strength of the new project was overwhelmingly the participation of the community in its development and implementation. Significant outcomes of the project that remain operational were:

- school council
- Year 9 receptionist
- reading partners scheme
- community drug centre
- parent–teacher association.

The need for the creation of a working group with new energy and vigour is now evident. Time has moved on, the school population has changed. History dictates that there is a need for further evaluation and a new initiative.

4

MANAGEMENT

The importance of effective management cannot be overstated. If schools are to adopt a multi-agency approach to the management of behaviour, there is a need to know and understand basic principles of education management. Teachers, support agencies and senior managers should develop the skills and abilities required to develop, implement and manage effective behaviour strategies. Highly committed professionals are needed to ensure that schools create a sense of community and achieve their goals. Successful schools are managed by successful teachers and senior management teams. Effective management of discipline does not just happen; it requires consultation, planning, commitment, and constant review and evaluation.

This chapter places the management of discipline within the context of education management. A shared understanding of education management will enable schools to design, implement and review a discipline policy that works within the school and reflects the needs of pupils, teachers, support agencies and the community. Key management issues that need to be addressed are:

- the principles of education management
- school development planning
- the management of change
- communication.

THE PRINCIPLES OF EDUCATION MANAGEMENT

A manager is someone who gets the job done, through other people (Everard 1986). A manager:

- knows what he/she wants and causes it to happen
- is responsible for the appropriate control of resources
- promotes effectiveness and continually searches for improvement
- is accountable
- sets a climate or tone conducive to enabling people to give of their best.

All members of the school community are affected by the management of the school through:

- leadership – sharing values and beliefs in creating a vision for the school
- management – consulting, planning, organisation, execution and deployment of resources
- administration – ensuring that all operational details happen.

The key functions of school management are to manage teaching and learning through policy, people and resources. The management of discipline encompasses all of the above. Teachers need to develop the skills required to (Spinks 1990: 121–2):

1 [develop] a relevant curriculum to meet the needs of the students
2 [develop] management skills to deliver the curriculum to students in the most effective and efficient ways possible through the available resources
3 [develop approaches to the management of] change as a natural phenomenon in schools.

Essentially, education management relates to where the school is going and why, how it is going to get there and then checking very carefully to see if and when it arrived. In essence, education management involves directing relevant members of the school community through six key phases:

- goal setting
- policy-making
- curriculum planning
- resource provision
- implementation of learning programme
- evaluation.

Each of these phases is as applicable to the management of discipline as it is to any other aspect of school management. Managers must adopt their own management style which fulfils the requirements of the post. Knowing what is required is the key. Courage and persistence are valuable tools; personal integrity is essential.

Teachers, managers and support agencies live in a practical world (Harrison 1995: 8). As a community, each school is self-centred, self-reliant and culturally 'different' from any other school. A school community will reflect its environment. In contrast, the management structure and organisation of the school will be similar to that of other schools. Communities and schools do not exist in a vacuum. There are generic responsibilities which apply to the management of all schools. These responsibilities are interrelated. Essentially, school managers are responsible for the management of people determined by the needs of:

- all pupils to learn
- all teachers to teach.

DECISION-MAKING

Discipline underpins every aspect of school life. A school without an effective discipline policy that encompasses strategies and support mechanisms that are available to all members of the school community will not function as a centre for teaching and learning. The process of developing and implementing a discipline policy will involve collaborative decision-making. Therefore all members of the school community should have the opportunity to participate in decision-making as appropriate.

Participation in decision-making is a relatively new phenomenon in schools. In previous generations, teachers have been autonomous in their classrooms and, apart from crises, have been responsible for the management of their classroom and not much more. Devolution of power through the local management of schools and the national curriculum has led to a greater level of participation in decision-making in schools. In practice, decisions may be beyond the mandate of individual teachers or working groups; however, participation in the process of decision-making will increase the likelihood of successful implementation of a discipline policy.

A confident, open manager will encourage participation that has meaning and relevance to daily practice. Teachers and managers should interpret participation in a genuine way. Participation can function in these forms:

- *consultation* – team members are invited to suggest ideas; decision-making remains the responsibility of the manager
- *consent* – team members, as a group, can veto any decision made by the senior manager
- *consensus* – team members are consulted, followed by whole-team involvement in decision-making through majority vote.

Deciding on when and how to involve members of the school community in decision-making will affect the quality of the decision, the staff's acceptance of the decision and the amount of time involved in the decision-making process.

> Participation in decision-making has two major benefits:
>
> a) an improvement in the quality of the decision
> b) improved motivation and commitment of those involved.
>
> (Fidler *et al.* 1991: 5)

The extent to which teachers, support agencies and members of the wider school community are consulted will depend, in part, on the management style adopted by the headteacher.

In some situations relating to the management of discipline, it would be impossible for members of a senior management team not to be autocratic. Crises occur and managers' decisions have to be made. I was once faced with a horrifying situation when a pupil's father had been shot. It was of prime importance to limit the threat of violence to the pupil, and a decision was made to remove the pupil from school to a 'safe house'. There was no time to consult colleagues or the pupil's family. The pupil's safety (and that of others) was the priority.

Management styles will differ according to several factors (Tannenbaum and Schmidt 1973). These can be identified as:

- *the leader* – his/her personality and preferred style
- *the led* – the needs, attitudes and skills of the subordinates or colleagues
- *the task* – the requirements and goals of the job to be done
- *the contact* – the school, its values and beliefs, visions and missions.

Selection of a style appropriate to the individual and the school is critical to the success of both. A manager should not adopt a style which is inapplicable or unsustainable, particularly in the management of discipline which requires consistency. Insincere sincerity is easily spotted.

MANAGEMENT STRUCTURES

The management of discipline in schools has to be placed within the context of the management structures that exist at governmental, LEA and school levels. In essence, discipline relates to:

- pupils
- teachers/senior managers
- general assistants/school meal service assistants
- parents
- non-teaching support staff
- governors
- support agencies
- education welfare officers/education officers/children's officers
- support teams/social services
- LEA advisory service
- educational psychologists
- medical teams
- judicial system
- police.

The extent to which each of the above is consulted is dependent on the pupil and issue to be addressed. What is important is that in the matter of discipline, teachers should not feel isolated. The management structure of the school, LEA and support agencies should be known by all members of the school community as shown in Figure 4.1.

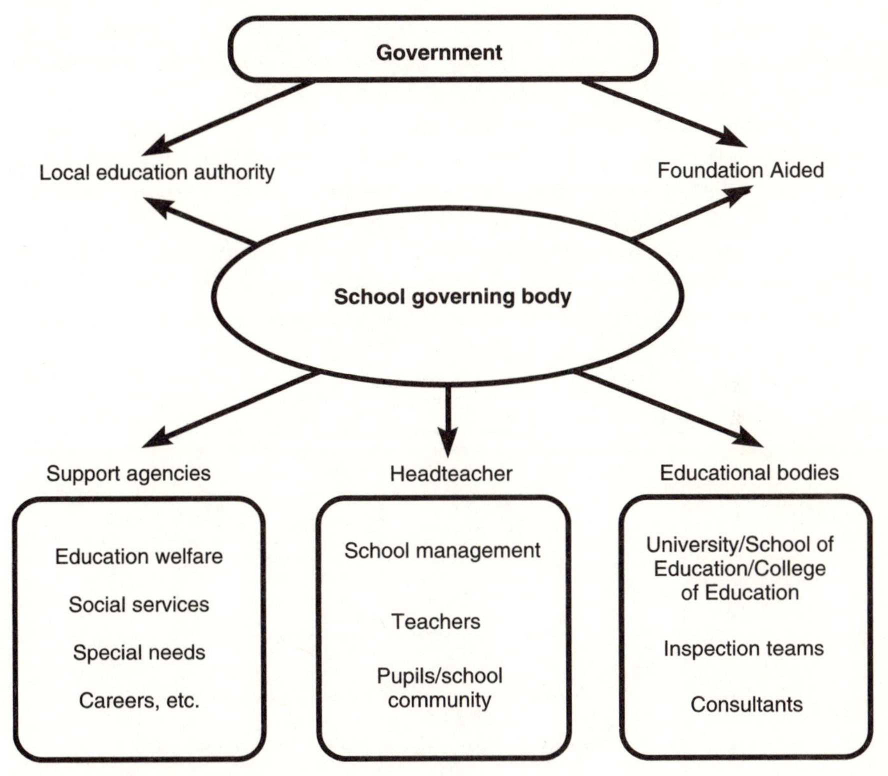

Figure 4.1 School management – external agencies
Source: Blandford 1997a: Figure 1.2

It is necessary for all teachers to know and understand the support systems available to the school. Every teacher has a pastoral responsibility for pupils. This involves regular contact with parents, members of the community and external agencies in addition to the more formalised agencies within the local authority. Areas of responsibility should be well defined within this often neglected area of school management. A framework for the management of discipline in schools should:

- be workable
- recognise the needs of the pupil
- recognise the needs of the school

- be understood and acknowledged by all staff (teaching and non-teaching)
- relate to the school's vision and school development plan
- allow teachers to develop knowledge and understanding skills and abilities
- include the management of discipline in continuing professional development and INSET programmes.

The position of pastoral coordinators in the management structure of the school will, in practice, reflect the level of importance placed on the management of discipline in schools. Where schools place an over-emphasis on academic issues and curriculum programmes, discipline and related issues may appear to be unsupported. While all teachers have a responsibility for discipline, a central role of the senior management team is the management of pupils. This role should be equal to the management of the curriculum and the management of resources. If a school is unable to fund deputy headteacher posts, roles and responsibilities in each of these areas should be delegated to middle managers. Figure 4.2 illustrates a school management structure that places equal emphasis on academic, pastoral and resource management.

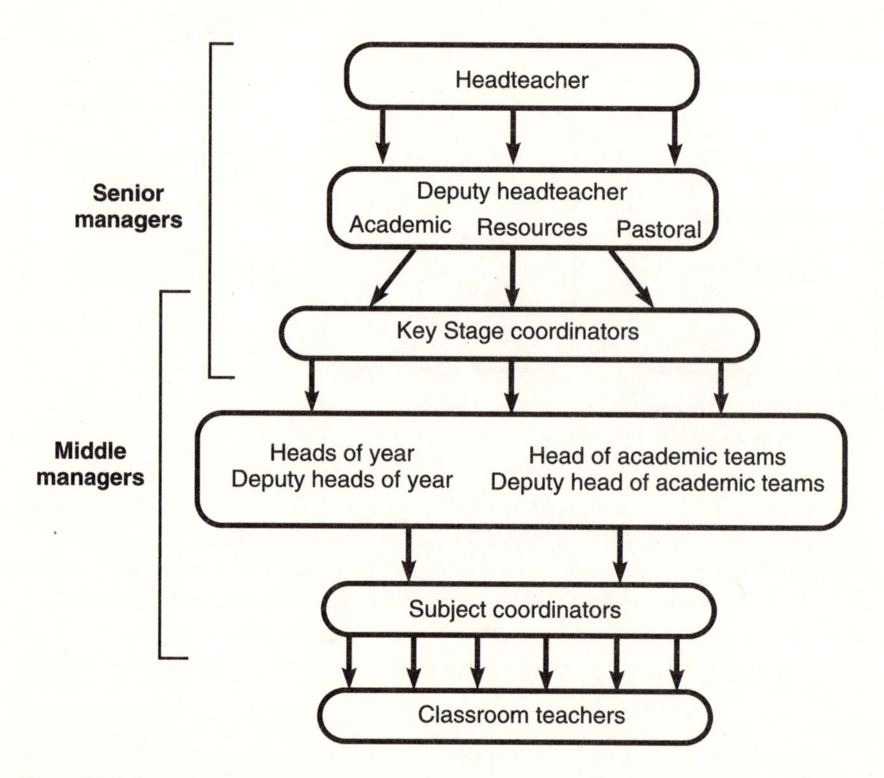

Figure 4.2 School management structure – large primary or secondary school
Source: Blandford 1997a: Figure 1.4

TEAMS

The management of discipline in schools encompasses an understanding of management structures and systems of communication. The management of teams within schools and the community is also a critical feature of the effective management of discipline in schools. There are many features common to all school management teams, across all phases of education.

There are also many differences as Wallace *et al.* (1996: 8) found in their study of primary and secondary school senior management teams. The study showed that secondary school managers tended to focus on school-wide responsibilities. This contrasted with the multiple responsibilities of primary school managers. Significantly, primary school managers do not have the luxury of pastoral, curriculum and administrative teams. Wallace concluded that the cultural and political (power) perspectives of primary and secondary teams are incompatible, which contrasts with the similarities in management structures and roles.

> A team is a group of people that can effectively tackle any task which it has been set to do. The contribution drawn from each member is of the highest possible quality, and . . . one which could not have been called into play other than in the context of a supportive team.
>
> (Everard and Morris 1990: 172)

The supportive and caring element of team work is fundamental to the effective management of discipline in school. In any challenging and demanding situation, teachers need the security of belonging to a strong team. Effective management involves sharing the pressures created by difficult pupils. Teams do not act as teams simply because they are described as such. Teamwork means a group of people working together on the basis of:

- shared perceptions
- a common purpose
- agreed procedures
- commitment
- cooperation
- resolving disagreements openly by discussion.

As with the creation of the school identity, successful teamwork depends on a clearly defined set of aims and objectives, and the personalities of the team members and team manager. Tuckman (1965) defined the stages of team development as:

> *Forming*: the team is not a team but a set of individuals. The focus is on the team's purposes, composition, leadership and lifespan. Individuals are

concerned to establish their personal identities in the team and make some individual impression.

Storming: having reached a consensus on the team's purpose, conflict arises as assumptions are challenged. Personal agendas are revealed and some interpersonal hostility may be generated. Successful handling enables the team to reach fresh agreement on purpose, procedures and norms.

Norming: the team seeks to establish its norms and practices – when and how it should work. As working procedures are established, there will be a communication of feelings, mutual support and a sense of team identity.

Performing: solutions to problems emerge, the team is mature and productive. Individuals and team are relaxed and confident.

As stated, teams are driven by tasks. The management of discipline in relation to community, visions and teams is a whole-school responsibility. Whilst the management structure of the school may define pastoral management and, as a consequence, the management of discipline as an independent area of responsibility, in practice discipline is the responsibility of all members of the school community. One function of all teams (multi-agency, pastoral, year, key-stage, department) is to ensure that all members of the community have a shared understanding of how discipline will be managed within the school.

The effectiveness of the team/individual responsible for the management of discipline in the school will be determined by the effectiveness of all managers, teachers, and support staff working together towards the achievement of a common goal. In practice this will involve (Coleman and Bush 1994: 279–80):

Explicit and shared values; translated into a vision for the school

Situational leadership; skills are more important than hierarchical factors, requiring a willingness by the designated leader to stand back and allow other team members to assume control according to the needs of the situation.

Pride in the team; commitment and involvement, team members have self-belief and confidence in others and in the team as a whole

Clear task; the outcome, or goal is clear, realistic and understood

Review; effective teams learn and develop by a process of continuous feedback and review. Openness, no hidden agendas, praise and criticism exist in equal measure.

Lateral communication; team members are able to communicate with each other without reference to the team leader. Networks are formed and nourished by the team.

Collaboration; decisions are shared and have full commitment.

Action; each team member knows what has to be done, by whom and *when*.

SCHOOL DEVELOPMENT PLAN

Every school should have a school development plan that provides a framework for strategic planning which identifies long- and short-term objectives. The plan should relate clearly to the school vision. As stated, the plan should be central to school management and involve all teachers in the process of identifying its aims and objectives. The plan should also encompass national, LEA and school initiatives. The plan will identify existing achievements and needs for development. The plan enables schools to manage themselves in an effective, coherent manner within both local and national contexts. The main purpose of a plan should be to improve the quality of teaching and learning for the pupils. In essence a school development plan should (Skelton *et al.* 1991: 166–7):

- demonstrate involvement
- provide a focus for action
- provide a means of presenting the plan
- provide a means of assessing progress.

Strategic planning occurs annually through the school development plan; this is a suitable time to review the effectiveness of behaviour policies and the management of discipline. Figure 4.3 illustrates the planning process in education management.

As can be seen, isolating discipline from education management would be unrealistic. Discipline is an issue that needs to be addressed. The management of discipline should be approached in a professional manner, similar to approaches adopted to other management issues in schools.

In order for the school development plan to be effective, all objectives should be **SMART** (Tuckman 1965).

Specific
Measurable
Attainable
Relevant
Time-limited

An example of an effective school development plan is shown in Appendix B prepared by all staff in a rural 11–16 coeducational comprehensive school with 900 pupils.

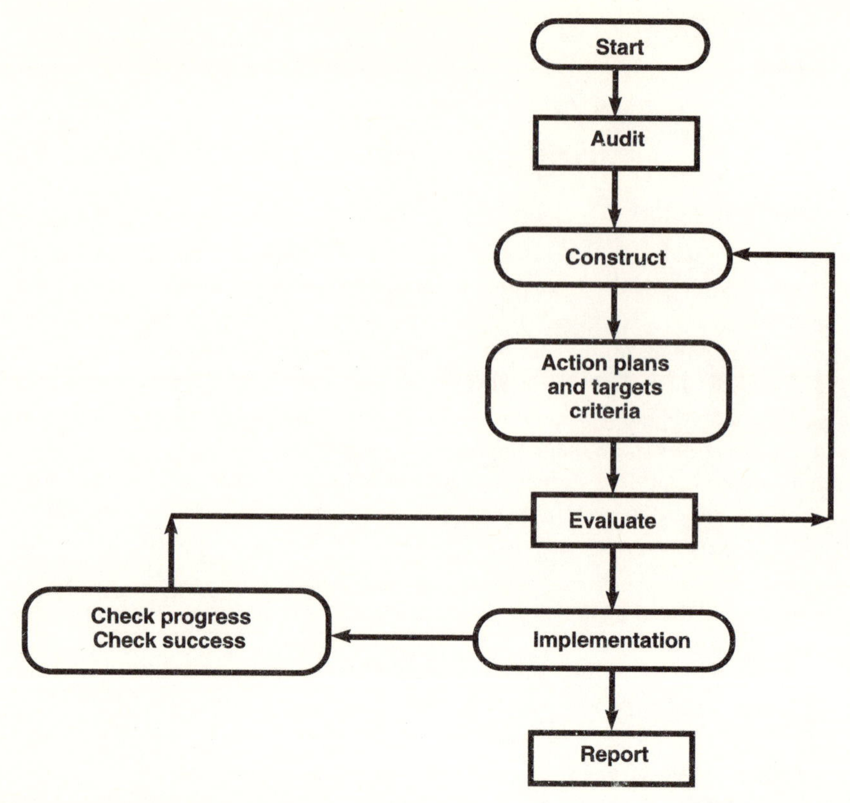

Figure 4.3 The planning process
Source: Blandford 1997a: Figure 7.4

MANAGEMENT OF CHANGE

The management of change is a recurring theme in education. It is axiomatic that, in society, change is on the increase.

> All institutions live and perform in two time periods, that of today and that of tomorrow. Tomorrow is being made today, irrevocably in most cases. Managers therefore have to manage both today – the fundamentals – and tomorrow. In turbulent times, managers cannot assume that tomorrow will be an extension of today. On the contrary they must manage for change, change both as an opportunity and as a threat.
>
> (Drucker 1980: 5)

In the context of the management of discipline, change will occur as a consequence of both internal and external pressures. Most changes are due to social,

technological, economic, political, market or chance factors. All these apply to the management of discipline in schools. In education, innovations involve a mixture of new 'things or conditions':

- policies
- knowledge
- materials
- techniques
- skills or behaviours
- attitudes.

(Hall and Oldroyd 1990a: 50)

In the management of discipline, a change may occur as the consequence of a change of pupil or teacher circumstances, a new pupil or a new management role. Change can take place at different levels: nationally, locally or in the classroom. During the process of change, each level should be identified. The level of change will impact on those who are involved in the process of change. Those who are uncomfortable with their new roles will view change as a threat. Every school will have a combination of people who view change on a continuum from threat to opportunity! There may be individuals who will not be threatened by the change, for example, a 'new' pupil joining their class, but will feel threatened by the change process, for example, the involvement of 'outside' agencies.

People will resist change, especially if it is someone else's change that has been forced upon them. Resistance to change can be a major restraining force that can be overcome with understanding. This can apply in equal measure to pupils, parents, teachers and other members of the school community involved in the management of discipline in schools. Change may incur resistance due to self-interest, misunderstanding, different assessments of the situation or a low tolerance to change. Common responses to change are poor behaviour, disagreement and/or excuses. The management of discipline in schools may involve choosing a change strategy that will enable the change to take place requiring:

- identification of the level of complexity and time needed
- identification of resistance factors
- selection of a method to overcome resistance
- evaluating management and teacher beliefs and values associated with the change.

A common mistake in the management of change is to move too quickly and involve too few people. Forcing change will have too many negative side effects. Equally, knowing and understanding change strategies will only go part-way to aiding and facilitating the change process. The management of change can be made more effective by providing support. This strategy is most effective when fear and anxiety lie at the heart of resistance.

Evaluation of changes associated with the management of discipline may be difficult to assess. There are often unintended outcomes, and defining criteria for success is problematic. If the objectives have been carefully constructed, evaluation should be possible. Evaluation should proceed simultaneously with the change programme; this should not be left until the end. Strengths, weaknesses, opportunities and threats should be identified within the school development plan. A model for change when managing discipline in schools might be:

- identifying the need for change
- identifying alternatives
- deciding on the most appropriate change
- planning the change
- implementing the change
- consolidating the change
- follow-up reviews – from *all* involved
- communicating the outcomes.

COMMUNICATION

All agencies involved in the management of discipline in schools need to communicate with colleagues, parents, pupils and others; communication is therefore central to effective school-based operations. In schools, teachers and managers use different methods of communication for different purposes; some are more successful than in others. Why is it that communication always seems to flow more smoothly in some schools, teams and departments than in others? One reason is the current and/or established communication climate. An open supportive communication climate promotes positive cooperative working relationships whereby all members of the school community will feel valued, trusted, secure and confident.

Communication is the exchange of information, which ranges from an informal discussion with a pupil, parent or colleague to a full written report to governors or the LEA on a discipline-related issue. Channels of communication are verbal or written. Verbal communication can be by telephone or face-to-face in a meeting. Written communication can be formal or informal. In the management of discipline it is essential to record the date, time, details and outcome of any relevant communication.

Problems that arise during the communication process are generally focused on: the message, encoding, the setting, transmission, decoding, and feedback. The message given may not always be the message received. Working in a pressured, pluralistic society creates a barrier to effective communication. Some people appear to have an innate ability to communicate; many others acquire skills through study and practice.

Verbal and non-verbal communication each involve listening and observing.

Being an effective listener is critical to the management of discipline at all levels. Listening is a skill that can be developed and practised in each new situation. Effective listening is non-judgemental allowing the pupil or teacher to say what is important to them (see Chapter 5).

Information technology is increasingly making information easier to access and share. Teachers, managers and members of the school community have a responsibility to comply with relevant legislation when dealing with sensitive information.

Meetings are becoming an important part of daily life in school. Teachers, managers and support agencies are required to plan, lead and participate in meetings. A shared understanding of the culture of meetings will help all participants to make better use of the opportunity to communicate in meetings. Networks provide support and are a useful means of sharing information. Education welfare officers can play an invaluable role in the support of pupils, parents, and teachers when preparing for meetings. All participants should aim to become valued members of meetings; prepare, think and listen – then speak and encourage others. It is essential for those present to know their audience, adopt accepted protocol and record their contribution. With good leadership, meetings can be effective.

Many schools have events when they communicate with the outside world. The management of discipline is critical in how schools are perceived and how members of the school community communicate with others. Dress code, basic manners, straightforward lines of communication and uncomplicated letters (without spelling/grammatical errors) contribute to communicating a positive image.

Parents, as clients, need to be attracted to the school and convinced that the school will offer a quality education for their child. Local industry and businesses will associate a good education with a positive school image. Public relations are important. All members of the school community need to be aware of how to promote the 'corporate image'. Each team within the school will need to participate in creating the image.

Schools hold many open evenings during the course of the academic year. These may be to deliver reports, select examination courses or to discuss behavioural or discipline issues. Members of the school community will need to adopt the appropriate protocol and practices involved in open evenings. It is important to:

- keep a record of appointments
- keep a record of letters and responses
- know where relevant colleagues will be for consultation/emergencies
- keep a list of problems/actions
- know whom to consult and the appropriate times for consultation.

All members of the school community have a role in how the school communicates internally, and externally to the outside world.

5

SENIOR AND MIDDLE MANAGERS

Teaching and management are roles adopted simultaneously by almost all middle/senior managers in their working lives. A manager in education is, in practice, a teacher, leader and team member. The multiplicity of tasks that teachers and managers are required to complete require clear strategies. Discipline is a fundamental aspect of the daily lives of pupils, teachers and members of the school community and, as such, it requires clarity of understanding, consistency of practice and sound leadership based on shared beliefs and values.

The effective management of the school community is central to the roles and responsibilities of senior management teams and headteachers. This chapter identifies the structures and mechanisms required for the management of discipline in schools, encompassing knowledge and understanding of pupil, parent and teacher needs. All teachers and managers have a responsibility to pupils to develop their self-esteem and self-confidence and to give them the opportunity to learn. As stated, teaching and learning should be experienced in all lessons at every phase of education.

School management is influenced by national and local factors. Table 5.1 illustrates, in broad terms, the impact of the Education Reform Act on school management, and provides a summary of the range of issues requiring management in schools.

Central to effective management, that is getting things done through people (see Chapter 4), is the ability of middle/senior managers to identify their roles at any given moment in the school day. For example, a headteacher who, as a drama teacher under pressure to complete practical examinations that are overly time-consuming, should avoid taking that pressure into a meeting with governors and parents to discuss the possible exclusion of a pupil. Middle/senior managers must have the ability to focus on the task in hand.

The framework for practice, teaching and management will be determined by the school as a community and organisation. Clear management structures will enable a complex organisation to function in terms of efficiency. However, with an intensely personal issue, as discipline is, there is a need for flexibility within the system. Dealing with immediate problems requires clarity of thought and action uncluttered by the need to inform a hierarchy of teachers and managers. Details

Table 5.1 The effects of the Education Reform Act (ERA) on school management

Aspect of ERA	*Affected area of school management*
Local management of schools	Budget
Parental choice	Marketing and development
National curriculum	Curriculum coordination
League tables	Pastoral and academic
Continuing professional development	Staff development, appraisal and selection
School development plan	Strategic planning
Diversity	Grant-maintained schools, selection and specialisation

can be communicated following the required action, colleagues need to know when such events occur. In all aspects of managing discipline other than those affecting the safety of the school community, pupil needs must be the priority.

Being an effective manager does not mean being 'all things to all people'. Middle/senior managers must adopt their own management style that will nevertheless fulfil the requirements of the post. Knowing what is required is the key. It is essential for middle/senior managers to identify their roles in terms of:

- tasks
- responsibilities
- relationships
- working conditions
- external influences.

SCHOOL LEADERSHIP

Headteachers and senior management teams have a multiplicity of tasks to complete in the course of their duties. Central to their role is the management of pupil and staff discipline within the school that they lead. 'It is essential to ask why schools function in the ways that they do, and consider how and by which means they have an impact on the behaviour and attainments of the children they serve' (Rutter *et al.* 1979: 177).

At a fundamental level, school leaders should reflect on what they do and how this affects discipline in their school. A headteacher should have sufficient management skills to support his/her staff and pupils in maintaining acceptable levels of discipline and behaviour.

We live in a multicultural, pluralist society which is not reflected in management posts in schools and local education authorities. Teachers and support agencies need to consider how power in society affects people differently. There are not many black people, women or disabled people in important positions in organisations such as schools, local government and local education authorities. The majority of headteachers and senior managers in large primary and all secondary schools are white men. Black people and white women are more likely to be in lower positions. This will influence the self-esteem of minority groups and may, ultimately, be the cause of the high exclusion rates among black pupils.

Preventative management is an absolute necessity in schools. Before the start of the academic year, schools should have in place measures, routines and practices that prevent unnecessary disruption and enhance classroom practice. Headteachers should lead teachers in the collaborative exercise of reviewing:

- how to provide adequate support for teachers
- how to establish good working practices that provide pupils with a stimulating and rewarding environment
- how to address pupils' needs.

Leaders should set a good example with clear aims and high expectations, matched by constant vigilance and a willingness to provide support, to identify in-service training needs and take action to meet them, and to encourage the professional development and maintenance of high standards (Badger 1992). Headteachers and senior managers need to reflect on:

- the growing unease and dissatisfaction with child-centred approaches to tackling disruptive behaviour in schools
- the economic climate and pressure on resources that have led to a decrease in the number of educational psychologists available and, consequently, in the number of referrals made
- the 1993 and 1997 Education Acts that emphasise the need to deal with all special educational needs children in mainstream schools
- the fact that, as society changes, the tacitly accepted rules in schools will also need to change.

Knowledge is the key. A lack of information detailing the background and needs of the pupil and the school discipline policy will result in inevitable difficulties.

> Far better for the student or teacher to learn everything possible about the children and the school as quickly as possible, and to show firm action and calm resolve in the face of the children's assaults upon his or her composure.
>
> (Fontana 1994: 59)

Teachers should not feel isolated when dealing with a difficult pupil or class, but should be able to discuss the problem in a professional manner with senior managers. In practice, senior teachers need to set up support structures for teachers with a particular class problem. Meetings to discuss details and preventative action will require planning. A senior teacher will need to collect information from colleagues to establish:

- who are the main problem pupils?
- is their behaviour a problem across all areas of the curriculum?
- what behaviour is causing the problem?
- what strategies have been successful in overcoming behavioural problems?

A meeting with all teachers concerned will help identify the problem and will also enhance their self-esteem. At the meeting, senior managers may have to deal with the anger and frustration of their colleagues. As with middle managers, personal integrity is very important: 'If the leader misleads, mistreats or misrepresents his or her colleagues in any serious way, he or she forfeits trust, respect and, in extreme cases, collaboration' (Holmes 1993: 104).

A useful approach to good practice is to keep the organisational aspects of school life as simple and straightforward as possible. The more complex the structure, the more complex the management processes required to maintain the organisation. All members of the school community should know what they should be doing.

Schools affect student behaviour and learning by their academic and social practices. As discussed in Chapter 4, structures that allow genuine opportunities for staff to contribute to and make decisions should be in place. Good practices will be nurtured by a collegial support framework.

The management of discipline in schools requires that effective communication systems should be established by senior managers in schools. Staff, parents and pupils need to know about matters that directly affect them. As detailed in Chapter 4, communication depends on the kind of processes set up, formal and informal. Senior managers need to consider:

- how are staff informed and consulted on major issues?
- how are staff meetings run?
- how much opportunity is there for staff, parent or student input in key areas such as curriculum, discipline and welfare?

It is axiomatic that school support networks and good communication will alleviate teacher stress. All practitioners benefit from encouragement and support. Acknowledgement of roles and contributions to the school as a whole encourages teachers to work more effectively and feel stronger socially. There should be a recognition of the good things teachers do. People work and behave better when they are well looked after and feel that those in charge understand and respond to their personal needs. Teachers feel secure if they believe that the headteacher is interested in their work and ready to provide support.

Meetings

Meaningless meetings that repeat processes and do not communicate essential information to teachers are a waste of valuable time in schools. Meetings need to be structured to ensure that relevant information pertinent to educational practice is given to all relevant members of the school community. As detailed in Chapter 4, meetings that focus on disciplinary matters should be recorded in detail and information/action points passed on to the necessary people. A professional approach to meetings will ensure that outcomes (decisions or actions) will be reached in a collaborative manner. Peer support will need to be built into meetings. Senior management in schools can help by adopting the following strategies:

- multi-agency meetings to discuss/share issues of concern, especially about discipline policy and difficult students
- cross-curricular meetings that focus on meeting pupil needs
- team-teaching opportunities that involve observation, monitoring, and evaluation of teaching and learning styles
- use of staff meeting times in small task analysis groups that have a specific problem to address and resolve
- staff-forum times to discuss policy-related issues
- invitations to set up inclusive, collaborative support groupings across the school.

When determining who should attend meetings, senior managers should consider:

- what is the purpose/function of the meeting?
- what are we trying to do?
- who needs to know?
- who needs to participate in any decision-making and/or planning activities?
- how will the meeting be valued, both by those attending, and those not attending?
- what will the outcome be?
- how will information be disseminated?
- who will report (when necessary) relevant information to pupils and parents?
- who will collate responses?
- where/when will the next meeting be convened?

Open-management

A good headteacher will be democratic when deciding on which methods are required to promote discipline in school. An effective headteacher ensures that everyone in the school community feels responsible for ensuring that discipline in the school is good. In essence, effective leadership is marked by a non-confrontational style, where decisiveness is combined with the ability to delegate, listen, enthuse, support and unite the team of staff (Rogers 1996: 31). Headteachers need to be listeners, and teachers and pupils should feel able to talk to them in confidence. Headteachers will aim to discuss discipline periodically with staff, pupils and the wider school community, emphasising the need for every person to keep the school functioning smoothly and to keep morale at a high level.

The continuous professional development of staff, teaching and non-teaching, is also the responsibility of headteachers and their senior managers. Staff should feel able to discuss the development of their knowledge and understanding, skills and abilities within the national standards set by the Teacher Training Agency. Discipline and the management of pupil behaviour are key elements in the training and education of future school managers and leaders, and headteachers need to be aware of these initiatives. A newly qualified teacher is a major responsibility of the headteacher. A clear discipline policy and supportive management is required to motivate and develop professional practice throughout a teacher's career.

GOVERNORS

In the 1980 Education Act, central government legislated that all schools must have their own governing bodies, including elected parent governors and elected teacher governors. The 1986 Education Act determined the type and number of governors according to the size and status of the school.

The 1997 White Paper, *Framework for the Organisation of Schools* (DfEE 1997b) stated that all governing bodies of maintained and foundation schools are to include representatives of the LEA, parents, teachers and representatives from the local community. Governors have specific responsibilities relating to attendance, and the exclusion of pupils for inappropriate behaviour (see Chapter 2). Governors and headteachers should also agree a discipline policy for their school (see Chapter 10). Teachers should be notified of all governors' meetings and consult with their representative on matters related to discipline.

There are too many pupils excluded from school and this contributes to higher incidences of crime. Exclusions have quadrupled since 1990. The government-commissioned report *Misspent Youth: Young People and Crime* (Perfect and Renshaw 1997) stated that there had been nearly fourteen thousand pupils permanently excluded from school in 1995/96. Many explanations have been offered for this deterioration, including the growing strain on children's family relationships, parents' inability to control their children and the increased pressure on schools to get rid of pupils whose presence adversely affects their reputation or their position in the league tables. The most common reasons for exclusions are:

- verbal abuse to staff

- violence to other pupils
- persistent breaking of school rules
- disruption
- criminal offences, usually theft or substance abuse.

Senior managers have to consider the consequences of excluding such a large number of pupils from school. Effective discipline policies, procedures and practices are considered by teacher unions to be the solution. Behaviour support plans are an effective multi-agency approach to support good discipline at a local level (see Chapter 9).

MIDDLE MANAGERS

The culture of school management is changing from a top-down hierarchical model to a flatter structure, which involves the majority of staff in the management of their school. Middle managers with responsibility allowances will manage a range of teams including:

- subject teams
- year/pastoral teams
- curriculum/faculty/department teams
- Key Stage teams.

A middle manager is required to have knowledge and understanding of whole-school issues. These are determined by central government, LEAs, senior management teams and governors. There are also other agencies involved in the daily management of the school: education welfare officers, educational psychologists, crisis support groups and independent consultants. A middle manager should know who these people are, how frequently they visit the school and their roles and responsibilities in relation to pupils.

Middle managers have to be able to identify the different influences on their job. The structure of the school as an organisation should give a clear view of their position within the management system. They should also be aware of their responsibilities in relation to pupils and teachers. Essentially, middle managers are responsible for:

- the implementation of school-wide strategies, structures and intentions. In this process, middle managers 'fine tune' strategies to suit the real world
- being role models for their staff. A middle manager's daily behaviour must represent the people-centred culture of the school as an organisation
- the passing on of practices which are learnt as a consequence of operational wisdom.

Pastoral care

Pastoral care permeates every aspect of school life. There should not be a conflict between the pastoral and academic domains in educational practice. The management of discipline in schools is fundamental to both pupil welfare, and teaching and learning. However the pastoral domain is not straightforward. Complexities and conflict may arise (Calvert and Henderson 1995: 71–2) because of:

- a lack of shared understanding and agreement as to the purpose and nature of pastoral provision
- the existence of an academic/pastoral divide with an overemphasis on academic results
- pressures of an overcrowded curriculum, limited resources for pastoral matters
- high level of stress in teaching, lack of time to provide support for colleagues
- a lack of consensus as to the aims, nature, content, skills and processes of the pastoral curriculum
- a lack of clarity of management roles
- inappropriate management structures
- difficulties in monitoring and evaluating the impact of pastoral management on the school community
- lack of support for pastoral care in education at national level.

Middle managers are responsible for maintaining good order and discipline within their areas of responsibility. The focus of a middle manager's work should be supporting teachers and pupils in the process of teaching and learning. Middle managers have a responsibility to inform their staff on the content of the school discipline policy and to ensure that all members of their teams are able to implement the policy.

Middle managers should be able to provide support to members of their team who are experiencing difficulties with a disruptive individual or class. As shown in the previous section, middle managers must be able to listen effectively to both pupils and colleagues. Holmes (1993) commented that 'maintaining a healthy professional community while focusing on learning can create its own conflict'. The job of a middle manager will always have problems and dilemmas. When managing discipline, it is important to resolve difficulties as they arise, remembering the advice given to teachers in Chapter 6. Courage, in measured doses, is required to deal with situations in a non-confrontational manner. How middle managers approach such situations often reflects their personal integrity. Middle managers are constantly watched by colleagues, and personal integrity is therefore very important.

PUPILS

School management should relate directly to pupils. Managers and teachers need to reflect on how pupils respond to the pressures placed on them by their encounters with teachers, managers and external agents.

All pupils should feel safe and secure in the school environment. In general terms, pupils should have access to the best quality education, that promotes equality of opportunity and rejects all forms of discrimination, including that based on disability, colour, gender, religion and ethnic or social origin. Pupils attend school to develop intellectually, physically, morally and socially. Fundamental to this process is the development of self-esteem and self-confidence. In practice, pupils have a right to skilled care and treatment, individual respect, and to be treated with dignity and fairness. Pupils should also be treated in a way that is appropriate for their age and be free from all forms of abuse.

More specifically, in terms of discipline pupils need to know and understand the rules and boundaries for their behaviour. If appropriate, they should also participate in the process of agreeing the rules and boundaries. Learning in the classroom requires an active commitment from pupils to participate in lessons; without this problems will occur. In essence, there needs to be a working relationship established between pupils, teachers and external agencies. Collaboration is the key: policies work when and if everyone has their opinion considered. From a pupil's perspective, discipline policies and codes of practice should be:

- consistent and genuine
- discussed and agreed by all parties
- practical, in that they should help people work together for the benefit of the school community
- re-negotiated and changed if they are not working effectively.

It would be wholly incorrect to focus the school discipline policy on the minority of pupils who appear to take up the majority of senior management time. As shown in Chapter 2, government legislation has produced a framework for practice relating to those pupils with emotional and behavioural difficulties. For various reasons, not all pupils who require additional support in the classroom will be provided with the necessary statement to release the funding needed to engage support staff. Obviously, one factor limiting the number of pupils receiving help is the time taken to complete multi-agency forms and procedures. Experience shows that many pupils excluded from school have not been afforded the appropriate support available within the educational system. This will be discussed in more detail later in this chapter.

For those pupils who disrupt lessons, by bullying, fighting or being generally abusive in some way, the sequence of events that follows their misdemeanour can be both ineffective and frightening. The sequence described in Figure 5.1 could be applicable to most state schools at any phase.

1 Disruption involving a pupil and *teacher*.
2 Pupil is sent to the *subject coordinator* and receives a verbal warning.
3 Pupil returns to the class, to be reprimanded a second time and isolated from peers.
4 Pupil repeats disruptive behaviour and is sent to the *head of year* for persistent bad behaviour receiving a second verbal warning.
5 *Subject teacher, head of year* and *subject coordinator* discuss the pupil's behaviour in the staff room. They report the two incidents to the *head of faculty/key stage coordinator.*
6 During the following lesson with the same teacher the pupil continues to be disruptive and is sent to the *head of faculty/key stage coordinator*, remaining there for the remainder of the lesson.
7 A report is written by the head of faculty/key stage coordinator and sent to *deputy headteacher/pastoral coordinator.*
8 The pupil is summoned to explain his/her actions to the *deputy headteacher/pastoral coordinator*. As this is now two days after the incident, the pupil becomes frustrated by an inability to remember what had happened and loses his/her temper.
9 The parents are 'phoned and invited to a meeting to discuss their child's behaviour.
10 A meeting is convened with the pupil, *class teacher, head of year, head of faculty* and *deputy headteacher*. Various accounts are given by staff, while the parents and the pupil sit and listen.
11 Headteacher excludes the pupil for uncontrollable behaviour.

Figure 5.1 Disruptive pupil – sequence of events

Consider that at no point was the pupil asked his/her account of what had happened, only why it happened. The 'system' took over and the pupil was removed, albeit temporarily. The pupil had learnt that following an outburst in the classroom it is best to say nothing and let teachers decide that non-attendance is the solution to his/her disruptive behaviour. This example is an extreme case that occurred in a large primary school in the centre of a major city in the centre of England. Critically, the teachers were following the school's discipline policy.

Much is to be learnt from pupils of the confusing, and apparently meaningless, procedures that are followed when disruptions occur in schools. Adults often fail to consider the consequences of their actions on a young person's self-esteem and self-confidence.

6

CLASSROOM MANAGEMENT

A child has only one opportunity to receive compulsory education. Schools have a responsibility to ensure that they provide an effective curriculum delivered in a safe and secure environment. Any behaviour that challenges a child's ability to learn should be managed. Teachers and pupils need support systems to deal with difficulties with discipline. Equally, all teachers and pupils need to recognise the significance of their role within the school community. All members of the school community should feel respected, safe and able to participate in the daily routine of school life.

Teachers are contracted to teach; in order to do so they must be able to manage their classrooms. Their ability to maintain discipline will impact directly on their ability to teach. Teachers should have the necessary knowledge and understanding of managing pupil behaviour before they enter the profession. When teachers require expert support and advice, this should be provided by a highly qualified and effective team of professional agencies. Communication is critical, as teachers need to know what is available to help them manage their classrooms effectively.

There are aspects of the culture of the teaching profession that militate against teachers being able to teach in an effective manner. Teachers are often wary of admitting that they have a difficulty with a particular class or pupil. This leads to tensions and pressure on all concerned. Teachers must be able to seek guidance and support when faced with the intolerable problem of disruptive behaviour in their classrooms. As professionals, teachers need to be able to discuss such problems with their colleagues and managers in an open, confident way. Fear of 'owning up' to a problem with discipline often leads teachers to experience severe stress that causes inevitable damage to their health.

Classroom teachers need to manage discipline in a caring, confident manner. They also need to be managed in a caring, confident manner. This chapter focuses on the stresses caused by indiscipline in the classroom and provides practitioners with positive mechanisms for dealing with disruptive behaviour. Aspects of teaching and learning styles and curriculum development are also examined. The need for all pupils to learn and all teachers to teach is emphasised throughout each section. Pupils need to attend schools, be respected, learn and become valued members of society. Classroom management provides teachers with the ability to create an environment whereby effective teaching can happen.

STRESS

A disruptive class or pupil will create stress for teachers, managers and other pupils. Rutter *et al.* (1979) noted that children exposed to multiple stresses were more likely to display unacceptable behaviour patterns than children exposed to isolated stresses. The same principle applies when determining the degree of stress teachers experience from disruptive behaviour.

A disruptive pupil is a reality that needs to be recognised by teachers within the context of teaching and learning (Galloway *et al.* 1982). If a teacher's energy in the classroom is focused on a pupil's, or group of pupils', indiscipline, teaching and learning will not occur. Pupils whose behaviour is continually disruptive need to be managed by support agencies, not by teachers who are unable to provide the necessary guidance and support to deal with individual problems.

Daily stress-inducing problems that confront the majority of teachers are often more to do with trivial, regular incidents of misbehaviour (Docking 1980). Seemingly unimportant events such as talking out of turn and general inattentiveness can create as much stress in a teacher's life as isolated incidents of violence and verbal abuse. The problem of indiscipline is further compounded by teachers' lack of training. Teachers do not have the mechanisms and tools to deal with disruptive behaviour in their classrooms. Rogers found that teacher stress is caused by pupil:

- resistance to teacher direction
- argumentativeness or procrastination
- defiance [and general] disregard of the teacher's role
- frequent 'lower-level' . . . behaviours such as calling out and talking.

(Rogers 1996: 4)

A teacher's capacity to address the challenges of disruptive behaviour will depend on self-esteem, training, knowledge and understanding, and skills and abilities. The ability to maintain an orderly, disciplined classroom environment is essential if teaching and learning are to occur. Any disruption will be stress-inducing for teachers and pupils alike. The daily demands on teachers are potential sources of stress. The level of support available from peers and other agencies will lessen stress and improve a teacher's potential to overcome the problem. Senior managers have a central role in the management of discipline and the management of stress.

Teachers need to know that they are supported by their peers and managers, even at the most trying times. The tendency to stay out of colleagues' classrooms and not to talk about discipline problems is ill-advised. The tradition of classroom isolation that persists in many schools places a barrier between teachers and colleagues. Teachers who do not seek help because they believe that a problem with discipline is an admission of incompetence will also fail to offer assistance, as this may feel like accusing a colleague of incompetence (DES 1989: 69).

As part of its remit, the Elton Committee (DES 1989) commissioned a survey into discipline in schools. Researchers from the University of Sheffield found that classes in primary and secondary schools were disrupted by a variety of behaviours, as Table 6.1 illustrates.

The manner in which teachers treat members of the school community will reflect their feelings about themselves. Pupils need to recognise self-esteem in their teachers if they are to develop a healthy self-concept (Rogers 1996: 5). Cleugh (1971) and Dunham (1992) found many factors that impact on the morale of teachers:

- public respect for the profession
- salary
- promotion and incremental rewards
- stability – redundancy and pension
- absenteeism
- senior management
- pupil behaviour

Table 6.1 Classroom disruption

	Frequency during lessons	
Type of pupil behaviour	*Weekly %*	*Daily %*
Talking out of turn	97	53
Idleness or work avoidance	87	25
Hindering other pupils	86	26
Unpunctuality	82	17
Unnecessary noise	77	25
Breaking school rules	68	17
Out-of-seat behaviour	62	14
Verbal abuse of other pupils	62	10
General rowdiness	61	10
Cheeky or impertinent remarks	58	10
Physical aggression – pupil	42	6
Verbal abuse of teacher	15	1
Physical destructiveness	14	1
Physical aggression – teacher	1.7	0

Source: Adapted from Elton Report (DES 1989: 224)

- school environment
- staff facilities
- level of support (perceived and otherwise)
- lack of resources.

All of the above are relevant and teachers are justified in their belief that morale amongst the profession needs a boost. However, teachers should not rely on others to create a feeling of self-worth.

> If teachers are going to give some strength to their self-concepts, . . . they will need to learn to balance the messages that:
>
> - they give to themselves
> - they give to others
> - they receive from others.
>
> (Rogers 1996: 5)

It is axiomatic that teachers with high self-esteem feel better and work more effectively. They have a positive sense of identity, security and belonging and, as a consequence, are able to deal with stress more effectively than those with low self-esteem. Teachers need to recognise that making unrealistic demands creates stress for others. They must also recognise when to ask for support and feel confident that support will be given.

STRESS MANAGEMENT

Teachers are exposed to many difficulties in their working life, and are constantly challenged within the workplace. However, challenges are on a continuum from excitement to excessive tiredness as shown in Figure 6.1.

A teacher's ability to monitor and evaluate is critical. Individuals should know their energy levels. If a challenge cannot be met and creates energy loss, inevitably

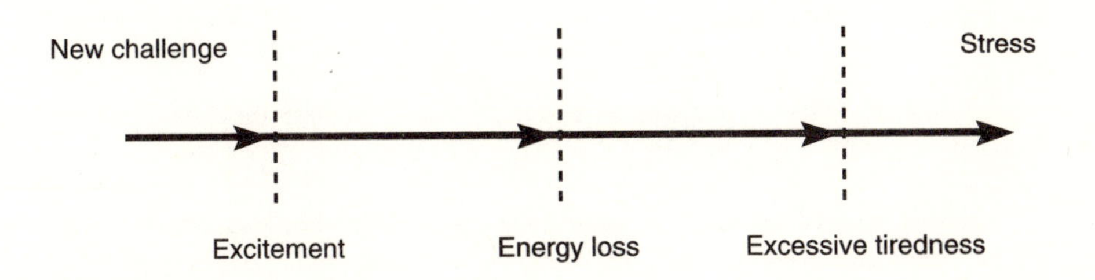

Figure 6.1 Stress levels

Source: Blandford 1997a: Figure 2.4

stress will occur. The consequences of stress can be debilitating. Stress can be exhibited in many ways, for example, irritability, tiredness, excessive drinking, depression. Teachers should be aware of stress in the workplace; it is important to identify and support those who find work stressful. Good relationships will lead to good practice. Identification of a problem in a culture of trust will enable an early resolution. Lengthy processes and negotiations will only lead to stress for all involved. It is also important to acknowledge personal stress levels.

Stress can be overcome if the imbalances that exist are redressed e.g., increase low energy levels. Teachers must look after their own welfare, and remain in control. Control may also mean evaluating how time is used, ensuring that no one activity makes excessive demands. Monitoring and evaluation are examined in more detail later in Chapter 10. More specifically, a model of stress levels as shown in Figure 6.2 will serve to illustrate the effect of stress in a teacher's working life.

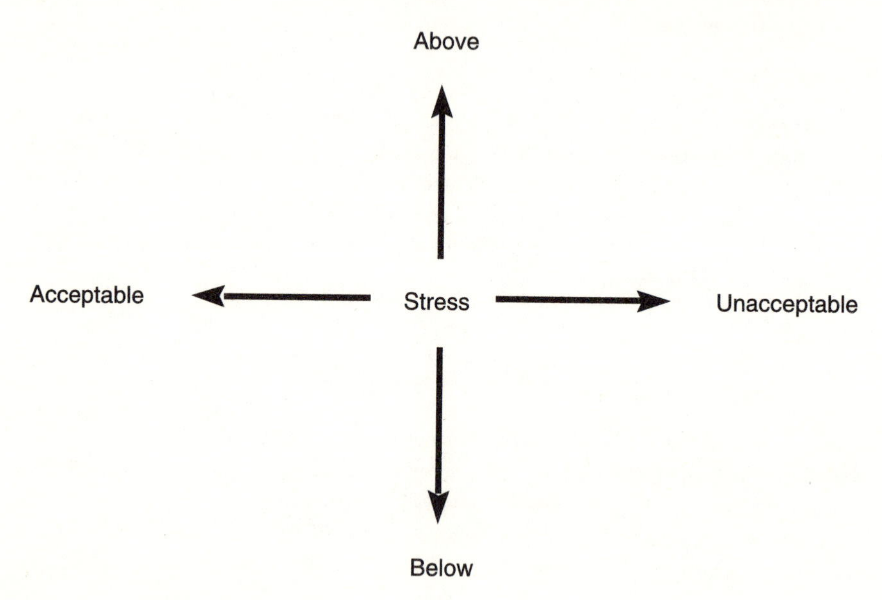

Figure 6.2 A model of stress levels

Source: Blandford 1997a: Figure 2.5

The following levels relevant to teachers' lives are described by Lifeskills Associates (1995):

> *Optimum level*: When teachers are at their optimum level they are likely to be alert and self-confident. In practice, they will think and respond quickly, perform well, feel well and be enthusiastic, interested and involved in the task which they will carry out in an energetic, easy manner.

Overstressed: Alternatively, when teachers are overstressed they are likely to have feelings of anxiety and mental confusion. In this condition they will not think effectively or solve problems clearly or objectively. They will forget instructions, and be inclined to panic. Physically, there will be symptoms such as increased heart rate and blood pressure, excessive perspiration, churning stomach and indigestion. In addition, coordination will be impaired and reflexes slowed.

Understressed: If teachers are understressed they are likely to experience a lack of interest or enthusiasm for the task. They can have feelings of futility or depression, and believe that nothing matters any more – even a simple job can seem a huge task. They will be bored and lacking in energy. To them the world will look drab and grey and it will be hard to summon up energy to start new jobs or create fresh interests.

In her Times Educational Supplement (TES) review of *What Really Stresses Teachers* (1996), Emma Burstall highlighted the following causes of stress in teachers:

WORK	HOME
Lack of time to do the job	Worries about own children
Lack of parental support	Worries about elderly parents
Lack of resources	Lack of time with family
National curriculum/ irrelevant paperwork	Untidiness of others
Rate of change	Family illnesses
Lack of LEA support	Housework
Poor status of profession	Guilt over not meeting all family's demands
Staff relationships	In-laws
Government interference	Having to take work home
Pressure of meetings	Lack of private space

Having identified the causes, a teacher should then attempt to manage stress. Brown and Ralph (1995: 95–105) offer the following advice:

> *Examining beliefs and expectation*: are these realistic and achievable? Is there a need to set more attainable goals?
>
> *Time management*: can time be used more effectively? Techniques such as prioritisation, delegation and objective-setting can be considered.
>
> *Assertion*: learning how to communicate more confidently at all levels and to deal positively with conflict.
>
> *Communication*: looking at patterns of interpersonal communication and self presentation skills.

Relaxation techniques of all kinds, such as physical exercise, meditation, yoga, aromatherapy, and collection of bio-data.

Support networks: it is important to build and maintain support networks of family, friends and colleagues, both within and outside schools.

Brown and Ralph also indicate the importance of how the school as an organisation can help teachers to address the problem of stress. They suggest a variety of ways in which middle and senior managers can approach this issue:

- Helping to *de-stigmatise* the idea of stress by putting it on the agenda for discussion.
- Encouraging the establishment of *self-help groups* to explore group problem solving of school stress factors and to develop appropriate solutions where possible.
- Developing an *empathetic ethos* and offering support for self-help management techniques.
- Identifying and liaising with *people who can help* within the local education authority and other relevant organisations.
- Drawing up a school action plan after school-wide staff consultation.
- Providing *appropriate staff development*, either within the school or at an outside venue.
- Making available information about *counselling services* and encouraging staff to use them where necessary.

In sum, Brown and Ralph found that teachers are unable to destigmatise stress and that organisational needs must be met before personal needs. Change issues also emerge as a significant factor in contributing to stress levels in schools.

Brown and Ralph (1995: 105) conclude that teachers 'need to recognise and analyse openly for themselves, signs [of] stress at work'. They emphasise the need for an organisational approach to the management of stress. In particular, 'teachers need to be reassured that they will not lose professional esteem or promotional opportunities by admitting to stress'.

Control, internal and external, is linked directly to stress. Individuals who believe that their lives are generally within their control (internal control) are less likely to experience high levels of stress than those who believe that their lives are generally outside of their control. The latter believe in external control – attributing events in their lives to luck, fate, people with power, or the unpredictable (Kyriacou 1981). The extent to which teachers manage stress is determined by how much they feel in control. Teachers must also acknowledge that there are many situations in life and within their profession over which they will have no direct control. In essence, a teacher can have negotiated control in school, never absolute control.

There is no doubt that pupils of all ages have a gift for 'detecting inadequacies in a teacher, and once detected, these inadequacies are likely to be used as a way of enlivening lessons' (Fontana 1994: 53). In practice, there is no easy option; children will find a way of demonstrating the power that they are able to wield over whoever represents authority. A teacher's ability to control pupils individually or *en masse* is at the heart of teaching.

In practice, the greater the teacher's level of control in the classroom, the greater the opportunities for involving pupils in the management of the classroom. Critically, the greater the level of control, the greater the opportunities for 'initiating and sustaining learning activities' (Fontana 1994: 3). Teachers need to know what is going on in their classrooms. Teachers also need to be able to create an effective climate in their classrooms. Getting a class quiet is central to starting to teach. Teachers should be able to prevent disruption in their classrooms by recognising the special behaviours of the groups within the classes they teach, and responding to them in an appropriate manner. The aim of control is to work towards a situation in which outward manifestations of control become less and less necessary. This kind of classroom control is based on the teacher's understanding of children's behaviour and their understanding of their own behaviour.

> Many of the forces originate from the teachers themselves. . . . Even when it is clear that a particular behaviour problem within the class is a direct consequence of the children themselves, teachers still need to look closely at their own response to this problem . . . self-examination by teachers of their own professional behaviours must not be attended by deep feelings of guilt or inadequacy.
>
> (Fontana 1994: 4–5)

ANGER

People respond to stress in different ways. Teachers should not lose their temper or show obvious signs of anger, unless anger is used for a strategic purpose (Comber and Whitfield 1978). Inevitably, teachers' responses to pupil behaviour have to be flexible, and strategies need to be planned to meet a variety of outcomes. As Rogers (1996: 42) comments 'anger as an emotion is not itself bad. But it is an emotion, and all emotions need some guidance'. Teachers need to plan for anger. The management of discipline within the school and classroom will be dependent on how successfully teachers evaluate the many variables in any situation, and study the effects of their own responses to each situation. Anger is, generally, a spontaneous reaction based on assumptions, prejudices or beliefs as to what individuals consider should be happening. Teachers need to develop the necessary objectivity and precision in dealing with their needs and the problems they sometimes generate.

Rogers (1996: 41) advises that teachers can learn to control their anger. They should:

- learn to perceive what is happening in anger-rousing situations, then aim to choose to get angry in a productive, pleasant way
- develop a plan to enable management of the situation, that which is awful and terrible can become annoying, disturbing and manageable
- act from the plan; consciously stand in a relaxed manner, focus on making feelings clear in a clear manner. Teachers must remember that they cannot be physically hurt by what pupils say or how they say it
- when unable to control anger, withdraw from the situation, state clearly why
- apologise; keep the apology clear, plan to get angry more effectively next time
- the goal in any anger inducing situation should be the workable resolution of the conflict.

Essentially, teachers must avoid reinforcing the behaviour problems that they are setting out to resolve. Teachers must be aware of the degree to which they influence many of the consequences of their pupils' behaviour. Individual teachers must decide which behaviours are required within the framework of the school discipline policy. All teachers have to personalise the approaches used to coincide with their beliefs and values with regard to influencing children's behaviour.

SUPPORT

Teacher and pupil behaviour is highly visible in, and beyond, the classroom. A teacher is at the centre of a number of people's expectations: parents, colleagues, headteacher, governors, LEA, central government, and pupils. When each agency is in agreement, a teacher will feel supported. When disagreement exists, a teacher will feel under pressure. When and if teachers fail to maintain an acceptable level of discipline in the classroom, they should feel confident in the support that they will be afforded by the relevant agencies. Rogers (1996) believes that failure should be considered as both an opportunity and danger; teachers should be able to fail meaningfully by redirecting emotional energy into the future. Teachers should be able to seek support. A supportive school environment legitimises natural failure and is tolerant of mistakes. No problem is so intractable that it cannot be talked through and something done about it.

A supportive environment is both formal and informal. The level of social support available in a school is a factor in alleviating stress. Teachers need to feel safe and secure in the workplace. In some schools, teachers and pupils label each other, adopting partial and limited views of each other. Such stereotypes are unhealthy and unprofessional. The passing on of inappropriate comments about pupils and colleagues in discussions and formal meetings devalues the quality of the school community.

Teachers should be confident in stating where there is a problem. Peer support is essential to good practice. Teachers cannot be effective if they work in isolation from their colleagues within the profession. All teachers need to know and understand the existence and nature of the support agencies available to them. They must also learn from good practice. A professional, supportive team will do much to enhance the status and confidence of the teacher in the classroom. Hargreaves (1984: 4) found that classroom misconduct does not stem entirely from teachers' poor management skills, but 'can and does arise from the failure to approach the central business of teaching and learning from the right perspective'.

Schools should have a discipline policy that will provide a framework for practice in the classroom. A discipline plan is needed in a supportive school environment, Rogers (1996: 47) commented that 'it is the corporate quality of classroom life that also determines the quality of a school as a whole'. The examination and evaluation of a classroom situation (or incident) can, and should, be positive. A team approach to particular events will take the immediate pressure off the individual teacher, who would otherwise be seen as the only influence in the classroom. This will also help teachers to develop different strategies for achieving classroom goals. Teachers will gain much from being able to communicate the complexity of the classroom to a wider audience.

In a culture of peer support, teachers should be able to reduce occupational stress through:

- development of discipline and management skills
- occupational and environmental support
- time management
- development of personal coping strategies.

Essentially, teachers need to know that they are not isolated and that their problems with disruptive behaviour will be resolved in a professional manner. Support agencies need to recognise that teachers are able to talk about disruption in an objective way, and that they are occasionally unsure about what to do and what not to do to correct disruptive behaviour. Internal and external agencies need to understand that teachers have very busy professional lives; they do not always have the time to create relationships within the profession in order to solve problems. Support agencies need to have a high profile within the schools they serve. In essence, teacher morale can be lifted by the involvement of support agencies with the skills to resolve discipline problems.

THE TEACHER

A complex issue in the context of managing discipline in schools is the personality of the teacher. Some teachers have little difficulty in controlling a class because of the qualities they have as people (Fontana 1994: 52). The way in which teachers talk to members of the school community is important. Teachers need to have an interest in and liking for pupils and their colleagues. Teachers must have advanced listening and evaluation skills.

It is inevitable that communicating with people in a curt and dismissive manner is inappropriate, and will result in a negative dismissive response. A teacher must relate appropriately to the individual pupil, class and colleague.

Teachers need to feel confident in their ability to govern themselves (Rogers 1996: 16). Any outward manifestations of uncontrolled, irrational behaviour are likely to result in an uncontrolled irrational response. Dysfunctional actions do not alleviate stress, nor do they resolve discipline problems. At a personal level teachers need to consider:

- the way in which they characteristically perceive, and reflect on, stressful events such as discipline problems
- their reactions and responses, and appropriateness of actions
- the skills required to minimise stress and achieve a positive, negotiated resolution to the problem
- the organisation of time, the classroom and self.

Where there are aspects of a teacher's personality that require change, this should be approached in a sensitive and caring manner. A range of issues that influence the degree to which a teacher is able to exercise the necessary class control may include (Fontana 1994: 52):

- appearance – dress or hairstyle
- annoying habit or gesture, for example pacing up and down
- speaking too loudly or softly, punctuating speech with errs or umms
- lack of knowledge about subject
- lack of teaching experience
- lack of training focused on pupils with emotional and behavioural difficulties.

PUPIL MANAGEMENT

In some schools, pupils are labelled failures through policy or practice. The process of labelling will, inevitably, result in the label becoming a reality. Very few pupils are in a position to ignore the label attributed to them by adults. Teachers must know and understand the contribution they make to pupils' development – beyond the subject and beyond the classroom. The significance of the interaction between pupils and teachers cannot be overstated. Teachers do make a difference to pupils' lives.

Pupils have sophisticated mechanisms for responding to individual teachers in schools. In the management of discipline, consistency is the key. However teachers' responses to pupil behaviour have to be flexible to meet individual needs; strategies need to be planned with colleagues to set boundaries and to meet a variety of outcomes. Teachers must be able to respond to each situation very quickly; appraisal and decision-making is rapid. Professional reflection on practice will take place at less busy times, unless strategies can be developed to enable this to happen.

Teachers need to monitor the events in their classrooms: learning, behaviour and social interactions. There is skill in monitoring more than one activity, just as there is a skill in choosing which to respond to and which to ignore: in practice, teachers must be able to accommodate the unpredictable. They should have the ability to set up routines that will provide structure to the day but which do not become restrictive or limiting.

Varying expectations by teachers of pupils in the same class, or from lesson to lesson, will generate insecurity and lead to disruptive behaviour. Experience suggests that many pupils have legitimate complaints when they are singled out and punished. Pupils dislike the following traits in teachers (Reid 1989; Dunham 1992; Rogers 1996):

- those who are inhuman, interpreting their role too literally, exerting power unnecessarily
- those who treat pupils anonymously, not as individuals
- those who are soft and/or inconsistent
- those who do not teach to goals, forcing pupils to underperform or underachieve
- those who barter for good classroom order
- those who are unfair, making unreasonable demands on pupils
- those who are insensitive to pupils with illness or learning problems
- those who bully or hold a grudge based on past misdemeanours
- those who do not listen.

If pupils consider their teacher to have all or some of the above traits, it is likely that they will manifest their unhappiness by disrupting lessons. Schools with a high number of disaffected pupils should examine their own practice.

Listening

It is important for all pupils to develop a positive sense of identity. There is no substitute for listening to pupils. While all pupils have the right to be educated, this can only happen if adults help them to participate in the process.

When listening, it is important to take the views of pupils seriously. Teachers and managers should not underestimate a young person's feelings of fear and confusion. All pupils need to be helped to develop a sense of personal responsibility. This is more likely to be achieved through mutual respect and trust, rather than control. The many points to consider when listening to a pupil with problems include:

- do not criticise
- do not be judgemental or negative about the pupil's views
- be aware that the pupil probably has divided loyalties: peers, parents, teachers, and so on
- value a pupil's need to be educated; exclusion, temporary or permanent, is not a solution
- let pupils bring up issues in their own time
- allow pupils sufficient time to make important decisions, check that they really mean what they say
- be an advocate and supporter, do not control
- do not attribute blame
- recognise that pupils have a right to expect discipline and security.

Sanctions and rewards

Behaviour that is rewarded tends to be repeated. In the classroom this basic principle has been expressed under various names including: positive feedback, reinforcement, operant conditioning, behaviour modification and assertive discipline. This approach requires teachers to have a strategy that focuses on pupils' here-and-now actions, with only those behaviours that can be seen and recorded objectively used in managing discipline. To focus on the positive aspects of professional practice will be far more rewarding for teachers than focusing on punishments and threats. There is a contradiction between engaging pupils in the process of learning and threatening to punish them if disaffected or disruptive.

In practice, a teacher must use rewards and praise and, if necessary, punishments and threats. Teachers must be realistic in their expectations of the class and individuals, and place more emphasis on rewards and encouragement than on blame and accusations. Teachers must be ready to learn from colleagues and pupils; they must be receptive to changing situations and new ideas. Above all else, a teacher must be fair and consistent. Newly qualified teachers must not be daunted by initial difficulties, since all teachers are apprehensive at the point of meeting a class for the first time.

The mechanisms used for managing discipline should be determined by the school discipline policy. In essence these will involve (Sarason *et al.* 1972: 10–12):

> *Positive reinforcers:* including smiles, verbal approval, tangible rewards, earned points, commendations, and the appreciation of peers and teachers. The only way a teacher knows whether a reinforcer is positive is to observe its effects on the behaviour that follows; a positive reinforcer is intended to encourage productive behaviour.
>
> *Negative reinforcers:* may be used to deal with unproductive behaviour. The problem with punishment is that, while it may reduce the limit of the questionable behaviour, it does not necessarily create produc-

tive results. Punishment can be a double-edged sword because of pupils' desire for attention. Pupils may become heroes to their peers for being reprimanded in class.

Whether positive or negative, the more promptly reinforcement occurs, the more effective it will be. Alternative strategies may be adopted, as appropriate:

Shaping: as a means of modifying behaviour. Teachers may choose to focus on a specific behaviour or aspect of behaviour in order to develop a pupil's ability to improve. For example, a child who may not be able to concentrate for the duration of a lesson may be encouraged to focus on the introductory session.

Extinction: whereby a teacher will ignore behaviour that is unproductive with the aim of extinguishing it.

The choice and manner in which a pattern of reinforcement is implemented needs careful consideration by all agencies. Schedules of reinforcement can be developed, so that teachers will know when a behaviour pattern has been learnt or reshaped. Thereafter continual reinforcement may not be necessary.

Good classroom management

Effective teachers work in a consistent manner that will allow pupils to learn, and develop self-esteem and self-confidence.

> Good management allows the children to get a clear picture of what is going on and what is expected of them, and allows them to see more clearly the consistent consequences of their own behaviour, both desirable and undesirable.
>
> (Fontana 1994: 122)

A few basic rules of good classroom management are suggested as follows:

- be punctual
- be well-prepared with appropriate material
- insist on full class cooperation
- be fair to all pupils and colleagues
- use the voice effectively, do not shout
- be alert to what is happening in the classroom/teaching space
- monitor and evaluate what is happening in the classroom
- have clear and well-understood strategies for dealing with crises
- allocate teacher attention fairly
- keep up-to-date with marking, be consistent within the school marking policy
- make sure all promises are kept

- make good use of questions: pupil and teacher-led
- ensure adequate opportunities for practical activities
- use a variety of teaching and learning styles
- wherever practical, delegate routine tasks to pupils
- organise the classroom effectively
- deal with children's problems
- be consistent in the use of positive and negative reinforcers
- conclude the lesson successfully, summarise key points and dismiss the class in an orderly manner.

The majority of the above are also applicable to the management of corridors, play areas, dining rooms and halls.

SCHOOL ENVIRONMENT

The school environment needs careful planning and nurturing. Poor working conditions contribute to poor behaviour, and both cause stress. The senior management team, in consultation with teachers, should create a positive environment conducive to good practice. Display boards and reception areas should reflect the quality of work and variety of accomplishments within the school. All open areas and classrooms should be a celebration of success. Teachers and managers should consider:

- who will see the display?
- for whom is the display intended?
- what will be communicated by the quality of the display and its presentation?
- how involved are all of the pupils?
- should all agencies have access to the display?
- is there a 'house-style' that should be adopted?

A positive environment that is clean and healthy will contribute to a positive atmosphere throughout the school.

The classroom

The term 'classroom' can be misleading when applied to schools. In the majority of schools, very few subjects are taught in a classroom with tables and chairs set out in regimented rows, with a blackboard at the front. A classroom seating plan that is effective is shown in Figure 6.3. The majority of classrooms in primary and secondary schools have their own character as determined by the teacher. There are subjects in the school curriculum that are taught in spaces that are not rooms at all. Classroom must be interpreted as the space in which pupils are taught.

Pupils need the right conditions to work. They must have access to books and

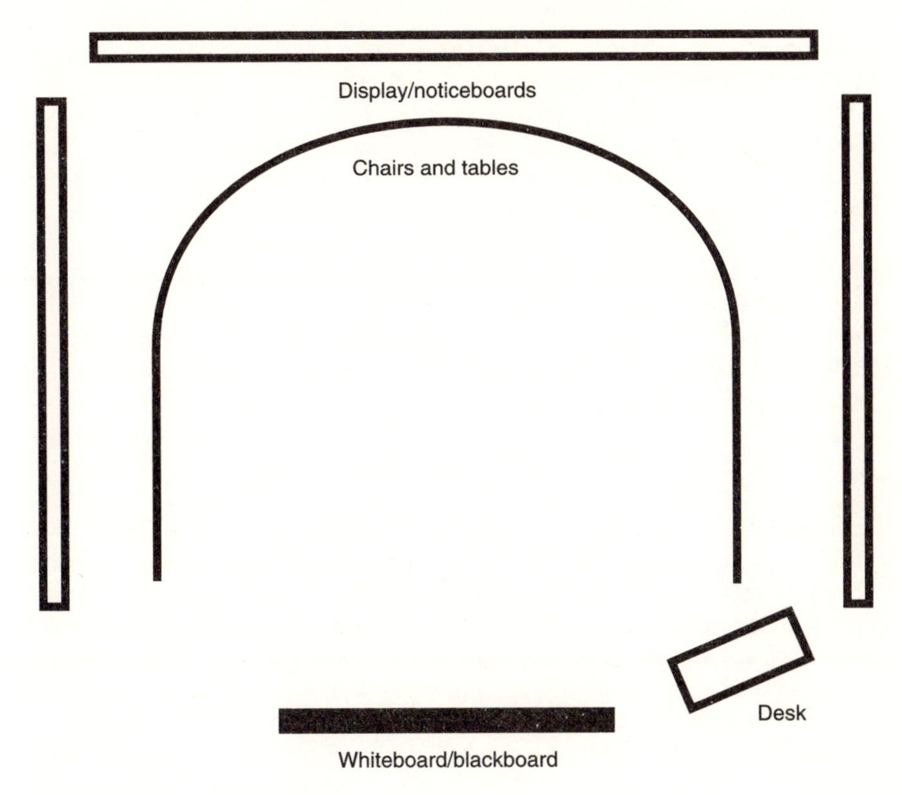

Figure 6.3 Classroom seating plan

equipment. Cramped classrooms are wholly inappropriate. Pupils also need to be able to see what the teacher is demonstrating. The design of the classroom also impacts on teachers. A teacher's personality will need to be considered when classrooms are assigned by management. The strain of working in an inappropriate space will affect the quality of teaching.

In practice, the effect of the physical arrangements of the classroom will impact on discipline. As a resource, classrooms need to be utilised as effectively as possible. Primary school classrooms will need to accommodate sufficient equipment for all national curriculum subjects, and provide ample space for thirty young pupils. The space must be appropriate to the subject and age-group. Teaching music in a room designed for home economics does not inspire the teacher to teach and the pupils to learn. The space must reflect the teaching and learning styles of the teacher and subject. A drama teacher in a studio will have a different approach from that of a science teacher in a laboratory. For drama, the room will require black-out facilities to accommodate lights and storage for costumes and texts. A science laboratory will require benches, chairs, storage areas and a preparation room for the science technician to produce materials for each lesson.

Once in the classroom, pupils should have ready access to all materials and equipment, as required. Pupils should respect classrooms and equipment. They should also be taught to share. Pupils need to know and understand that they are members of a school community that respects its environment.

Having established the parameters within which both pupils and teachers work, there should be as few interruptions as possible to the period of teaching and learning. School notices and other messages should not be sent for delivery during lessons. Classrooms are busy places. Teachers need to be able to control timing effectively and smoothly; effective routines are essential for effective practice.

CURRICULUM

The most effective deterrent to disaffected or disruptive pupils is a well-planned curriculum with relevant activities. A curriculum must be challenging, rewarding and appropriate to pupils' age, ability and intellectual development. A class will be difficult if the curriculum is demeaning or devaluing. A teacher is a skilled manager of a unique environment, a conductor of learning. It is fundamental that teachers should have the ability to plan, select and arrange activities. Planning appropriate activities for pupils is the central skill of teaching.

When assessing the appropriateness of the curriculum, it is important for a teacher to be able to predict pupils' responses to work, pacing of work and all aspects of pupil behaviour. In practice teachers need to be consistent in the specific expectations of their pupils. Within the curriculum framework a teacher should be alert to the content of other subjects and be able to differentiate when necessary. As school management, the curriculum and pupil behaviour have a direct relationship, teachers should think in terms of the whole curriculum and work closely with other schools and colleges for mutual support. The successful management of the curriculum: planning, delivery, monitoring and evaluation, are vital for ensuring a positive response from all pupils. Clearly, all teachers must be committed to teaching and take the education of all pupils seriously.

The essential ingredients of the curriculum, schemes of work and teaching styles, are all relevant to the management of discipline in schools. Fontana (1994: 54) indicates the importance of the way in which a teacher presents a lesson and the lesson's suitability for the pupils' ability levels, age and interests. Teachers need to consider the balance between written and practical work, pupil participation and lecture.

The management of the curriculum should, as with all matters in school, be negotiated. Teachers should not feel pressured into teaching material that they are uncomfortable with. All participants in the classroom should have a shared understanding of the purpose of each lesson. Teaching and learning should be meaningful and relevant to teacher and pupil experiences, past, present or future.

Pupils need to be excited by the curriculum, and it is essential that teachers do not become bored by a repetitive curriculum that lacks direction and cohesion. A creative approach to teaching should be tempered by the need for pupils to learn. Pupils need to be stimulated by the curriculum and not just learn to sit still in lessons. Successive lessons involving similar activities will contribute to discipline problems. The context of the curriculum – how the school approaches the central task of curriculum planning and the organisation and delivery of learning – is critical to effective teaching. Balance and coherence is essential.

Curriculum problems, content or delivery, need to be managed collaboratively. Discipline problems can be overcome through the introduction of remedial measures introduced into the curriculum. Teachers and curriculum planners need to understand that there are children who do not learn as expected and that they need special interventions. The meaning and application of remediation need to be understood by teachers in order that it becomes an effective curriculum tool to aid children with identified learning and behavioural problems. Methods for motivating pupils, remediation and special support need to be developed, implemented, monitored and evaluated. Collaboration is the key to curriculum management.

7

SUPPORT AGENCIES

An effective multi-agency approach to support good discipline and behaviour at local level is vital (DfEE 1997a). The 1997 Education Act requires schools to prepare behaviour support plans. The government has prompted LEAs to review the range of their provision in this area and to improve coordination with social services and other agencies locally. The government also intends to develop home-school links in fulfilment of its drive to raise standards in schools. The main areas to be developed are:

- LEA support for schools in improving the management of pupil behaviour, with a view, amongst other things, to preventing unauthorised absence and exclusions
- the type and nature of provision available outside mainstream schools for pupils with behaviour problems
- arrangements for supporting the education of excluded pupils
- arrangements for effective co-ordination between relevant local agencies, and for involving the youth service and the voluntary sector.

(DfEE 1997a: 57)

This chapter aims to provide teachers with an introduction to the support agencies funded by the government and local education authorities. There is also a brief description of the range of independent support agencies and consultants available for specific behavioural and disciplinary problems.

The need for multi-agency communication is self-evident, as the aim of each agency is to provide support for pupils in school. The level of consultation that actually happens in practice is dependent on the relationship between each agency within the LEA, and the communication skills of those involved. It is evident that teachers and school management teams need to develop a comprehensive understanding of the role of each agency in relation to the management of discipline.

Following the Education Reform Act (1988), many LEA agencies were reorganised. This was a direct response to the devolution of resource management under the local management of schools (LMS). LEAs are responsible for the provision of four general kinds of service to schools, each relevant to the management of discipline:

- coordinating the introduction of national initiatives – LMS, national curriculum, inspection, appraisal, target setting and monitoring and providing advice and support for the development of government initiatives, the performance of schools and school improvement
- providing a range of personnel services including professional advice to governors for appointments and dismissals, in-service training, staff appraisal and staff welfare
- providing client-based services for individual pupils, parents and teachers including education welfare and psychology services, alternative provision for disturbed or difficult pupils and youth and careers services
- long-term planning of educational provision including organising schools placements, managing school building programmes and the structural repair of school premises.

Local education authorities are therefore responsible for funding support agencies including: education welfare officers (EWO), support teachers for pupils experiencing emotional and behavioural difficulties (EBD), and educational psychologists. They are also responsible for funding out of school units and child and family units. Schools are responsible for contributing funds to EBD and educational psychologist initiated programmes, learning support assistants and lunchtime supervisors. Schools are also responsible for establishing and maintaining home-school contracts as a means of improving communication and teacher-parent relationships. The wealth of support available to pupils and teachers for the management of discipline in schools is a significant reflection of the need for schools to provide a safe and secure environment for all members of the school community.

LUNCHTIME SUPERVISORS

The Elton Report (DES 1989: 122) commented on the difficulty of supervising pupils during lunchtime in schools. It suggested that the risk to lunchtime supervisors was significantly greater than to other staff, particularly when intervening to stop fights in the playground. The Report advised that the most effective lunchtime supervision is that provided by teachers. Having acknowledged that this is no longer possible in many schools, the report recommended (DES 1989: 123) that 'LEAs and governing bodies which employ school staff should ensure that midday supervisors are given adequate training in the management of pupils' behaviour'. In practice, it is the headteacher's responsibility to provide adequate supervision of pupils during lunch breaks. The employment of lunchtime supervisors is now commonplace in the majority of schools in England and Wales.

The management of pupil behaviour at lunchtimes is a priority in every school. For most pupils this is often an important time of the day, when they have an opportunity to develop their social skills. For some pupils lunchtimes can be lonely, or a time when arguments escalate into fights. Critically, it is a time when children can feel at risk of bullying and intimidation (Avon EBD Special Needs Support Team 1996). The responsibilities of supervisors are to provide an organised and structured lunchtime and, through promoting positive behaviour, provide a safe and secure environment for all pupils. As members of the local community, lunchtime supervisors have much to bring to their job.

In practice, lunchtime supervisors organise pupils in the eating area, managing the queue for meals, trays, tables, cleaning and tidying after the meal. They are also responsible for managing pupil behaviour in the eating and play/social areas during the lunchtime break. Lunchtime supervisors are often untrained, and unlikely to have knowledge of behaviour management strategies other than from the experience of situations with their own children or those observed on the job.

The need to train supervisors prior to their contact with pupils is essential if schools are to have an effective regime for lunchtime supervision. It is also necessary for schools to have open lines of communication between teachers and lunchtime supervisors. In order to be effective, lunchtime supervisors need to develop knowledge and understanding, skills, and competencies encompassing:

- behaviour management
- conflict resolution
- dealing with difficult situations
- child protection
- child abuse
- bullying
- dealing with parents and visitors
- first aid and emergencies
- monitoring and evaluating their practice.

Lunchtime supervisors also need support from senior managers and teachers. Encouragement from teaching staff will go a long way towards alleviating the pressure of managing the pupil population during lunchbreaks. This will also impact positively on pupil behaviour in afternoon lessons.

EDUCATION WELFARE SERVICE

The education welfare service is usually funded and managed by the LEA. The service provides specialist support which aims to ensure that all school-age children access the maximum benefit possible from the education system, appropriate to their age, ability, aptitude and any special educational needs they may have. The service employs education welfare officers with social work skills, expertise and techniques and specialist knowledge of the education system. The service works with pupils, families, schools and other sections of the LEA and with outside agencies, such as the social service department, in seeking to achieve its overall aim.

A typical mission statement is given in Figure 7.1 from Bristol City Council's education welfare service (EWS).

> The mission of the EWS is to promote achievement by ensuring that all children receive the maximum benefit possible from the education system, appropriate to their age, ability, aptitude and any special educational needs they may have.
>
> The EWS believes:
> that the education and welfare of children are of paramount importance;
> that our staff are our most valuable asset.
>
> - Our service aims to promote a partnership linking schools to parents and other agencies and organisations to work in the best interests of the child's education.
> - Our service strives to be accessible, responsive, reliable and effective.
> - Our service will seek to further develop its professionalism and flexibility, focusing both on individuals and on the agency as a whole.
> - Our priority at all times will be to protect children from abuse of any form, from exploitation and to support their basic rights, in particular, their rights to education.

Figure 7.1 Mission statement

Source: Bristol City Council Education Directorate 1997a

The education welfare service works within a legal framework and also assists the LEA in discharging its own legal obligations as set out in the 1944 Education Act and the 1993, 1996, and 1997 Education Acts. The service is also concerned with those sections from the Children and Young Persons' Acts, 1933 to 1969, that relate to the employment of children and to their engagement in public entertainment, and with the sections of the Children's Act 1989 that relate to care proceedings.

More specifically, the service is also actively concerned with the provision of special educational needs programmes for pupils under the provisions of the 1981, 1993, 1996 and 1997 Education Acts. Schools may expect the EWO to undertake core functions in relation to:

Attendance:

- visit the school at regular and agreed intervals to meet appropriate senior members of the school's staff

- discuss with staff those children who have irregular attendance at school (including persistent lateness), whatever the cause
- assist the staff of the school to devise plans which will help overcome attendance problems
- work directly with pupils and their parents, where appropriate, to help overcome attendance problems
- evaluate the outcome of action plans, maintain records of work undertaken, and provide regular feedback to the school on progress
- initiate court action, on behalf of the LEA, in order to carry out its statutory duties should the problems remain unresolved
- check the attendance registers at regular and agreed intervals, following up matters which appear to be of concern, even if they have not been referred to the EWO by the school
- act as liaison officer between the school and other helping agencies when appropriate.

Exclusions:

- ensure school staff, parents and children are aware of their rights and responsibilities with regard to exclusions
- assist all parties in thinking through the issues to be raised at governors' meetings to consider permanent exclusion, and assist all parties in accessing appropriate support systems
- maintain contact with permanently excluded pupils and their parents to ensure the child is admitted to another school as quickly as possible.

Child protection:

- advise the school about the child protection matters in accordance with the Joint Child Protection Committee's handbook.
- attend child protection case conferences and other relevant meetings whenever possible, where the EWO has had direct involvement with the child
- monitor the school attendance of children on the child protection register.

Special education needs (SEN):

- where the EWO has had direct involvement with the child, to support parents and children in the process of formal assessment.

Welfare benefits:

- assist parents to obtain their entitlement to state and other benefits at times of crisis. Assist parents to obtain their entitlement from the LEA of free school meals, clothing grants, and maintenance allowances.

General:

- advise and support schools in relation to general welfare issues affecting pupils, which can include breakdown in communication between school and home, under-achievement which could be caused by a domestic problem, and/or the child not being properly cared for at home.

Additional services are available to be negotiated with the school according to priorities and time available, these include:

- raising the priority of attendance with pupils and parents by addressing them in meetings and assemblies, by giving talks to tutor groups or by displaying and distributing relevant posters and literature. In addition, providing opportunities for group work for disaffected pupils and responding to requests for help from individual children on matters such as problems at school, bullying and relationship difficulties.

Education welfare officers will also support pupils and families where behaviour difficulties are likely to lead to exclusion from school. For effective use of the service, schools should have a policy on attendance, including a known system for prioritising pupil referrals. They must also maintain attendance registers accurately where in existence. Teachers should use the official referral form to bring cases to the notice of the EWO providing relevant, up-to-date information outlining concerns and actions taken by the school, as part of its own initial procedures for dealing with school non-attendance and other welfare matters prior to referral to the EWO.

Senior managers must allow the attendance of appropriate members of staff at an agreed programme of regular timetabled meetings with the EWO to discuss referrals and on-going cases. They should also inform other school staff of the EWO involvement. It is essential that staff welcome back with care pupils who have been absent (for whatever reason).

When meetings are held in school they should be in a suitable room to enable the EWO to discuss, in private, matters with pupils, parents and staff. Senior managers should make arrangements for any other appropriate members of staff to be available to discuss the referral/action taken by the education welfare officer.

The education welfare service in the majority of LEAs are active in their consultation with specialist agencies within the authority, including social services, medical and legal services. The complexity of each of these agencies is such that a detailed description of each would not be appropriate in the context of this book. However teachers and school managers should be aware of the existence and status of such agencies in relation to the management of discipline in schools.

EDUCATION OFFICERS

LEAs provide a service to support pupils and parents with admission, exclusion and special educational needs procedures. Education officers have a responsibility to oversee all decision-making for children in their area. They are also responsible for the application and development under the direction of senior officers of the Education committee's policies concerning provision for children.

In practice, education officers represent the LEA at admission, exclusion, statement and special educational needs meetings within their geographical area. This involves working closely with parents, carers and other agencies concerning the placement of children. They are also responsible for the education of children other than at school.

Education officers liaise with staff from other local authority directorates to ensure open lines of communication regarding pupils' needs, as appropriate. They also coordinate children's service teams to ensure that they work together and manage children's case work at a local level. An education officer will lead all consultations with parents and the area community on education matters, and will be the point of contact for the chief education officer in the authority. This will involve regular and close liaison with headteachers and governors on all matters affecting their schools. Education officers will also coordinate support for schools in difficulty.

Education officers have specific expertise in the management of discipline in schools. They are able to advise on the development and implementation of discipline policies and provide training for staff, teaching and non-teaching. Assistant education officers and education officers will have detailed knowledge of the local community, its needs and the range of support available for children in the local area. Both are central to negotiations concerning emotive issues involving parents, children and the LEA.

EMOTIONAL AND BEHAVIOURAL DIFFICULTIES SUPPORT TEAM

Emotional and behavioural difficulties (EBD) teams do far more than their title implies. EBD teachers are specialists who provide a range of services to mainstream schools and specialist schools. They are experts in the management of discipline in schools, a necessary and, at times, undervalued resource. As Elton (DES 1989: 156) advised 'it is essential that EBD teams have sufficient status to work effectively with headteachers'. EBD staff are highly qualified professionals able to deal with difficult pupils. They are also able to deal tactfully and effectively with teachers in mainstream schools who need their help, yet may feel defensive about seeking it. EBD teachers have a variety of professional skills in counselling, negotiation and in-service training. Within the EBD team there will be a team leader, specialist teachers, special needs support assistants and administrative support staff.

EBD teams were set up to provide a service to schools to support pupils experiencing emotional and behavioural difficulties in their mainstream placement. Their purpose is to enable these pupils to maintain their places in mainstream education and to access the national curriculum by:

- providing direct support to individual pupils experiencing emotional and behavioural difficulties
- providing practical advice on support strategies to school staff working with pupils experiencing EBD
- working in partnership with parents/carers in supporting their child's educational placement
- assisting schools in developing their own support structures and expertise in relation to pupils experiencing EBD
- working in partnership with social services, health and other education agencies to encourage continuity of support and exchange of information for all pupils experiencing EBD.

In practice, support will include (Bristol Special Needs Support Service 1996):

- advice on individual behaviour management programmes
- advice on classroom management strategies
- use of counselling skills with individuals and groups
- social and interpersonal skills with individuals and groups
- curriculum-focused work
- break-time, lunchtime and after school groups
- in-class support
- home-school liaison.

In addition to direct pupil support, EBD teams may provide whole-school focused advice and support, including:

- working with schools to develop whole-school policies for the management of pupils' behaviour
- working with schools to develop expertise in action planning for pupils in stages 1 and 2 of the Code of Practice (DfE 1994a)
- INSET on group work, behaviour management, counselling skills, classroom management, bullying and conflict resolution
- working with schools where pupil behaviour and discipline has been identified as a cause for concern as a result of school inspection.

In the majority of LEAs, pupils may be referred for EBD support with or without a statement (see Chapter 2). Support for non-statemented pupils considered to be at Stage 3 or 4 of the Code of Practice (education welfare, psychology service or health) can be obtained when the pupil's school placement has broken down. Referrals will also require evidence that the pupil, after receiving support from the school still exhibits inappropriate behaviour. Evidence that the educational performance of the pupil or his/her peers is seriously affected by the inappropriate behaviour will also be needed.

The direct support to pupils will be managed in a range of ways within the following framework by:

- gathering information from pupil, school, home, community, other agencies
- assessing the pupil by identifying patterns
- understanding and observation
- planning for school, home, the community
- defining intervention procedures, including:
  - one-to-one work
  - group work
  - work in classroom
  - work off-site
  - continued observation
  - a combination of approaches
  - a watching brief
- reviewing dates planned well in advance, especially those required in the Code of Practice (DfE 1994a) – see Chapter 2.

EBD teams approach their work with the core value of non-directive counselling: encompassing the value of empathy, respect, and unconditional positive regard in promoting personal growth. EBD teams offer space, time, a variety of skills, support and approaches to pupils to grow in self-esteem and to make positive changes in their lives. For the work of the EBD team to be successful, it will be necessary for there to be planned, consistent time and space in schools, which is uninterrupted, allowing as much privacy for the pupil as needed. Effective communication is also necessary. Communication is the key to ensuring that pupils receiving support are afforded the essential requirements of consistency and privacy. Teacher, parents/carers, support staff and other agencies need to work collaboratively in order to meet pupil needs.

Teachers and senior managers need to understand that the pupils referred to the EBD team will usually have experienced distress, hurt, unhappiness or difficulties for some time. Because the process of their reparation, change, confusion-sorting and/or establishing an integrated sense of identity and feeling of self-worth is a slow one, there is a need for patience and understanding.

EBD teams need to evaluate pupils' progress in terms of their feelings of well-being and their own perception of progress in relation to the concrete observations and experience of those teaching members of staff who have most contact with them. Teachers need to be aware of slight shifts and patterns of behaviour and being, that might be recognised, acknowledged and discreetly encouraged. Observation will form the basis of the more formal evaluation that takes place through review meetings. The focus of review meetings is to consider the extent to which the pupil's needs are being met by their individual education plan.

In practice, EBD teams provide support for pupils in mainstream nursery, primary and secondary schools. Most pupils referred to the service are statemented or selected by the headteacher. Support will usually span two terms and include between thirty minutes and an hour one-to-one contact each week. For some pupils of secondary age, support may be supplemented by EBD teachers working in Child and Family Support Centres. The range of pupil support includes:

- classroom observation
- lunchtime and break observation
- one-to-one counselling
- social and interpersonal skills group work
- anger management and conflict resolution group work
- friendship groups support work
- lunchtime clubs and playground support
- therapeutic use of art, drama, play and music
- cooperative games
- home-school liaison
- support for parents
- classroom focused support work
- off-site curriculum focused work.

EBD staff also provide in-service training for learning support assistants, lunchtime supervisors, special educational needs coordinators, teachers and senior managers (see Chapter 11). Qualified counsellors within LEA teams also provide a counselling service for professionals coping with disruptive pupils in mainstream education.

LEARNING SUPPORT ASSISTANTS

The relationship between academic achievement and disruptive behaviour is evident in mainstream schools. Pupils, frustrated by a lack of understanding and inability to access the curriculum, are likely to behave badly. In many cases learning and behaviour difficulties apply. In general, support for statemented pupils is provided on-site. This has inevitable consequences for teachers and other professionals. The inclusion of pupils in mainstream classes will also impact on the school-life of other pupils. Mainstream teachers may find it difficult to be able to give the necessary time to support a disruptive pupil effectively without assistance. Teachers should not have to spend the majority of their time in the classroom trying to maintain order.

As shown, educational psychologists can provide professional advice for teachers; EBD teachers can also advise and withdraw disruptive pupils from the classroom for a range of much needed support and counselling. Class teachers are provided with additional support for pupils experiencing EBD by the least qualified members of the teaching staff: learning support assistants. Many members of this invaluable team have not been trained in dealing with pupils with emotional and behavioural difficulties. Funding generated by statemented pupils may not always provide the necessary or appropriate support.

Learning support assistants require training to meet the needs of the pupils in their care. Classroom teachers also require training in the management of support staff. Clear targets need to be established and communicated and implemented by relevant professionals for support mechanisms to be effective and to achieve positive learning outcomes.

SPECIALIST UNITS

The Elton Report (DES 1989: 154) commented that on-site units for disruptive pupils were limited in their overall impact on pupil behaviour throughout the school. Research in this area (Galloway *et al.* 1982; Graham 1988) found that the presence of on-site units did not lead to a reduction in temporary or permanent exclusions. The isolation of pupils from their peers may result in an improvement in attitude and motivation, but this has to be balanced with the effect this has on their learning. The alternative to on-site provision is costly. Each LEA will have a range of specialist units to meet the needs of their pupils and community. The Child and Family Support Centre is an example.

The aim of CFSCs is to attempt to modify the demands made by a pupil or his/her school. These demands are understood to relate to the pressures on the pupil, from home and community, and the developmental needs of the child which relate to his/her previous life experiences. The centres may encourage the school to modify its demands on the pupil. This necessitates the school being well informed about the individual circumstances of the child within the family setting. The underlying principle to the CFSC approach is based on the notion that a pupil's development and self-concept is primarily formed by his/her family and educational experience. At the heart of the centre's philosophy is the concept of attempting to develop a total home/social environment capable of responding to the pupil's developmental needs.

The multi-disciplinary teams at the centres have experience of working with young people and their families while simultaneously building strong links with local mainstream schools. The majority of the cases referred to CFSCs are at an impasse in the agency and family systems. The Centre attempts to rebuild the relationships between home and school which may have become hostile and blaming. CFSC teachers are involved in helping schools to effectively use referral systems. The task of the CFSC teachers' input to pupils is to define and understand the educational aspect of their difficulties and to identify, in collaboration with schools, parents, pupils and social services, strategies for resolving these difficulties, thus enabling pupils to achieve their educational potential (Avon Education Department 1995).

Mainstream teachers and senior managers should be aware that many of the pupils and families involved with CFSCs have little energy and low self-esteem. The pupils may also have lost any sense of enjoyment or reward from learning, and see school work as irrelevant or as a reminder of their failures. It is crucial to overcome such feelings if they are to begin to succeed within school.

EDUCATIONAL PSYCHOLOGY SERVICE

A highly specialist area of the education service is that of educational psychology. An educational psychologist provides psychological support and advice for pupils, to schools, parents, the education department, social services, health services and to the pupils themselves.

Educational psychologists are trained experienced teachers bound by professional codes of conduct to act in the best interests of the individual pupils referred to them. They work with parents, teachers and other professionals to help pupils succeed and to prevent or minimise difficulties. Their work is concerned with:

- learning, language and literacy
- specific learning difficulties
- behaviour, emotional or social problems
- physical or sensory difficulties.

The role of educational psychologists is central to the assessment and statementing of pupils with learning and behavioural difficulties. The educational psychologist provides an effective consultation, assessment, advice and intervention service for pupils who may have special educational needs and for other pupils about whom there may be concern.

Educational psychologists also provide in-service training and support research projects involving teachers, other professionals and parents in fulfilling their aim to promote a wider understanding of pupils' needs.

In legislative terms, an educational psychologist will inform and advise LEA officers regarding the needs of pupils in relation to Section 167, 1993 Education Act and the related Code of Practice (see Chapter 2). As such, they will be in contact with pupils, parents, headteachers, governors, LEA and social services officers and a wide range of professional and other staff from all agencies providing services to the local community.

Educational psychologists work within a team led by the senior educational psychologist. The team will be responsible for the provision of a high quality psychological support service. The service provided will be evaluated, reviewed and adapted in response to the changing needs of pupils, parents, schools, LEAs and the community.

In practice, educational psychologists will be assigned a number of nursery, primary and secondary schools. They will then consult with the headteacher to establish priorities according to the needs of the pupils in each school. At Stages 1 and 2 of the Code of Practice (see Chapter 2) they will consult with the headteacher and class teacher only. At Stage 3 the educational psychologist will also work with pupils and their families to assess, advise, and support action planning for pupils with emotional and behavioural difficulties. When the Code of Practice (DfE1994a) is working effectively, an action plan will be in place prior to Stage 3.

Educational psychologists will offer advice to headteachers and teachers on the implementation of the Code of Practice. They will also assist schools with the process of developing, implementing and evaluating their discipline policy. The educational psychologist will also provide a range of in-service courses for parents and professionals that focus on:

- pupil needs
- action planning
- individual and whole-school behaviour policies
- mediation and negotiation
- assertive discipline for teachers and parents
- development of teacher self-esteem.

The educational psychology team is central to the planning of multi-agency support for pupils and families with behaviour problems. They advise the LEA on the allocation of the funding that will provide schools' EBDs with teachers and learning support assistants. The level of service available will vary according to available funding. Teachers need to know and understand the role of the educational psychologist in relation to their school, if pupils are to receive preventative support that is needed.

ACTION/INDIVIDUAL EDUCATION PLAN

The Code of Practice (DfE 1994a) for special educational needs advises that all statemented pupils, at Stage 2 or above, should have an individual education plan. This is a plan of action focusing on individual pupil needs following a period of consultation with all relevant agencies. A multi-agency report will set the parameters for the action/individual education plan. The plan will identify targets and strategies for pupils and teachers in order to achieve success.

Action/individual education plans are a useful mechanism for evaluating the needs of pupils with problems, learning or behavioural. Educational psychologists, EWOs, EBD support teachers and education officers value the inclusion of action/individual education plans in school discipline policies. Senior managers should provide teachers and support staff with guidance in preparing and implementing an action plan. To do this, they would need to:

- identify the problem, individual teacher or team
- understand the problem, gather as much information as possible
- identify pupil needs and teacher needs, try to balance these
- generate possible strategies
- negotiate a feasible strategy, agreed by the team of professionals, as appropriate, that will address the problem
- create a time-scale for action
- determine desired outcomes
- monitor progress
- evaluate outcomes.

In practice, action plans are the detailed planning of short-, medium- and long-term goals for pupils with behavioural or learning difficulties. Many schools have concentrated on creating action/individual education plans focusing on learning difficulties and neglect the need for action plans for pupils with behavioural problems. Action/individual education plans should be developed and implemented at Stage 2 and 3. Advice and guidance from support agencies is available and should be utilised to the full. An action/individual education plan, well-prepared by multi-professional agencies, should prevent the escalation of problems that often result in exclusion.

Action planning should be supported and enhanced by clear record-keeping systems. The process should formalise specific behaviour/learning targets and provide a written basis for action. As a pupil-centred mechanism for improving behaviour, action plans must consider:

- feelings of all involved
- strengths and weaknesses of all involved
- areas to develop
- what must be done
- who should do it
- when it should be done by.

For pupils with serious difficulties, an action/individual education plan presents a useful opportunity for discussion between pupil, parent, child and other professional agencies, as appropriate. Action planning is based on the principle of a contract, an agreement entered into by all involved. As with all plans (see Chapter 4) the targets set within an action plan will need to be:

Specific	clearly stated
Measurable	all must agree on how success will be assessed at the Review
Attainable	pupils and teachers must act on the identified problem
Realistic	targets must be possible within the home/school

Time-limited	everyone must be clear about the time-scale within which the targets are to be reached.

Critically, all targets must be positive and meaningful. Once agreed, the action plan must be resourced in order to achieve the targets set. The three main areas of resourcing are likely to be:

- people
- time
- materials/equipment.

The management of resources must be established if adequate support is to be given (Blandford 1997b). Monitoring is often a neglected area in education (see Chapter 10). Monitoring should provide the means of keeping a running record of observations of progress made as a result of targeting and intervention; what worked well, what did not work and why? The format will need to be straightforward in order that it can be used for individuals and groups. Monitoring should be referred to in the review meeting.

Reviews must happen. It is important that the Review date is adhered to and that each participant is given the opportunity to report back, leading to an overall discussion of progress. The most common outcomes should be the identification of:

- what worked well and why
- the difficulties and how such difficulties can be overcome
- new areas of concern and new targets for action.

A successful action plan will leave all participants feeling that they are in control and are confident of achieving their goal for the pupil.

8

ALTERNATIVE MODELS

The management of discipline in schools is a complex area involving all members of the school and wider educational community. In schools where discipline is a problem there is little chance of pupils receiving an education that meets their needs. If pupils are to develop academically, they also need to develop socially. Pupils need self-esteem and self-confidence in order to reach their potential as members of the school community.

There are accepted practices that are common to most schools. These include:

- responding positively to all pupils' needs
- defining the parameters for acceptable behaviour
- providing a safe and secure environment for all pupils
- adapting discipline policies to meet the needs of a pluralistic society
- effective communication between all agencies
- open management.

Yet, the majority of practitioners encounter discipline problems within their classrooms that are beyond their experience and expertise. In response to this need, teachers, researchers and educationalists have attempted to find a solution. This chapter examines examples of practice that have been introduced to schools in England and Wales. Each is described and evaluated by teachers, parents and pupils. Addresses are given in Appendix C.

PEER MEDIATION

Peer mediation in schools was developed in the United States of America, Australia and New Zealand and is now spreading across England. It appeals to pupils with a sense of social responsibility, and provides an opportunity for others to develop this. It offers useful practice in facilitation and extends their self-esteem and confidence.

The *Mediation UK Education Network* (1996) defines school peer mediation as 'when selected and trained pupils are encouraged and given space by staff to mediate the less difficult of interpupil conflicts'. Two or more pupils in conflict may be invited by mediators to withdraw from an audience to a more private place and, after confidentially exploring facts, feelings and options, come up with a joint solution that they are willing to implement. Mediators are not arbitrators or advice-givers, but non-judgemental caretakers of the process and recorders of any confidential written agreement. A more formal mediation process may take twenty minutes or longer, but sometimes the peer mediators may arrive early enough on the scene to pre-empt the need for formal mediation.

Peer mediation can be beneficial to schools, as it encourages all involved to take an active part in looking constructively at peaceful solutions. Through the emphasis on personal responsibility and thinking carefully about ways of dealing with conflict, pupils can be taught that solutions to conflicts need not be violent ones.

The Bristol Mediation Schools Project (BMSP) was set up in 1990 at the request of several schools on a local estate, shortly after the community neighbour mediation service began. Several training schemes were piloted in response to the expressed needs of the schools. One such pilot involved the Schools Project Team working with lunchtime supervisors, helping to raise their self-esteem, and to integrate them into the school community. Another involved a series of sessions for infant classes and a special needs unit, in developing conflict resolution skills. As with their current work, the team used a wide variety of activities appropriate to the age of the children – ideas storming, paired listening, visualisations, singing, drawing, puppets, being silent and active games. With little emphasis on writing this approach is popular with less able and special needs pupils.

In 1995 the EBD support teachers, in collaboration with mediators from the Bristol Mediation Schools Project, identified two schools in Bristol where the Schools Project Team could pilot the peer mediation training they had developed. The project aimed to enable children to deal positively with conflict and solve their problems without violence and intimidation and to improve their behaviour towards each other, their community and society. This received a very positive response and the Schools Project Team were then able to attract funding from national organisations. Since then the Team has worked in thirteen primary schools with Year 5 and 6 children where it has been enthusiastically received by teachers and pupils.

The Schools Project Team have valued collaborating with the emotional and behaviour difficulty teachers. The continued support of the EBD team for the project has been an important factor in its success. EBD teachers identify schools which are likely to be able to nurture and develop the peer mediation scheme once they have received the initial training from Bristol Mediation. Where possible EBD teachers working in those schools have been involved in the training so that they can provide ongoing support to the schools and in particular to the teacher who manages the scheme.

Bristol Mediation's comprehensive training manual describes how to use peer group mediation effectively in primary and middle schools. It offers ten sessions with the class and their teacher. The first six sessions enable pupils to develop their communication skills and raise self-esteem. They explore conflict and cooperation, learn effective listening skills and how to express their feelings. They become skilled at seeking different points of view and at not taking sides. They are helped to apply these skills to their friendships and their relationships with others as well as in their role as mediators.

The four mediation training sessions were designed to teach the class: 'A process of peer mediation in which those in conflict are guided by an equal through a series of steps so that they can find their own solution to the problem' (Bristol Mediation 1997: 15).

The aim was to enable a fresh start and to improve future relationships. The members of the class were then able to use these skills working in pairs as mediators on duty in the playground, to help other children solve their disputes. Mediators do not mediate incidents involving fighting or bullying. Mediators are only involved if both disputants want to solve their difficulties and choose to go to a mediator, and both agree to work through the process. This is in addition to the duty teachers' and lunchtime supervisors' roles in the playground.

An integral part of the training are the sessions with teaching and non-teaching staff with separate sessions for the lunchtime supervisors, in recognition of the crucial role they play in supporting the mediators on the job and in encouraging disputants to seek the mediators' help. Staff support and participation are very important to a successful scheme. The support of the headteacher, senior management team teachers and lunchtime supervisors is necessary. At least one committed member of staff is required to liaise with the Schools Project Team and take part in the training. It is crucial to the success of the scheme that a member of staff supervises the mediators on a regular weekly basis in order to pick up any problems and to reinforce good practice. It is intended that all staff will model the necessary skills and help the pupils enhance their skills throughout the school. Circle work forms the basis of the programme so that each person can make their contribution or pass if they wish. As with their earlier work a variety of methods are used, with emphasis on role play in the mediation sessions. Each session ends with an evaluation of its enjoyment and usefulness. At the end of the training the children prepare a presentation at assembly about the scheme. They volunteer to work on a rota, the teacher pairing stronger candidates with those who need help to improve their skills.

Teachers found that working together through peer mediation benefits both the teacher and the outside mediator. It gives the mediator valuable school experience, and a teacher valuable meditation skills.

As the results begin to show in the classroom, other teachers in the school want to know more about the project. Teachers found that a structure of formal mediation stages created a safe and disciplined atmosphere in which conflicts can be solved.

Feedback has been positive. An improvement in school atmosphere has been reported along with raised self-esteem and confidence in pupils. Where an adult needs to arbitrate the children are more receptive to the process. Pupils from two schools have appeared on a local BBC TV and radio news programme, and pupils from one school have presented a role-playing mediation situation to Bristol Mediation AGM.

There is much to be learnt from peer mediation; the process empowers children to solve some of their own problems and thus reduces the need for adults to become involved or impose solutions. Through setting up a dialogue between those involved in a conflict, issues are aired and ways forward found and agreed. This is an adventurous and innovative process for schools to set up, since it allows the pupils to take more responsibility and teaches them transferable life skills. It releases staff from these problems and leads to a more settled, quieter atmosphere in which learning can take place.

SCHOOLS OUTREACH

Schools Outreach is a charity that trains pastoral care workers to look after pupils' welfare and personal development. Pastoral care workers are placed into schools to complement the relationship which exists between parents and teachers and the children in their care. A Schools Outreach worker offers friendship to pupils in the school in which the worker is based as a non-official adult, without any official powers within the school organisation.

Within the friendships offered to every pupil, there will be the encouragement and motivation of pupils towards personal wholeness, a continuing attention paid to the child's developing aptitudes, the stimulation of an enthusiasm concerning positive relationships with others, the promotion of health and well-being and the prevention of personally and socially destructive difficulties. This work will be entrusted to high-calibre and appropriately trained persons who live in the community where they work. They will normally be linked to only one or two schools. The work is local, long-term and wholly child-centred.

Having earned the affection, respect and trust of the pupils, the workers are ideally placed to exert a positive influence on the pupils. The workers employ their skills and talents in the building of deep relationships with the pupils by means of a mix of classroom and one-to-one work. Pastoral care workers are free to devote their time exclusively to relationship-building though they are, at all times, accountable to the school's headteacher and are expected to work with and complement the work of the teachers.

A report from the headteacher of a middle school to the LEA chief education officer described the considerable impact of the Schools Outreach project on a large number of pupils as well as on the staff and governors. While it is very difficult to quantify work of a pastoral nature, the headteacher was able to show that two years after the placement of a Schools Outreach worker:

- the number of temporary and permanent exclusions had dropped from fifty to three
- staff turnover had reduced from over fifty per cent to none
- there was a marked improvement in attendance
- there was a reduction in disruptive behaviour in the classroom
- pupils had learnt how to defuse situations that had previously led to bullying
- anger management training had a significant influence on staff attitudes to pupils
- group and individual self-esteem had improved
- parents were more frequent visitors to the school.

The headteacher believed that the project was of tremendous value to the school and the pupils and their community because it addressed the whole child in a preventative and positive way, enabling teachers, parents and community workers to work closely together.

The Schools Outreach project would appear to be effective, perhaps due to the qualities that are essential in a pastoral care worker. These include:

- an appearance, personality and character which would be attractive to a pupil
- a sense of vocation to a caring, long-term commitment to children
- ownership of a firmly-held sense of self-esteem
- a gentle, humble and sensitive attitude to others, in particular those who are experiencing difficulties
- a sense of awe and wonder concerning the privilege of being involved with and contributing to the development of children
- a balanced approach to life
- the ability to operate effectively as a member of a team, while able also to function as an individual.

In practice, pastoral care workers offer each individual unconditional acceptance, respect and trust. The project team works together with a school towards the production of a schedule that will be suitable for the pupils (Hinds 1997:13).

PRIMARY EXCLUSION PROJECT

The Bristol Primary Exclusion Project (BPEP) was created in response to the significant increase in exclusion figures in schools. The increasing figures raised many concerns about the damaging effects on young pupils of exclusion, permanent or temporary, from school (see Chapter 2). In particular, a child whose behaviour is constantly challenging, when at home for twenty-four hours a day, can cause enormous tensions within already vulnerable families. Furthermore, when pupils are not accessing the national curriculum, they are likely to fall behind, thus compounding the problems of low self-esteem which may have contributed to the exclusion.

The Project was started in September 1995 in response to the rising numbers of children of primary age excluded from school. It was piloted during the autumn and spring terms 1995–6. The project adopted a multi-disciplinary approach with specialist teachers, support assistants from the EBD team, and support from an educational psychologist, EWO and social worker.

Permanent exclusion from school is likely to lead to a downward spiral of behaviour and an increased likelihood of further exclusions from alternative placements. Long periods out of school increase the opportunities for delinquent or criminal behaviour as the pupil gets older. Increasingly, schools are meeting the needs of pupils by achieving successful School Attainment Tests (SATs) and external examinations results. Schools need to provide excellent learning opportunities for all pupils, and the presence of a pupil with very demanding or disruptive behaviour is expensively time-consuming. Exclusion is, therefore, a reasonable option in the context of the school as a whole.

The BPEP was established to provide a trained multi-agency team to support schools where a pupil was in danger of being permanently excluded. The aim was to reduce exclusion levels of children of primary age in Bristol schools by working with targeted pupils using clear referral criteria. The project's objectives were:

- to support schools in their capacity to cope with children who are at risk of being permanently excluded
- to provide a practical coordinated approach between school, home and various support services
- to offer direct support to the individual child, the class teacher, headteacher and parents, coordinated by a specified key worker in each case
- to increase the confidence and morale of school staff, in relation to their ability to work with such youngsters
- to produce relevant, pragmatic information for schools and key agencies on issues pertinent to exclusion.

(Bristol Special Needs Support Service 1996: 14)

The aim is to provide intensive short-term support to stabilise crisis situations, to offer support to children to re-enter school after a period of exclusion and to help schools develop new strategies or systems which could make a long-term difference to the pupil's school experiences. The BPEP team work in a coordinated way, with the main emphasis being on the building of good relationships with schools and parents. Work with pupils focuses on the development of their self-esteem. Limits are set on behaviour in accordance with the whole-school policy. Careful action planning ensures that these are properly differentiated to the needs of the child and are used consistently in a non-punitive way. The BPEP team is aware of the difficult balance between dependency on external support and the need to ensure that any changes can be maintained after a short-term intervention.

All members of the team are experienced in working with difficult pupils. The team works with the pupil, family, teacher and relevant agencies to provide the most appropriate support. The BPEP team also works jointly with class teachers and learning support assistants on the development of useful materials for supporting children in schools. Schools are also offered INSET from the team on issues such as restraint and action planning. Typical roles and responsibilities that could be taken on by the Project Worker in school may include (Robinson 1997a: 2–3):

- relationship building with pupils
- direct teaching of social skills, for example, turn-taking and sharing
- support in academic work, for example, keeping on task
- withdrawal from stressful activities, such as assembly, to avoid activities that trigger unacceptable behaviour
- helping the pupil to calm down after an outburst
- building self-esteem through systematic rewards
- offering counselling support
- working with another group to allow the class teacher time with the pupil
- teaching playground skills through structured clubs or other activities
- liaising with parents about home/school plan
- liaising with teachers about the effectiveness of the action plan (individual education plan).

In addition the EWO, educational psychologist and social worker work with parents on improving behaviour at home. The team aimed to support fifteen to twenty children over a relatively short two to three term period. It offers short-term support from either a support teacher with specific expertise in EBD for at least one half day a week, or a support assistant specialising in behaviour management for up to four sessions a week, an EWO and social worker to offer specialist help to parents and carers. The educational psychologist coordinates referrals and allocations to the team and provides immediate support to headteachers who may be under pressure to exclude a child. The team supports schools helping to structure individual educational plans and behaviour plans at regular review meetings. It supports teachers with ideas and strategies for management of behaviour in the classroom and provides the child with in-class support, establishing a good working pattern for the child in the context of the whole class.

Small group work aims to build self-esteem and develop the child's social skills, with activities and games to develop empathy and social awareness. Individual work provides the child with the opportunity to express concerns on a one-to-one basis and to explore alternative reactions to difficult situations. The team liaises with parents and carers to encourage home-school links. Home visits aim to give ideas on behaviour management for parents and carers.

The evaluation of the project by schools after the three terms showed that there had been successes. It highlighted a decrease in frequency of behavioural outbursts in the child and less dependence on adult support. Teachers felt the input had benefited the child, helped them with their own strategies for working with children who have difficulties and had a positive impact on the relationship between home and school.

In practice, the schools involved have felt very supported by the project and have seen behavioural progress in the majority of the pupils who have received support. Schools have valued the excellent learning assistants' support and also the multi-agency team, with its wide range of expertise. The BPEP team has increased communication, held regular reviews and monitored each pupil's progress. The project has also enabled the team to share and develop ideas. All schools have valued the additional support in the classroom and play areas, the rapid response to crisis situations and the additional work carried out with parents and families. Critically, the BPEP team has contributed to a forty-six per cent reduction in primary school exclusions within its LEA.

ASSERTIVE DISCIPLINE

The government White Paper, *Excellence in Schools* (DfEE 1997a) stated that schools should be 'well-ordered communities'. This emphasises the need for every school to have a clear discipline policy. In particular, the government advocates the benefits of assertive discipline in schools. 'This involves the whole school in a concerted effort to improve and maintain discipline through a clearly understood behaviour framework, emphasising positive encouragement as well as clear sanctions' (DfEE 1997a: 56).

Assertive discipline is an approach to the management of discipline in schools developed by Lee and Marlene Canter in the United States of America during the 1970s. It was introduced to primary and secondary schools in the United Kingdom in the late 1980s and early 1990s. Following this period, there were revisions to the programme (Canter and Canter 1992). The initial enthusiasm for assertive discipline was rooted in the widely-held view that school discipline had seriously deteriorated and that a number of schools were at breaking point. However there is little evidence to support this view (Robinson and Maines 1994: 30). The Elton Committee (DES 1989: 59) found that, when surveying the problems of discipline in schools:

- while the survey results presented to us by the professional associations showed the strong concern felt by many of their members, these results could not be used as reliable estimates of the extent to which such problems affect schools across the country
- we could provide no definitive answer to the question of whether things are getting worse.

Although there was little agreement among educationalists as to the effectiveness of existing discipline policies, assertive discipline was adopted by a significant number of inner-city schools.

Assertive discipline focuses on the emotional motivation of teachers to implement a plan that asserts their right to teach. The programme stresses the need for a positive discipline system that is readily integrated into the teacher's routine teaching of the curriculum, so that it becomes fundamental to the classroom atmosphere, and not something added on for the benefit of the misbehaving pupil. In practice, assertive discipline is an approach to school discipline that helps teachers to 'learn more effectively to express their wants and feelings, while at the same time not abusing the rights of others' (Canter and Canter 1976: 2). The assertive discipline technique has three essential components:

- clear unambiguous rules
- continuous positive feedback when pupils are successfully keeping these rules
- a recognised hierarchy of sanctions which are consistently applied when the rules are broken.

(DfEE 1997a: 56)

In order for teachers to have their needs met in the classroom, they must be in a position to influence the behaviour of the pupils. Canter and Canter (1992) consider that the majority of discipline problems in the classroom are caused by children who do not have a positive self-esteem. They recommend three assertive actions when misbehaviour occurs:

- tell the child to stop the particular behaviour
- set out the sanctions that will occur if he/she does not
- offer the child a choice.

Sanctions are graded and recorded (Martin 1994) and take the form of warnings which lead to detentions and letters to parents. Simultaneously, positive behaviour is noted and rewards issued. Assertive discipline encourages teachers to be consistent in order that pupils come to believe that, when they behave in an unacceptable manner, they will be treated appropriately. For assertive discipline to work successfully, the rules must be clear, and the teacher must be assertive in insisting on adherence to them. When evaluating the effectiveness of the programme, the following needs to be considered:

- are the rules clear, negotiated and age appropriate?
- does the teacher consistently expect the pupils to follow them?
- how many rewards and sanctions are given? Is there a balanced response?

In preparation for the implementation of assertive discipline, all agencies involved in the management of discipline in school need to be trained. The training focuses on how to build a positive relationship with pupils and increase their self-esteem, encompassing:

- how to guide pupils towards constructive behaviour by identifying when and why they misbehave
- the development of whole-school behaviour plan based on pupil needs
- the handling of pupils' anger and attention-seeking behaviour
- learning how to stay calm and assertive when pupils undermine a teacher's ability to teach
- how to succeed with pupils who do not respond to the school discipline policy
- developing and recording action plans.

Assertive discipline cannot be introduced effectively to schools where the curriculum is inappropriate for pupils and does not meet their needs, personally or culturally. The assertive discipline plan requires consistency in order for pupils and teachers to succeed. Key elements include:

- building trust, establishing a positive relationship
- responding to pupils in a proactive manner
- identifying the primary needs of difficult pupils: attention, motivation, boundaries
- developing rules stating expected behaviour
- teaching appropriate behaviour through practice, demonstration and praise
- looking for positive behaviour and praising pupils when they succeed
- using sanctions that are effective, not vindictive
- working with parents, senior managers and external agencies as appropriate.

Canter and Canter (1992: 13) believe that pupils' rights in the classroom include:

- a teacher who will set firm and consistent limits
- a teacher who will provide them with consistent positive encouragement to motivate them to behave
- knowing what behaviours they need to engage in that will enable them to succeed in the classroom
- a teacher who will take the time to teach them how to manage their own behaviour.

Assertive discipline has been effective in schools where the school community has been involved in its implementation and development. Changes to pupil behaviour have been noted, particularly in primary schools (Moss 1995). With success, teachers inevitably become more positive towards pupils and other members of the school community. The evaluation of assertive discipline in some of Liverpool's primary schools showed that training teachers to use this technique had at least four positive outcomes (DfEE 1997a: 56):

- an increase in appropriate, i.e. 'on task', pupil behaviour
- a decrease in the frequency of disruptive incidents
- a dramatic increase in the amount of praise given by teachers
- a marked decline in how much pupils needed to be [reprimanded].

The difficulty of introducing an externally generated innovation cannot be overstated. Assertive discipline may not be congruent with the demands of the adopting school's community. Equally, when headteachers or senior managers openly support the introduction of a new policy, it is very difficult for other members of staff to challenge it. Cultural assumptions need to be considered before imposing rules and agenda (Hoyle 1986). When approaching the possibility of introducing assertive discipline, headteachers need to recognise that schools will have their own clearly defined cultures and sub-cultures that will employ political techniques to protect themselves (Willower 1986). External innovations will fail if staff are not fully trained and ready. Effective training involves theory, demonstration, practice, feedback and coaching (Joyce and Showers 1982).

Any analysis of the existing situation is likely to discover only some of the variables and there are no easy answers. Robinson and Maines (1994:34) considered that the application of assertive discipline:

> neglects some of the rights of pupils and parents, the right to be listened to, the right to participate in the teaching/learning structure and the right to express needs which may conflict with school or classroom discipline without fear of punishment.

THE 'NO-BLAME' APPROACH

The prevalence of bullying in schools led Barbara Maines and George Robinson to develop an approach to bullying that enables both bully and victim to deal with the problem. Many of the strategies previously adopted in schools may have been ineffective in changing the behaviour of the bully. Teachers and adult members of the school community approach each situation with strong feelings of anger and frustration towards the bully and sympathy for the victim. Maines and Robinson (1994: 1) believe that teachers have a responsibility to pupils and their parents to respond effectively and the measure of the success of the intervention is the degree to which it stops the bullying. Some of the responses, often made by teachers, are not successful in achieving the above. 'Bullying is an antisocial behaviour resorted to by inadequate people and we must respond in a way which will be helpful to their learning of improved behaviour. Increasing their anxiety and alienation from us is not likely to work' (Maines and Robinson 1994: 2.

The stages of the 'no-blame' approach are as follows:

Step one: Interview the victim. When a teacher finds out that bullying has happened he/she should talk to the victim about his/her feelings. The teacher does not question the victim about specific incidents but does need to know who was involved.
Step two: Convene a meeting with the people involved. This will include some bystanders or colluders who joined in, but did not initiate any bullying. Maines and Robinson advise that groups of six to eight people work well.
Step three: Explain the problem. The teacher explains the way the victim is feeling using a poem, prose or drawing to emphasise the victim's distress. At no time are details of particular incidents discussed or blame attributed to members of the group.
Step four: The teacher does not attribute blame but states that he/she knows that the group are responsible and can do something about it.
Step five: Ask the group for their ideas. Each member of the group is encouraged to suggest a way in which the victim could be helped to feel happier. The teacher gives some positive responses but does not go on to extract a promise of improved behaviour.
Step six: Leave it up to them. The teacher ends the meeting by passing over the responsibility to the group to solve the problem and arranges to meet with them again to see how things are going.
Step seven: Meet them again. About a week later the teacher discusses with each pupil, including the victim, what progress has been made. This allows the teacher to monitor the bullying and keeps pupils involved in the process.

The application of the 'no-blame' approach to school practice has received a mixed response. Many EBD teachers and educational psychologists believe that the impact of the programme is short-lived. There are inevitable problems in changing the existing mindset of pupils, parents and teachers (see management of change, Chapter 4).

Training is required for all members of the school community. Consistency is the key. A school which has a clear, written policy on anti-bullying procedures is not likely to incur disapproval from the community.

In extreme cases of bullying, when a pupil is seriously assaulted by another member of the school community, Maines and Robinson (1994: 7) consider that the usual sanctions must be applied, involving the police if appropriate. This implies that the 'no-blame' approach should be integrated into existing discipline policies. In practice, the 'no-blame' approach has achieved positive results when adapted to meet the needs of the pupil and school. Following training, teachers feel more positive about themselves and their ability to deal with the problem of bullying in their school. A case study of a school adopting the 'no-blame' approach can be found in Chapter 9.

9

GOOD PRACTICE

Teachers need to feel good about their practice. There is a tendency within education to criticise practice and, in doing so, belittle the professional status of practitioners. A paradox exists between the celebration of examination success and a dissatisfaction with pupil behaviour. Good practice is not an imaginary phenomenon, it happens in the majority of schools on a daily basis. There is much to be celebrated. Teachers should feel confident that they are able to provide a safe, secure environment in which children learn.

This chapter describes the good practice which exists in a range of primary and secondary schools. It provides an insight into the relationship between theory and practice. Based on what actually happens, and how and why it works, the examples shown should give teachers and other education agencies the self-confidence and belief that there are effective methods for the management of discipline in schools. Each example is set within its own culture and practice and should, therefore, be considered not as directly transferable to other schools, but more a framework for practice. As the government states: 'We will support local initiatives to tackle behaviour problems, take more active steps to spread information on good practice emerging from these, and expect LEAs to offer schools proactive support in tackling unacceptable behaviour' (DfEE 1997a: 56).

The chapter begins by describing the development of a behaviour plan, then focuses more specifically on timetable and curriculum, morning and break supervision, bullying, attendance, home-school contracts and early intervention, for example, LEA guidelines and peer support.

BEHAVIOUR MANAGEMENT PLAN

This example is taken from a small inner-city coeducational secondary school. The pupils were from the local community, a socially disadvantaged area, where many were sent to the school as a last resort, having failed at the more academically successful local comprehensive schools in the area. The deputy headteacher had been in post for five years, the majority of staff were reasonably accepting of the challenges with which they were confronted. The deputy headteacher, with the support of the LEA and governors, worked with a colleague to develop and implement a behaviour management plan for the school.

The school had previously based the management of discipline on the principles of assertive discipline. The newly appointed behaviour coordinator considered assertive discipline, 'to be worse than no discipline at all'. He believed that many teachers could not deal with discipline issues effectively because assertive discipline had become known as a system based on management structures, rather than a philosophy to be shared by all. Inevitably, where systems and structures exist they could be leant on by some teachers who believed that they were no longer responsible for the behaviours in their classrooms. If the system was allowed to decay, teachers would feel disempowered to respond to pupil needs. Further training and development was required to create a system based on shared expectations.

The behaviour coordinator interviewed most members of staff to discuss the issue of managing discipline. Many of the staff were keen to contribute, seeing the need for solutions to the behaviour management problems that were evident throughout the school. There was a developing belief that the majority of pupils wanted to behave and needed an environment in which they could learn. Expectations of pupil behaviour and work levels by staff and pupils required clearer defined boundaries. The lack of esteem in the community compounded the problem; pupils needed to be made aware that they were able to succeed.

There needed to be a change in perceptions and attitudes in order to raise expectations and, consequently, standards. The behaviour coordinator decided to develop a Code for Success (Wardle 1997) in consultation with all members of the school community. The Code for Success includes expectations for behaviour and attitudes for the whole-school community. The management team is also reviewing teaching and learning styles as, in common with schools with a significant discipline problem, pupils were low-achievers academically.

Pupil-teacher relationships were good. A positive feature of the school was its work as part of the local community. This had triggered funding for support mechanisms for pupils and teachers. The structure for a multi-agency approach to school-based initiative was in place. The extra funding available for EBD and family support reduced pressure on staff enabling them to assist pupils and parents in these areas. In practice, however, there was a need to increase the level of communication and the effectiveness of support.

The school had a very full schedule of extra-curricular activities which built on the evident community strengths. Pupil behaviour during these alternative activities was generally good; they wanted to do well and it was possible for them to succeed. This positive behaviour was not transferred to the classroom or school corridors. Many pupils lacked self-discipline in school, reflecting their lack of self-esteem in a learning environment. The consequence was disastrous; there were a high number of permanent exclusions in 1996/1997. A behaviour management plan was considered, by all, as a significant means of resolving the problem of managing discipline.

The aim of the behaviour management plan was to create and maintain the environment and expectations required for a learning community as defined in Figure 9.1. The diagram shows how a behaviour management plan should encompass all aspects of a pupil's experience in school. The plan relates the elements of teaching and learning to expectations.

The behaviour management plan was shaped by three strands of activity within the school: systems, expectations and support:

- Systems: behaviour management plan, clear guidelines, constant review and evaluation, consultation (pupils, parents, governors and staff), clarity and simplification and agreed criteria
- Expectations: Code for Success, assemblies, teaching expectations, parental contracts and meetings, staff discussions, clear guidelines and expectations for specific times of the day
- Support: staff, development for class teachers, heads of faculty, tutors and new staff, directed support for difficult pupils.

As shown, emphasis was placed on clear guidelines; pupils should know what is expected of them in order that they develop self-confidence. Every pupil was given a pupil guide explaining how they should behave generally and a specific description of how they should behave in lessons. This was developed through the school council, a body that represented all members of the school.

Teachers and support staff were trained in behavioural management techniques based on care studies within the school. A key element was the support for staff to help them develop their own classroom management techniques. Class teachers took responsibility for the management of discipline in their lessons. The

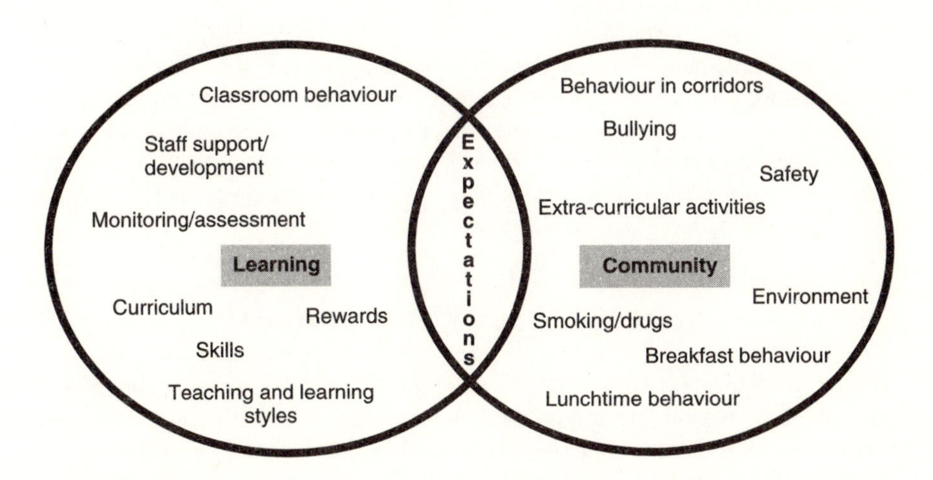

Figure 9.1 The learning community – behaviour management

Source: Wardle 1997

behaviour coordinator believed that, as an outcome of the consultation and training programmes, teachers were becoming more reflective.

Teachers were now in a position to try new approaches to their work. They were reviewing teaching and learning styles, considering accelerated learning programmes, developing pupil self-confidence in learning to learn, reviewing schemes of work to ensure a relevant curriculum, increase motivation and were also engaged in academic monitoring. As pupils and teachers have found, there is much to be gained from the first phase of introducing the behaviour management plan.

The behaviour management plan recognised that not all pupils were able to remain in class throughout the day. There would be those that would continue to disrupt lessons in an unacceptable manner. The behaviour coordinator had devised a scheme for 'parking' disruptive pupils in host lessons in order to avoid further disruption. The pupil is taken to a designated area in the host classroom; the principle being that when 'parked' they will, in time, be ready to leave and rejoin their class. A pupil will be placed in 'parking' only after all agreed classroom strategies and sanctions have been applied and failed. There is an agreed system to follow up the original incident that draws on the further expectations from the expectation sheet; the aim being to reduce the likelihood of the incident happening again. Figure 9.2 illustrates the pattern of events leading to, and from parking. Further documentation has been prepared to support the plan including:

- parent guidelines
- senior management team guidelines
- letters to parents
- rewards and sanctions
- procedures for placing a pupil in parking.

Having implemented the behaviour management plan, the coordinator and senior management staff are confident that it will succeed. The behaviour management plan includes an automatic review system which is considered to be a very important part of the plan. This will take place every two months and will later be reduced to three times a year. If the plan fails the process will be changed; the review will form the basis of any future plan.

TIMETABLE AND CURRICULUM

The Elton Report (DES 1989: 121) advised that timetables should be constructed with pupils' behaviour in mind. The lengths of lunch, morning and afternoon breaks and movement between lessons should be considered when planning the structure of the school day and the timetable. Curriculum content should also be considered; a pupil who is expected to carry to school physical education kit and

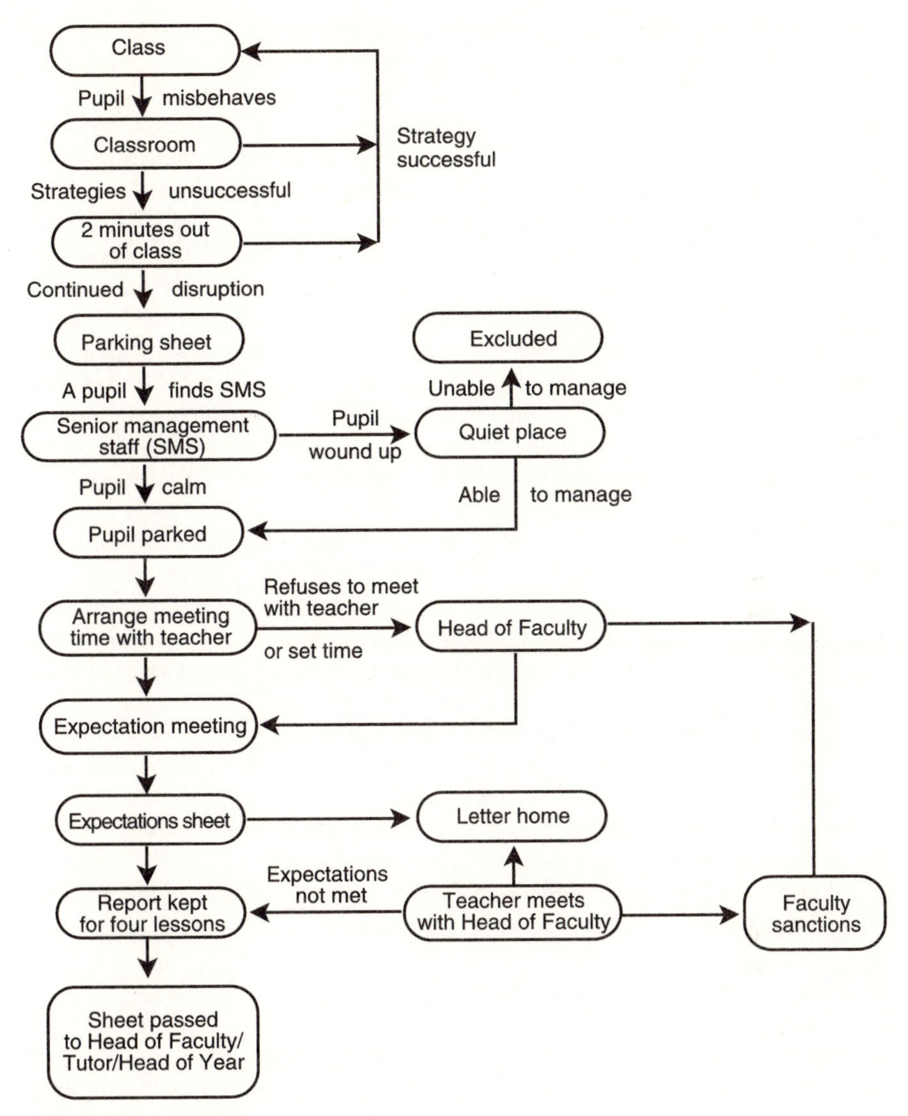

Figure 9.2 Behaviour management plan

Source: Wardle 1997

food for technology on the same day as his/her double bass is going to have problems!

In all schools bottlenecks can occur in narrow corridors, or stairwells. Badly placed queues can lead to behaviour problems. Pushing, jostling and bad language can lead to more serious problems such as fights. Physical aggression is a problem in schools that can in some cases be avoided by improved timetabling.

A possible solution to timetable and curriculum issues related to the management of discipline in schools is the introduction of a modular curriculum. This system of curriculum planning was first introduced to England and Wales by the curriculum team of a small girls' comprehensive school in an urban area of London. Much of what follows is described in full in *Modular Curriculum* published by the Centre for the Study of Comprehensive Schools (Blandford *et al.* 1991).

A module is a short course that is spread over nine weeks and lasts for forty-three hours. In Key Stages 4 and 5, pupils select two different modular courses during each nine-week block. In the example given, it is possible for pupils to complete sixteen modules during a two-year programme. All modules culminate in some form of recorded assessment and the unit credits produced are an integral part of the school's profiling system. The new school year timetable begins in May for Year 9–13 pupils, thus allowing two modules to be completed in the summer term. This provides Year 7 teachers with the opportunity to develop and maintain links with feeder schools, critical to effective transition between Key Stage 2 and Key Stage 3.

A module is a self-contained course in its own right; modules of several types can be considered:

- A single, self-contained unit which is a complete nine-week autonomous course. This type of unit does not lead directly onto other modules. Despite being a self-contained unit, the assessment is formative, providing part of the basis for decisions about the pupil's future learning needs.
- A complementary module linked to examination subjects. This would allow pupils to develop their skills where appropriate.
- Related sequential modules for those courses that require pupils to complete modules in a particular order.
- Cluster modules: independent modules that can be taken in any order, but come together to form a complete examination course.

There are many advantages to a modular curriculum:

- By dividing up the courses into modules and by offering two modules only at one time, pupils wanting four GCSEs out of the module system are never taught their full range of courses at any one time. They are always two subjects light. The school has moved from 'drip feed' teaching, where pupils get constant small doses, over two years, to an approach where they receive four concentrated doses often with breaks in between. Initially, one concern was over the amount of knowledge that the pupil may forget between cluster or sequential modules. Whilst it was important to produce a modular structure which minimised large time gaps between related modules (rather than fragment the learning process) it appeared that such short courses could, in fact, enhance it.

- Many syllabuses offered an above minimum level of coursework as counting towards part or all of the examination process. Coursework could be evenly spread over the period of the GCSE course by building it into the final assessment of each module, thereby avoiding some of the coursework pressures on pupils that were seen to build up in the second year of GCSE.
- With a modular approach, the starting and ending points of a GCSE course were flexible. Courses could start at any of four points during the year and could be completed in a minimum time of thirty-six weeks. This flexibility is one of the system's strengths. Year 10 pupils could be entered for examinations at any of three points within the final two years, or could delay entry until the sixth year, without having to repeat a complete GCSE course. If pupils were not satisfied with their grades, many would take the opportunity to improve them. Pupils finding modules difficult could repeat them later, in order to strengthen their chances of gaining good grades.
- Pupils not ready for a particular course could delay entry to it. The possibility exists for courses to be left, and taken up again later if there are factors working against the pupil's successful completion of the module, for example, peer group pressures or staff/pupil relations. Pupils would not be left to experience inappropriate courses, as is often the case within the option system. They could change at the end of the module and still pick up a complete GCSE course. New pupils entering the school in Years 10/11 could select a course more appropriate to their needs and were not left with a mismatch of courses as normally happens with such transfers.
- Long pupil or staff illnesses could be catered for; in the case of the former, by building in repeat modules so that whole sections of courses are not lost and, with the latter by redirecting pupils from within a module (emptying it) and placing it back in the structure at a later date. Because of the intensity of the learning, pupils do not have as many subjects to work on at any one time as under the old system. It was soon realised that many pupils would not have large gaps between modules, and that the starting and ending points of most GCSE courses could be less far apart than in the two-year option scheme.
- The intensity of the learning and the short-term goals of the nine week modules were seen as powerful motivating factors. It was considered important to enter pupils for a GCSE examination as close to the end of their final module as was possible, and to consider running some related modules 'end on', should a time gap be considered detrimental to learning.
- There was some concern over the maturity of some pupils who might complete a course early. It was felt that some pupils completing courses by Year 10 might be disadvantaged compared with those completing the same courses over two academic years. This factor is very difficult to gauge, because pupils within any one year differ greatly and it is further complicated by the maturity levels of the same pupil appearing to differ between subjects. To offset this, it must be remembered that, as the modular groups are identical, the level of learning is the same and all groups contain pupils from several

> different year cohorts. This latter factor tends to bring wider experience to groups than may have previously been the case.

If, however, a subject teacher feels that a pupil would be better taking additional modules the next academic year, the system will cater for it. In addition it could be argued that, for some pupils to take examinations at the end of Year 11 is too late. Demotivation and dissatisfaction with school can prevent many pupils from achieving their full potential. Any system which offers early entry must benefit these pupils.

Teachers found that a partially modular curriculum could lead to the avoidance of many of the organisational and administrative limitations of a traditional curriculum. Cost-effective in terms of resourcing and staffing; it is flexible and allows a greater degree of choice to pupils and parents than a limited option system. It requires a detailed analysis of syllabuses as well as a review of teaching styles. Short courses lend themselves to the introduction of a profiling system culminating in a record of achievement. It provides a means by which the educational benefits of vocational courses can be shared by a greater proportion of the school.

There are many advantages of a modular curriculum that are also transferable to Key Stages 2 and 3. Curriculum coordinators in all phases of education should consider the impact of an inappropriate curriculum on the management of discipline in schools, and the possibility of changing to a modular structure.

BULLYING

Bullying is an experience no pupil should endure.

> As part of their behaviour policies, all schools need effective strategies to deal with bullying. These work particularly well when the whole-school community, including pupils, is involved in their development and application. The emotional and mental distress caused by bullying can have a severe adverse effect on pupils' achievement – both directly and where it leads to truancy.
>
> (DfEE 1997a: 56)

The following example shows how a primary school responded to bullying in a positive manner when faced with a problem created by their own community. The closure of a large factory, the major employer in an already deprived area, triggered a period of social unrest. The housing estate's junior school was to witness some of the worst cases of bullying in the experience of its headteacher and his well qualified staff. The headteacher, in collaboration with his staff and governors, introduced the 'no-blame' approach (see Chapter 8) developed by Maines and Robinson (1994).

The process began when the school community was invited to an open meeting to discuss the function and meaning of the 'no-blame' approach. Bullying was defined as a person or group behaving in a way that does not recognise or meet the needs and rights of other people, who are harmed by the behaviour. Victims were defined as persons or groups that are harmed by the behaviour of others and who do not have the resources, status, skill or ability to counteract or stop the harmful behaviour. The school was advised that using 'bullying' and 'victim' as labels was unhelpful. To call pupils by any name other their own will affect their self-image and will be difficult for them and their parents to accept.

The 'no-blame' approach advises teachers to listen to both the bully and victim, to develop an understanding of how they feel. The school decided that teachers would need to be trained in basic counselling techniques in order to listen effectively. The LEA EBD team was contracted to lead INSET courses during one term, to enable teachers to develop these skills.

The staff members were asked to abandon punishment as a response to the bullies. In order to encourage disclosure and to work positively with bullies and their victims, everyone in the school community must know that effective action would be taken but that it would not lead to punishment. The key principle was then communicated by letter to parents. Following the INSET course, staff felt confident about the 'no-blame' approach in school. Pupils were introduced to the idea in an assembly performed by the school drama group. Their enactment of the bully/victim scenario was clear and the headteacher was able to explain the 'new' course of action that would follow.

The school was able to review the impact of the 'no-blame' approach on its community at the end of the academic year. Teachers felt that the process had enabled them to tackle a difficult problem in a constructive manner. They appreciated the value of the support given to them by the area EBD team and the relevance of the counselling skills to their practice. The occurrence of bullying had decreased significantly and pupils appeared more confident with each other. The need for an anti-bullying policy remained for the few extreme cases that still occurred. Teachers believed that the greatest benefit of the process was the opportunity to discuss discipline matters in a secure, supportive environment.

ATTENDANCE

There are significant variations in attendance rates between different schools. These would appear to relate to pupil age, (older pupils 'vote with their feet' against the curriculum), the locality (inner-city schools have a higher truancy rate (DES 1989: 166)) and the quality of dialogue between the EWO, parents and headteacher.

Shadowing a highly successful EWO from an inner-city area illuminated many of the issues relating to non-attendance, or truancy. The EWO concerned is responsible for five primary schools, a large 11–18 coeducational comprehensive school and a large 11–16 community school. This constitutes a total of approximately four and a half thousand pupils in a highly populated area covering five miles of the city. The EWO is from the city and has worked in the area for eight years. She has been allocated her current schools for two years.

Good practice can be defined in many ways: administration, interpersonal skills, communication skills, knowledge and understanding of people and legislation all relate to the very demanding role of an EWO. The more personal attributes that distinguish good practice from someone 'doing their job' are tenacity, strength of personality and the intangible effective traits that pupils relate to instantly.

An EWO is responsible for the welfare of pupils in their area, ensuring that they have access to education in order to fulfil their potential (see Chapter 7). In practice, an EWO will attend a number of meetings covering attendance, pastoral care, exclusion, pupils at risk and team work. An EWO is the advocate for all pupils, a link between parents and the school and an LEA representative. This multiplicity of roles and responsibilities could, if not managed effectively, create a number of dilemmas. The effective EWO will:

- be there for all clients, teachers, pupils, parents, LEA, headteacher and governors
- be non-judgemental in his/her relationship with the school community
- be able to represent parents and pupils in an unemotive manner
- be a confidante and friend to all pupils
- be known and trusted in the community.

The EWO described in this section displayed many of the characteristics, professional and personal, that determine good practice. In her approach to pupils, she is firm, fair, friendly and supportive. Pupils 'know' that they are to attend school and that continued absences will lead to a home visit from the EWO. There are regular meetings with key members of the pastoral and senior management teams to discuss pupils' problems and to plan a strategy involving all relevant members of the school community.

Critically, the EWO places pupils' needs on the agenda of every meeting. She spends many working hours talking to pupils, their families and friends in order to establish a positive relationship with each pupil. This involves walking into amusement arcades to identify under-age players who should be at school, visiting a pupil's house-bound grandparents to locate a missing pupil and following a pupil to her boyfriend's high-rise flat. The range of activities is exhausting, requiring an energetic approach to an extremely demanding job.

The EWO is professional at all times, communicating, informally and formally, with LEA support agencies. Within the legislative framework (see Chapter 2), she works towards the development of pupil-esteem and self-confidence. A major element of her practice is working at being a high-profile member of the local community. She is known and respected at all levels. Her working relationship with

the senior management team and governors is of the highest quality. In essence, she is valued and respected by all who meet her, including pupils who have been the subject of education supervision orders (see Chapter 7). The early intervention of the EWO is very effective. The rapid communication of a pupil's absence from school or a lesson and immediate follow-up result in effective action by all agencies. The schools served by the EWO are also developing home-school contracts, following the implementation of more effective legal sanctions by central government regarding parental responsibilities for ensuring regular and punctual attendance (DfEE 1997a).

HOME-SCHOOL CONTRACTS

One EBD team serving a highly populated area on the outskirts of a major city has developed the effective use of home-school contracts. Relating directly to the management of discipline in school, home contracts are for all pupils attending the schools in their area. When evaluating the home-school contract, the EBD team found that in the past there had been a tendency for action plans (see Chapter 7) and other home-school agreements to 'be done to' pupils. Contracts were imposed as a condition of continuing placement. The EBD team believed that there should be two levels of agreement, whole-school and individual plan.

Home-school contracts should present to parents a clear statement of what they can expect from the school and what the school expects from them and their children. An example is shown in Appendix A. Schools should provide opportunities for parents to discuss their expectations with teachers. The EBD team believes that this is very important for nursery schools and primary schools, as this is the first school contact for parents. To this end the EBD team advises that headteachers should ensure that their schools have effective induction arrangements for parents of new pupils. They also advised that senior managers should ensure that their schools' behaviour policies are communicated fully and clearly to parents, who should be reminded of them regularly and informed of any major changes to them throughout their child's school career.

At the point where a more detailed individual education plan (action plan) is needed (Stage 2), this should be negotiated between the parties involved. Action plans should follow the guidelines contained in the Code of Practice (DfE 1994a) (see Chapter 2). An action plan is a useful mechanism to employ when dealing with particular difficulties between pupils and schools. The EBD team advises the following:

- a home-school contract should set out what the school will provide for the pupil and parent
- the contract should state what the school will expect from the pupil in terms of effort and behaviour, and from the parent in terms of support

- the home-school contract should be signed by the pupil, parents and class teacher.

More specifically, the EBD team considers that it is necessary to establish targets for the pupil, based on the observations of all involved. Targets should emphasise and build on the pupil's strengths, celebrating success and achievement, but only employing a reward if the pupil values the reward given.

The EBD team found that the implementation of an action plan is therefore uncomplicated in primary schools, where the class teacher has the majority of the teaching time. In secondary schools, however, there are far more members of staff interacting with the pupil and consistency is far more difficult to achieve. The EBD team advises that it is imperative that the contract/action plan is communicated and explained to staff. Teaching and non-teaching staff need to understand the reasoning behind requests for monitoring, the nature of rewards/sanctions and to be dedicated to following the contract/action plan. The EBD team explains that, while the contract/action plan is designed to help the pupil, improvement in the pupil will result in decreasing stress and tension in the classroom thus helping the teacher.

The EBD team states that, with all home-school contracts, it is essential to monitor behaviours and for all agencies involved to have the opportunity to review their effectiveness. In practice, the purpose of a contract is to set out clear boundaries for behaviour: what the school does to help the pupil remain within these boundaries and, where necessary, the consequences of the pupil overstepping those boundaries. The EBD team believes that imposition rarely fosters respect or compliance, a negotiated contract is far more likely to succeed.

Following the advice given by the EBD team, the head of Year 7 in a large 11–16 coeducational comprehensive designed and implemented a *target book* shown in Appendix D. The target book is issued to pupils once a home-school contract has been negotiated. The head of year piloted the use of the book with twenty-three pupils, involving parents, teachers, senior management and outside agencies in the process. Pupils valued the book (which had a bright gold cover) and were enthusiastic in engaging teachers in their development. With the exception of two teachers, all completed the relevant sections on a regular basis. Parents were pleased to have a lesson by lesson account of their child's progress. Subsequently, the target book has been adapted for use in other schools.

EARLY INTERVENTION – LEA GUIDELINES

The multi-agency approach to managing discipline in schools is effective in providing quality advice and support to pupils, parents, teachers, senior managers and governors. In practice there is a need for teachers to know how to implement whole-school, class and individual pupil discipline policies and behaviour plans. An LEA in the west of England (Bristol Special Needs Support Service 1996) approached this problem by producing documented advice for school-based intervention on primary pupils experiencing behavioural difficulties, summarised as follows:

> Teachers should build a relationship with pupils by showing a particular interest in how they are. It is also essential for teachers to gather as much information as possible from the pupil and their parents. In practice, teachers should really listen to pupils and acknowledge how they feel. The aim should be to problem-solve together without blaming. Teachers should try to avoid the triggers which set off the behaviour that they want to change by:
>
> - adjusting the length and nature of learning tasks
> - adjusting pupil groupings – to provide support for all pupils
> - checking that all pupils have understood the instructions required to complete the task
> - structuring unstructured time, lunchtime clubs or groups
> - recognising that anger is a secondary emotion: identify and deal with the primary emotion instead (usually humiliation, frustration or fear)
> - avoiding activities that cause problems, for example, assembly
> - setting targets that are achievable, and reward success
> - avoiding power struggles
> - adapting use of language, trying not to be confrontational
> - being creative.

The LEA also advised teachers on how to identify any skills the pupils need in order to change their behaviour by teaching cooperative group work skills and helping the pupils to recognise their flash points. Teachers should teach turn-taking, listening, sharing and choosing through group games and work on friendship skills with small groups. Isolated pupils should be given opportunities to work in pairs or groups. A class teacher can also teach pupils how to behave in a specific school situation using modelling, practice and praise.

Central to good practice is building pupils' self-esteem. In order for this to happen, teachers need to create situations where pupils can succeed. Teachers need to know what pupils are good at, providing support when difficulties arise. Teachers can help the pupils to become experts, or develop an interest by providing the opportunities for pupils to participate in extra-curricular activities, or by giving them responsibilities in the classroom. Pupils should be given praise and rewards appropriate to their needs; teachers should highlight achievement in behaviour or learning.

Target setting will enable teachers and pupils to recognise and record changes in behaviour. Pupils should be encouraged to record one success at the end of each day. The school discipline policy provides the framework for success or failure in the classroom. If it is not working for a particular pupil, change it (see Chapter 10).

This is acceptable when it is clear to all pupils that there are consistent rewards and sanctions in operation. It is possible to differentiate a whole-school discipline policy. Rewards for individual pupils can include:

- choice of play activities
- game with teacher or chosen friend
- first out to play
- doing a special job
- being a leader of an activity
- time with a busy box
- time on computer
- time with a special adult in school, for example, the caretaker or secretary
- going to help in a younger class
- badges, stickers, stamps, certificates
- notes home.

Rewards need to be placed within the context of practice; teachers need to 'catch' pupils being good. They also need to decide on which behaviours to ignore. Teachers need to work with parents in being consistent; parents will also need to know what behaviours to ignore or reward. Peer support is also valuable. Teachers ask pupils to nominate a peer as a special helper, to remind them of expected behaviours and praise when it happens.

The LEA also advised that teachers should make the time to share with a sympathetic colleague or staff group, feelings of exhaustion, frustration, disappointment and worry as a result of pupil or class behaviour. Teachers need to recognise that they have a right to such feelings and they need to be expressed and recognised. If not, the feelings will hinder a teacher's ability to support the pupil or class with appropriate strategies.

In practice, the staff at the local primary school felt confident about the advice given. Following an INSET course developing the ideas detailed in the document, teachers set a programme to review the discipline policy in their school. They also established pupil support teams for each year group. Perhaps the most significant outcome was the coming together of a staff support group that was to meet weekly in order to share discipline-related problems and suggest possible practical solutions.

PEER SUPPORT

An article in the *Times Educational Supplement* (Carlton 1997: 17) focused on a scheme that enabled sixth-form pupils to provide counselling for Year 10 and 11 pupils. While the emphasis was on enhancing academic achievement, the fundamental cause of the problem was discipline. Boys, in particular, were under-achieving owing either to lack of self-discipline, or lack of self-esteem. The overall plan to develop boys' learning skills was based on ten strategies that included a mentoring scheme by teachers for under-achievers and of peer-counselling by sixth-form pupils.

Peer-counselling involved pairing sixth-form students – those with 'street cred', who had been in trouble themselves for not working hard – with Year 9 pupils requiring support. The pairs met regularly throughout the year and were encouraged to become friends. The principle idea was to get the Year 9 pupils to see their work from a different perspective in order that they would be more interested in their personal performance, organise time more effectively and not leave the completion of coursework until it was too late. The benefit to the sixth-form pupil was that they had to evaluate their own practice in order to help their younger colleague. They were also able to mention peer-counselling on their university entrance form.

In practice, peer-counselling was effective because of the closeness in ages of the pupils and relevant shared experiences. The pupils were able to reflect on the time wasted in the classroom through distractions and lack of concentration. The pupils were also able to consider how to organise their time in a more effective way by not 'mucking about'. Peer-counsellors were able to examine the more negative aspects of school friendships that discourage pupils to concentrate in the classroom. Boys were further supported by teacher mentors to help those who had a particular problem with their behaviour, academic work or study skills. The senior management team has created an achievement board in the school's entrance hall to celebrate success and staff have become more positive in class.

In practice, peer-counsellors feel valued and respected members of the school community. They are able to relate their own experiences to the needs of their partners. The pairs have developed a good understanding of the need for self-discipline in school. The strength of the scheme is the impact on the self-esteem of both peer and partner.

SCHOOL COUNCIL

Researchers and practitioners believe that schools that give pupils positive responsibilities achieve better standards of behaviour (Rutter *et al.* 1979; Mortimore *et al.* 1988). Headteachers and teachers should give pupils every opportunity to take responsibility and to make a full contribution to behaviour in the school community.

The following example of good practice defines the aims, structure and management of a school council established in a large inner-city, 11–16 coeducational community school.

Definition

The student council is a representative meeting of the school community through which the needs and concerns of students can be voiced on matters regarding school life, working in a partnership to improve the quality of learning and the environment of the school.

Aims

- to provide a forum through which students can raise issues which concern them and make suggestions about aspects of school life
- to provide a means of communication between students and staff and the wider community
- to create a structure through which students can be consulted
- to encourage student responsibility for involvement in school issues
- to encourage action on areas of identified need.

The structure of the student council is shown in Figure 9.3. The term of office should last for a whole year, for both school council representatives and year council representatives. New year councils will be elected by the end of the first half of every autumn term. The first meeting of the council in each new academic year would be of the remaining existing members. This meeting would be used to review the work and progress of the council. The first meeting of the new school council, including new Year 7 representatives, would be held shortly after the half term break in the autumn term. New officers (chair, secretary) are elected at the first full meeting of the school council in the new academic year.

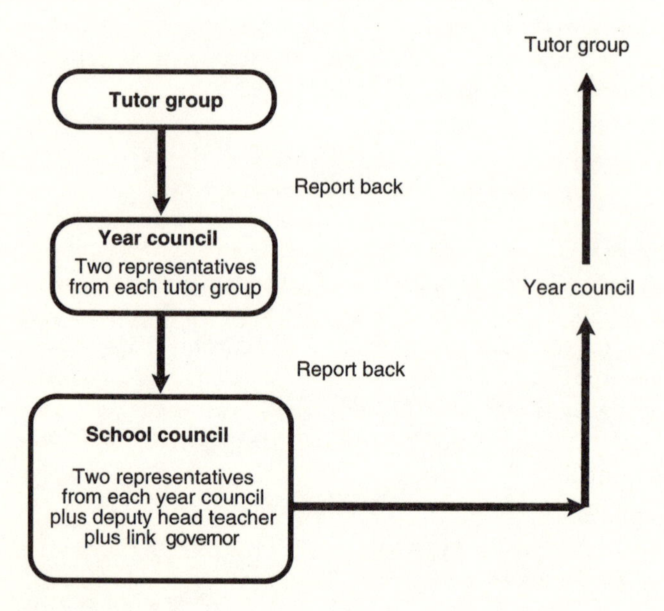

Figure 9.3 Student council structure

Frequency of meetings

School council meetings need to be held during the week following the year council meetings and every half term. In the event of it being necessary to call an additional meeting, representatives are to liaise with the chair and arrange for a briefing sheet to be issued to year teams for their comments before the meeting. School council meetings will be held at different times in a week throughout the year to avoid pupils missing the same lesson. All meetings are planned for one hour.

The minutes of the school council meetings are issued to tutor group representatives, as soon as possible following the school council meetings and displayed in year areas. The issues are discussed at SMT following the school council meeting, and an agenda item for governors' meetings – achievement and guidance and main governors.

The work of the school council is reviewed annually, during the summer term to include Year 11. Changes to the constitution can only be made following a majority vote by year councils. The structure works well as it allows all pupils' views to be presented in year councils in addition to the whole-school perspective of the full school council.

PARENTS: COPING WITH KIDS

A very successful project focusing on parental skills, Coping with Kids (Robinson 1997b) aims to help children to develop the motivation, self-control and responsibility necessary to be effective future members of society by providing support to their parents through a short series of workshops and discussion groups. The aims of the project are:

- to provide a network of workshops for parents in [the local area], focused on managing children's behaviour successfully
- to involve all the helping agencies, [that is] education, health and social services, together with voluntary and charitable organisations, to work at a multi-agency level to provide workshops and venues in a variety of community locations and to support the most vulnerable families to attend the sessions
- to allow open access to all parents in the locality, irrespective of income, ethnic background, gender or disability
- to provide leader training on a regular basis to enable suitably qualified and interested adults already working in the community to lead the workshops
- to continue developing and adapting training materials to provide the best possible support for both parents and leaders.

(Robinson 1997c)

Individual workshops are held to support and encourage positive, caring and happy family life in order to enable parents to cope effectively with challenging behaviour, within the principles laid out in the United Nations *Convention on the Rights of the Child* (1989). Each session provides an opportunity for mutual discussion and support between parents.

Workshops are open access and available to parents locally within the community. The project would benefit from research on effective recruitment, leading to focused recruitment of parents from a wide range of cultural backgrounds. In addition, increased publicity and a higher profile would raise awareness of the programme's advantages and potential.

There is a need for continued regular leader training, and increased secretarial and coordinator time. Each course is evaluated by the participants and leaders at the end of the third session. It has been suggested that consideration is given to longer-term evaluation; higher education establishments could be approached in order to involve potential research students in the evaluation.

In practice, over two hundred families have benefited from Coping with Kids courses during 1996–97, with fifty per cent of these being drawn from the lowest income sector. Evaluations by both participants and leaders have been very positive and the quality of the workshops is demonstrated by the very low 'drop-out' rate of only 7 per cent. There is now an increasing demand for more workshops and many course leaders are beginning to run them on a regular basis from their own centres.

Recruitment to the courses is becoming easier as publicity and 'word of mouth' reaches more and more parents. Regular courses at convenient venues and the inclusion of Coping with Kids as part of ongoing parent involvement programmes have also encouraged recruitment and helped to establish viable groups.

Funding for Coping with Kids has been received from Safer Cities, the Gulbenkian Foundation and from charitable donations. Additional funding is generated by course fees and the sale of books and leader training. More funding will be needed, though, to enable the development of support materials and videos, and to provide time for the proper administration and management of the project as it increases in size.

FAMILY CONNECTIONS – A PROGRAMME FOR PARENTS AND THEIR PRE-SCHOOL CHILDREN

The Family Nurturing Network, a registered charity which is part funded by social services, the Pre-School Teacher Counselling service and an Educational Psychologist in Oxford City have combined their skills in order to support children and their parents.

The Family Connections programme is aimed at families where the pre-school child (estimated 15–20 per cent) is showing signs of developmental, emotional or behavioural disturbance of clinical severity (Oxford County Council Education

Department 1997) which can undermine successful transition to school. These children are likely to have experienced some or all of the following: lack of stimulation, inconsistent and ineffective discipline, lack of good shared experience, parental hostility and rejection, violence in the home, corporal punishment, and parental absences and mental illness. They may also suffer from undetected sensory or physiological impairments. If not addressed, the child's problems (particularly when they are multiple) and detrimental style of parenting do not spontaneously resolve. They are known to reduce the child's potential to benefit from education, to relate to peers and to become well-adjusted adults. For example, 50 per cent of pre-school children showing emotional and behavioural difficulties at home go on to present these problems in primary school. Therefore, the strategic approach to the prevention of EBDs in schools needs to start at the pre-school stage.

The Family Connections project is designed to help parents of pre-school children who are showing early signs of emotional and behavioural difficulties to develop more effective parenting skills, to enhance children's ability to play and communicate, and to provide baseline assessment of children coming into school.

Parents learn about the principles of play and praise, how to set limits, how to deal with misbehaviour without resorting to harsh or punitive measures, and how to develop communication and problem-solving in families. These principles and skills are illustrated in a series of video vignettes showing parents and children in everyday situations 'doing it right' and 'doing it wrong' and what effect this has on the child's behaviour and feelings. Participants watch and discuss the vignettes and then practice the principles in role-plays with each other during the sessions, and with their children during assigned home activities between the sessions. Throughout the programme, the team emphasise that there is usually more than one way to solve a problem, that parents need to have realistic expectations of their children, that each child has a unique temperament and that parents will get more of what they pay attention to. The team also encourage parents to stop and think before responding 'instinctively' in conflict situations, to develop a set of skills for use in the future and to feel empowered to help their children learn and be confident.

Children are provided with a range of activities in a well equipped nursery setting. They are encouraged to play and explore these activities with the support of an adult according to individual need. The sessions have an established routine of individual play, group activities, snack time, outdoor play and, finally, play with parents. They adapt activities to suit the children's developmental needs. The last thirty minutes of each session when the parents join in, provide an excellent opportunity to observe, encourage, praise and give advice on play activities, etc.

The parents' group is led by a clinical psychologist/coordinator of the Family Nurturing Network (FNN) and a co-leader, often a health visitor wishing to develop further their skills in assisting families. The children's group is planned, run and supervised by pre-school teacher counsellors who guide several volunteer 'key workers' (usually health visitors or psychology graduates) specifically trained for their role with the children. An educational psychologist coordinates observational assessment of children and preparation of reports for parents. The pre-group assessment of families, evaluation questionnaires, hire of the venue, programme materials, equipment of nursery and recruitment of key workers for children have been provided from the FNN.

Evaluation

Two programmes were run with twenty families in total. Three families were on the child protection register and two families had a statemented child in the primary school. Only the pre-school children attended with their parents though many also had older siblings.

The families came from very varied social and educational backgrounds, however, this was not found to be detrimental in any way to forming a very supportive group. Many parents were at the end of their tether, trying to do their best but not succeeding with their children. Often, their relationship with their children has broken down and they felt they did not have much affection left for them. They were very keen to find out first of all how to control the children but they did readily accept that the team should begin by concentrating on strengthening the attachment with the children through play. The team found that the parents often had inappropriate/unclear expectations of their children and 'erred' by being either too harsh and punitive or too permissive instead of authoritative (not authoritarian).

10

POLICY

Good discipline in schools is dependent on a shared understanding of what is accepted behaviour among members of the school community. In most cases, if a class or pupil is deemed to be of little value to the school community, the response will be to behave in an unacceptable manner. A fundamental element of good discipline is self-esteem of pupil, teacher and senior management. Without self-esteem pupils and teachers will not function in the school community.

Many of the strategies and approaches to the management of discipline described throughout this book relate directly to the development of self-esteem and self-confidence in the individual and school. This emphasises the need for every school to have a discipline policy that focuses on personal development and growth, not punishment and blame. A discipline policy should reflect the ethos of the school and contribute to the fulfilment of its mission.

In practice, a discipline policy should reflect the values and beliefs of the school community. It should also relate to the social development of pupils as appropriate to their age and personal needs. School values (OFSTED 1994: 12) should include:

- telling the truth and keeping promises
- respecting the rights and property of others
- acting considerately towards others
- helping those less fortunate and weaker than ourselves
- taking personal responsibility for one's actions.

School values should reject:

- bullying
- cheating
- deceit
- cruelty
- irresponsibility
- dishonesty.

For schools to develop their own ethos and sense of community they will need to have a view on what behaviour they wish to encourage. Schools will also need to encourage the development of desirable attitudes and personal qualities and the way in which these skills can relate to the knowledge and understanding, skills and abilities members of their community will acquire.

Pupils should be able to move from taught discipline, which is characteristic of the very young, and an essential prerequisite of personal development, to a position where their values, judgements, behaviours and attitudes spring from internal sources and allow them to be mature, autonomous, decision-making and responsible individuals. However, it is necessary to reflect that human beings often move between such stages of development in a seemingly random manner; those who are perfectly capable of self-justifying, autonomous action may often act irrationally, for example, out of fear or loss of self-control (OFSTED 1994: 13). The period of compulsory schooling is a time when many pupils increasingly subject their family and community values to an intense, critical scrutiny. Schools should aim to help pupils to establish their own values, and also help them to develop the self-confidence and resolve to maintain those values against peer group and other pressures.

The development of personal values is an outcome of an effective discipline policy that relates to the social function of schools. Schools complement and extend the functions of the home and wider community by helping to prepare their pupils to live in society. Pupils need to learn the obligations that go with membership of a group and a community (OFSTED 1994: 15). Pupils also need to become aware of their own identity as individuals and of the importance of taking account of the feelings and wishes of others.

In practice, teachers provide a range of opportunities for pupils to learn and develop social skills and attitudes. The process of social development is continued throughout primary and secondary education, in school rules and codes of practice, in school councils and clubs and in the encouragement of pupils' responsibility for themselves and others.

The precise content of a school's behaviour policy must be determined by the school community. The process of developing a policy is discussed later in this chapter. Following the recommendations from the DfE (DfE 1994b), whole-school discipline policies should:

- be simple, straightforward and based on a clear and defensible set of principles and values
- provide for the encouragement of good behaviour and for the punishment of bad behaviour
- be specific to the school
- have a minimum number of rules that are expressed in positive, constructive terms, so that all are absolutely clear how members of the school community are expected to behave.

Encouraging respect for others should be promoted within the framework of a discipline policy. A school's moral code will underpin its behaviour policy and will be reflected in the style and atmosphere of the school itself, and the manner in which members of the community relate to each other. If all pupils are to have their chance to learn, the ethos of the school should include a clear vision of the values which it wants to teach its pupils. Staff and pupils should have a clear sense of what is important, what will be valued and what is not acceptable. In practice, everyone should have a clear understanding as to what kind of behaviour is expected of them and how they can expect others to behave towards them.

The local community will pay great attention to the behaviour of individual pupils and how they treat one another, since pupils will be seen as representatives of their schools. This applies equally when pupils are away from the school premises.

As indicated throughout this book, improvements in behaviour are more likely to follow if self-esteem can be enhanced and if the pupil can be brought to recognise the effects of his/her behaviour on others. Schools have a role in developing a sense of responsibility in pupils and in promoting consideration towards others. This can be accomplished in a number of ways:

- informally, by regular positive recognition of everyday acts of consideration
- by older pupils being actively encouraged to look after younger or disadvantaged pupils, particularly those pupils whose special circumstances may make them vulnerable to bullying
- teaching time can be devoted to an examination of the issues of mutual respect
- commendable behaviour can be drawn to the attention of parents
- the celebration of success, including rewards for individual pupils who have distinguished themselves by their attitude and conduct towards members of the school community.

Teachers should be able to feel that their work to maintain discipline in the classroom takes place within the framework of the school's overall policy. The contribution of teaching and non-teaching staff to the development of a policy on the systems and steps to be taken to resolve a disciplinary crisis is important. For example, teachers will need to know the range of options available to them, which may involve other members of staff when a pupil needs to be removed temporarily from the classroom. It is also helpful if teachers dealing with pupils who cause particular difficulties discuss common problems and develop consistent strategies for dealing with them (see Chapter 6).

Schools need agreed and effective systems of support for individual teachers. Teachers should not be blamed for failures in maintaining good discipline if the necessary support systems within the school for providing practical advice and help are absent. Individual teachers have, in turn, a responsibility to contribute to those support systems which depend for their success on school endorsement.

Teachers will benefit greatly from a clear and agreed discipline policy that has expectations of them as practitioners. Effective teachers operating under clearly understood guidelines will feel confident in giving clear instructions and presentations, have precise work requirements of pupils, handle misbehaviour quickly and calmly, ensure that work is appropriate to pupils' abilities, set clear goals, start and end lessons on time and minimise interruptions.

In sum, the management of discipline in schools requires schools to have a clear policy that all members of the school community are prepared to stand by. The alternative is indiscipline that will impair the efficiency of the school and create considerable stress amongst pupils, parents, teachers, senior managers and members of the wider school community.

DEVELOPING A WHOLE-SCHOOL DISCIPLINE POLICY

A policy should be a living document that both determines and reflects good practice. Policy documents that are not created by those who have responsibility for the practical implementation of policies are worthless. A whole-school approach to discipline (Lowe and Stance 1989) will encompass the characteristics of an effective school:

- commitment to commonly identified norms and goals
- collaborative planning, shared decision-making within a framework of experimentation and evaluation
- positive leadership in initiating and maintaining improvement
- staff stability
- continuing staff development linked to the school's pedagogical and organisational needs
- carefully planned and coordinated curriculum, catering for the needs of all pupils
- high level of parental involvement and support
- the recognition of school-wide values
- maximum use of learning time
- the active and substantial support of the LEA.

Research (Merrett and Jones 1994) has shown that headteachers feel that they are working in isolation and would like to have clear guidelines on how to formulate a whole-school policy. More guidance is required from other headteachers or support agencies.

In practice, a discipline policy should be a comprehensive and assertive statement intended to guide the school community (Johnson *et al.* 1994: 262). The policy should be the outcome of a democratic decision-making process involving all members of the school community. Participation is the key to an effective policy. Senior managers should begin the process of developing a policy by:

- identifying the stages of development
- identifying key personnel; a coordinator for chairing meetings and a team responsible for writing the policy
- deciding on a timescale for short-, medium- and long-term objectives
- identifying achievable outcomes related to the school vision and development plan
- identifying professional development support and INSET needs for key personnel and the whole staff
- considering the material resources needed
- deciding on a review structure for the completed policy.

Participation in decision-making is critical to the success of any policy (see Chapter 4) and time must be allocated accordingly. Effective policies require careful planning, implementation and review (see Case Study B on page 137). Factors influencing the success of discipline policies include:

- pupil misbehaviour: the extent of the problem
- self-appraisal: teachers' and pupils' perception of their worth
- morale and psychological distress measures that contribute to teachers' quality of life
- perceived programme outcomes; when implementing policy teachers need to be aware of these outcomes (Hart *et al.* 1995: 27–8)
- monitoring pupil exclusion rates, as these indicate a school's need to remove perceived disruptive pupils from their school roll.

RULES, REWARDS AND SANCTIONS

Rules, and the reward and sanction systems which uphold them, are central to the good order of all organised groups including schools. Whilst the majority of schools have quite elaborate systems, very little research has been carried out in order to examine the nature of these systems, how they become established, how they are changed and how effective they are (Merrett and Jones 1994; Robinson and Maines 1994).

Rules should be kept to a minimum. They should be agreed by all members of the school community and the main reason for each rule should be clearly stated. Obscure and irrelevant rules will discredit the system. Rules of behaviour should be constructed in such a way as to ensure that pupils learn to expect fairly and consistently applied rewards and sanctions when merited. Such rules should be designed to promote good behaviour and should make apparent the distinction between serious and minor offences.

It is helpful in the implementation of the discipline policy to recognise and reward good behaviour. Rewards should cover the broadest possible range of achievement and will need to be consistent with a pupil's chronological age and individual needs. Examples of good practice include:

- public commendations, in assembly
- merit marks
- letters home
- appropriate entries in target/homework/exercise books
- prominent displays of pupils' work
- personal logs, target books or day books (see Chapter 9).

In addition, quiet praise from the teacher to a pupil who demonstrates improvement from previously unacceptable behaviour can be a powerful motivator to maintain improvement. Recognition need not be confined to school; community service may be rewarded.

Parents expect, and respond well to, fair play and an ordered atmosphere. Rewards and punishments should be seen by them to be fair and consistent. Headteachers and teachers have legal authority to impose reasonable punishment. Pupils and parents need to be aware that bad behaviour is unacceptable and will be punished and that punishments will be in proportion to the offence. Where punishment is necessary, the following general rules should be observed:

- headteachers and teachers should avoid the punishment of whole groups for the activities of individuals
- ringleaders should be picked out where appropriate
- conversely, individuals should not be made scapegoats for the activity of a group
- punishments which are humiliating or degrading, such as ascribing labels related to personal characteristics or traits, must not be used
- punishments should be in proportion to the offence.

Sanctions short of exclusion take a variety of forms. They may include measures designed to ensure that the pupil makes some form of reparation for his or her misbehaviour, such as:

- withholding break or lunchtime privileges
- detention
- withholding privileges such as participation in school trips or sports events, where these do not form an essential part of the curriculum
- completion of additional written work
- carrying out a useful task in the school.

In addition to the straight reprimand, measures used by schools which help to prevent a recurrence of the misbehaviour include steps such as:

- moving the pupil's position in class or isolating a pupil from the peer group
- enlisting the support of senior staff
- contacting parents.

Schools should have agreed and understood procedures for the use of detention, covering the circumstances in which it can be used and the arrangements for notifying parents. Although it is not compulsory (1997 Education Act), it is generally good practice to provide parents with at least twenty-four hours' written notice for detentions lasting longer than thirty minutes. In primary schools, parents meet their children up to a certain age, and therefore have a right to expect their children to come straight home. With concern about child molestation, parents need to know where their children are at all times of the day.

Whatever sanction is employed, teachers should act quickly and pupils should be left in no doubt as to why they are being punished and how, through improvements in behaviour, they can avoid a recurrence. If a child does not acquiesce to the punishment, the teacher should feel free to consult a senior member of staff without this being regarded as a failure. It is important in such cases not to allow the child's refusal to escalate into an issue in its own right. Teachers should be able to feel confident that they have support and guidance available when they need it. But in many situations forethought, preventive action and positive interventions can avoid the need for sanctions.

Good behaviour, as well as bad, should be drawn to parents' attention, and early notice given of particular difficulties with an individual pupil. Each school's behaviour policy should make clear the matters considered to be of sufficient importance to require notification of parents. Exclusion should be used sparingly (Lloyd-Smith 1993); the costs to school and community are enormous.

There may occasionally be very serious incidents in which a pupil commits a criminal offence in school, for example by causing criminal damage. Where a young person is convicted of a criminal offence and the court decides to make a compensation order, Section 55 of the Children and Young Persons' Act 1993 places duty on the court to order the parent or guardian of the young person to pay the compensation awarded, unless the parent or guardian cannot be found or it would be unreasonable in the circumstances to make such an order. If a school or LEA suffers loss or damage as a result of a criminal offence committed by a pupil, the court may award compensation to be paid by parents.

TRUANCY

Truancy should be prevented; it is essential that pupils attend school and remain learning throughout the day (see Chapter 7 and Chapter 9 – EWO). Prevention of truancy is an integral part of a school's policy. Governors and teachers should consider how to maintain good attendance.

Children who truant, or who are otherwise absent without good reason, are more likely to grow up under-qualified and unfulfilled. They may damage their future chances of adult happiness and employment. They may also place themselves at greater risk of being drawn into crime. Governing bodies and headteachers should consider how best to reflect this in their behaviour policy and the need to establish and maintain good attendance.

Effective monitoring of attendance is essential, but more than this is needed. Many factors can contribute to truancy. The factor over which schools have complete control is the experience which pupils have in the classroom. Good practice in teaching and discipline is also likely to be good practice in preventing truancy. Schools which seem most likely to prevent pupils drifting into truancy are those which are well-ordered places, where teaching is interesting and effective and, where expectations of pupil achievement, attendance and behaviour are high. Guidance to schools on the categorisation of absences is provided in DES Circular 11/91 and the DfE publication *School Attendance: Policy and Practice on Categories of Absence* (DfE 1994h).

BULLYING, RACIAL AND SEXUAL HARASSMENT

Bullying remains a major concern for both pupils and parents. Schools should be *seen* to act firmly against it. Racial and sexual harassment is also unacceptable and must not be tolerated (see Chapters 8 and 9). Bullying may be distinguished from other unacceptable forms of aggression in that it involves dominance of one pupil by another, or a group of others, is pre-meditated and usually forms a pattern of behaviour rather than an isolated incident. Many pupils experience bullying at some point. The fact that incidents have not been reported to staff does not mean they are not happening. Bullying or other forms of harassment can make pupils' lives unhappy and hinder their academic progress, and can sometimes push otherwise studious children into truancy. It can lead to hypochondria, psychosomatic illness, and in extreme cases, it has led to pupils taking their own lives.

School staff must act – and, importantly, be seen to act – firmly against bullying wherever and whenever it appears. School behaviour policies and the associated rules of conduct should, therefore, make specific reference to bullying. Governing bodies should regularly review their school's policy on bullying.

Similar considerations apply to racial harassment *and* bullying. Racial harassment takes many forms. The Commission for Racial Equality's definition (which is a working, not a legal, definition) is 'violence which may be verbal or physical, and which includes attacks on property as well as on the person, suffered by individuals or groups because of their colour, race, nationality or ethnic origins, when the victim believes that the perpetrator was acting on racial grounds and/or there is evidence of racism'.

All incidents must be taken seriously and, as with bullying, it must be made clear to pupils that such practices are unacceptable and will not be tolerated. Racial harassment does not happen only in schools with large ethnic minority populations. Schools may wish to make explicit reference to racial bullying in their behaviour policies, in order to make clear the seriousness with which they view the issue. Schools should explain how pupils can bring any concerns they may have to the attention of staff. Staff should, in turn, be alert to emerging patterns of racial harassment.

Schools may also make explicit reference in their behaviour policies to sexual harassment. Incidents should again be taken – and be seen to be taken – seriously. Schools should seek to foster appropriate and responsible behaviour between the sexes, and to deter and address offensive behaviour. This might readily be done through their programmes of pastoral and social education and sex education, where these are provided. Schools should bear in mind that precocious or otherwise inappropriate sexual behaviour may be a sign that the pupil is being abused.

POLICY – PRACTICE

The government has advised that assertive discipline is an appropriate approach to the management of pupil behaviour. The following case study shows the development and implementation of a discipline policy in a small 11–16 coeducational comprehensive school based on assertive discipline principles.

Case study: School A

Discipline policy

The school aims to maintain good order and discipline. This is established in the context of:

- a positive school ethos which recognises, values and rewards as appropriate all forms of pupil achievement and provides a wide range of opportunity for involvement in extra-curricular activities
- a curriculum which is broad, balanced, differentiated and which aims to meet the needs of the individual child
- the identification and assessment of, and provision for, pupils with Special Educational Needs, including those who exhibit emotional and behavioural difficulties
- clearly defined standards of behaviour which are understood by pupils and consistently applied throughout the school
- the positive reinforcement of acceptable and desirable forms of behaviour through a structured rewards system.

The school believes in the importance of respect. This includes self-respect, respect for others: respect for race, culture, religion and gender; respect for learning and achievement, respect for the school rules and guidelines and respect for equipment, property and the environment.

Acceptable or desirable behaviours are those which show:

- regard for self
- care and consideration for others
- understanding and tolerance
- a positive attitude including regular attendance, arrival at school and lessons on time with equipment, good effort and taking a pride in work
- sensible and orderly behaviour
- a willingness to keep the building and grounds tidy and in good order.

Unacceptable behaviours are those which show:

- a lack of respect for self
- a lack of concern for others including acts of verbal or physical aggression
- racism, sexism or intolerance
- irregular or poor attendance, late arrival and a negative attitude to work reflected in a lack of effort and under-achievement
- disregard for the school rules and guidelines resulting in disorderly and disruptive conduct
- a lack of care for equipment, the building, grounds or personal belongings of others resulting in litter, graffiti or damage.

This list is not intended to be exhaustive, but serves as an example of the types of behaviour which will result in disciplinary action. The school views aggressive behaviour, acts which endanger self or others and extreme rudeness to members of staff to be serious breaches of school discipline. The school takes a clear stand against any form of bullying and is in the process of formulating an anti-bullying policy.

The school has five school rules and a series of guidelines which it expects all pupils to follow. These are based on the principles of orderly and safe conduct, good behaviour and respect for the building. In recognition of the importance of well-ordered lessons, the school has introduced a whole-school approach which is based on the assertive discipline model (see Chapter 8). This is designed to promote consistency, praise positive behaviours and give clear warnings to pupils when their behaviour is becoming unacceptable.

The school has a senior member of staff on call throughout each period of the day to assist classroom teachers and has a unit to which pupils can be withdrawn. This allows the pupils concerned time to reflect on their own behaviour and to work quietly under close supervision, while allowing others to work free from interruption.

The school is committed to giving pupils responsibility, providing a wide range of extra-curricular activities, and to the reinforcement of desired behaviours. Each faculty has a structured rewards policy which gives credit for behaviour, attitude, effort, completion of homework, presentation and individual achievement. Whole-school rewards include attendance and punctuality certificates, a range of commendations based on an accumulation of plus marks and positive attitude awards which are based on respect for the school rules and guidelines. In responding to disciplinary incidents the school seeks to be firm, fair, clear and consistent:

- firm in that incidents are followed up; action is taken, the pupil is made aware that their behaviour is unacceptable and serious incidents are dealt with accordingly, which includes use of the exclusion procedures
- fair in that the nature of the punishment suits the offence; a distinction is made between minor and serious infringements and the system is established on the principle of escalating sanctions. Allowing for individual circumstances, there is consistency of approach
- clear in that on entry to the school every pupil is given a copy of the pupil guide which outlines basic routines, expectations, informs pupils of the various rewards and spells out the consequences of poor behaviour
- consistent in that the assertive discipline model helps promote consistency of approach while the principle of escalating sanctions ensures that consistent measures are applied.

The school uses a range of disciplinary sanctions. These include correction of behaviour, additional writing tasks, additional work, short and longer length detentions, withdrawal to the unit, referral to another member of staff, contact with home, withdrawal of privileges and acts of community service. Use of exclusion is made for serious infringements of school discipline and for persistent poor behaviour. Short fixed-period exclusions are used for single-act breaches of discipline such as fighting, aggression, endangering the safety of others, abuse directed at staff or for failing to respond to the warnings built into previous sanctions; the formal warning or staged exclusion procedures are used for serious offences and for continued disruptive behaviour over a period of time where the pupil fails to respond to supportive or lower level disciplinary measures. This list is not intended to be exhaustive, but serves as an example of the types of behaviour which will result in exclusion.

The school recognises that the ultimate sanction of permanent exclusion is an extremely serious measure which must be used sparingly. A permanent exclusion may occasionally be applied for one major offence, more usually this sanction is applied when all reasonable steps to support or correct a pupil's behaviour have been exhausted and the pupil continues to exhibit challenging forms of behaviour culminating in a further serious incident, or when allowing a child to remain in school would be seriously detrimental to the education or welfare of the pupil or others.

The school has clear procedures on the use of exclusions which meet the legal requirements and which are in line with the LEA's guidelines. These have been adapted to meet the school's needs in response to the abolition of indefinite exclusions and will be further revised in the light of any new guidance by the LEA.

In recognition of the pupil's behavioural difficulties, the school seeks to make the exclusion process a positive learning experience. This includes a parental interview and the involvement of the pupil in setting targets for improvement in all cases of exclusion and building in an additional warning known as a cause for concern, the setting of a review date and the formulation of an action plan when responding to formal warnings or staged exclusions. These steps ensure that the pupil is given every opportunity and the necessary support to improve.

The school recognises that some pupils may require additional support. The school has a structured referral system for pupils with special educational needs and is currently in the process of responding to the Code of Practice (DfE 1994a). In the context in which these pupils have been identified, their needs assessed and help offered within the resources available, including referral to support agencies, the school expects all pupils to demonstrate behaviours which are safe, show due regard for authority and which allow others to work free from interruption. The school therefore seeks to establish a balance between assessing and meeting the needs of the individual while maintaining a well-ordered environment for all.

The school believes in acting and intervening quickly on small-scale problems and in the active involvement of parents. The school has a wide range of merits, praise letters, certificates and commendations which demonstrate to parents positive achievement and welcomes parental support through establishing early contact and through the use of telephone calls, letters and meetings in responding to disciplinary incidents.

It is through the combination of a positive school ethos, the recognition of pupil achievement, the delivery of a balanced curriculum, the identification of and provision for pupils with special educational needs and the active involvement of parents in commending and correcting behaviour and through decisive disciplinary action that the school seeks to maintain good order and discipline.

In case study: school A, the emphasis on sanctions relates directly to assertive discipline (see Chapter 8). However, there is much to be commended in the document, including the commitment to self-respect and consistency. The system, in focusing the responsibility of maintaining discipline on a senior member of staff, has a clear sense of direction and focus. The school is currently in the process of reviewing the policy and aims to move towards a more pupil-centred approach.

In contrast to the above, the following example, case study: school B states clearly that the responsibility for classroom management, in the first instance, must be with the class teacher. The emphasis is on pupils owning their problems and the school helping them to manage their behaviour. The policy celebrates success and limits the impact of inappropriate behaviour on the pupil, class and teacher by providing a safe, secure environment.

Case study: School B

Behaviour policy

This behavioural policy document is underpinned by the school's vision statement: 'The Community School aims to provide a warm, purposeful, secure learning environment in which achievement is shared and the opportunities provided reflect comprehensive education at its best.'

The school has high expectations of its pupils, teachers and other members of the school community to ensure that the school both enhances and contributes to the community in which it exists. All relevant documentation is sent to parents, teachers and governors. The rights and responsibilities of pupils and the school rules are printed in their planners.

Purposes

- to ensure that all staff, pupils and parents are aware of the aims and expectations of the school in terms of behaviour
- to encourage good orderly behaviour and self-respect as well as respect for others and the environment, based on a recognition of rights and responsibilities agreed by the whole-school community through the school council
- to provide consistent and effective support for staff and pupils
- to promote a positive attitude to learning and provide a learning environment that is attractive and stimulating so that pupils are enabled to realise their full potential
- to support pupils in achieving success and encourage patterns of good behaviour through a range of rewards
- to deal with incidents of unacceptable behaviour with appropriate sanctions
- to ensure that all pupils are treated equally and fairly with regards to rewards and sanctions.

Rights and responsibilities

My rights as a member of school are:

- to learn to the best of my ability
- to be treated equally and with respect
- to learn in a clean, safe and secure environment
- to have lessons start on time.

My responsibilities as a member of school are:

- to learn and let others learn
- to treat others equally and with respect
- to respect the school and the property of others

- to get to lessons on time.

Rights and responsibilities – consequences

If you accept and follow the rights and responsibilities agreed with the School Council you will help the school reach its vision for the future.

The reward scheme is to encourage you in your work at school. You should expect your rights to be considered by all at the school, but you have responsibilities too. If you do not carry out your responsibilities you may be punished by:

- detentions
- being sent to the quiet room
- contact with parents
- being excluded from school.

It is up to you to be responsible for your own behaviour so that everyone can learn.

Rules

The school expects pupils:

- to do as requested by all staff
- to have the correct equipment and be on time for class
- not to use language which offends others
- to line up outside the classroom with coats and hats off
- to settle to work quickly and to stay on task
- not to eat, chew or drink in class
- to leave the classroom in a sensible and orderly way
- to move around the site in a sensible and orderly way
- to follow the dress code.

Rewards

Most people respond to rewards, rather than sanctions. This documentation is presented to staff and governors only.

In the school we support pupils in achieving success in a variety of ways:

Subject certificates:	available in most subjects, for specific skills, attributes being mastered. May be presented in class or year assemblies.
Dragon Points:	coloured, self adhesive labels (from Reprographics) – signed by the member of staff – are stuck into the Pupil Planner. Written comments on marking.

Letters home:	commendable work may warrant this. Families and pupils find this most motivating.
Weekly newsletter:	it is worth passing on information about pupils' successes for distribution to all families.
Verbal praise:	in class.

All of us achieve in our daily lives. We can identify much in our pupils' experience which is worth noting: *catch them being good.*

Half-termly awards are issued – nominations are asked for from all faculties. Certificates are then issued.

Headteacher's monthly awards – staff are asked to nominate pupils.

Sanctions

Young people have to own their behaviour. They are ultimately responsible for their actions. As classroom teachers, we are responsible for managing that behaviour.

Primary responsibility lies with the classroom teacher who will be supported in implementing the teaching code of practice by faculty strategies, for example, buddy system, the quiet room and duty teacher. Follow-up by the classroom teacher is empowering, as is *certainty not severity*. Severely disruptive, violent, unacceptable behaviour may lead to exclusion. In all cases of unacceptable behaviour an information slip should be completed.

Cooling off: it is sometimes appropriate to send a pupil out of the class *for a few minutes* to cool off. It is essential that such pupils can be seen by the teacher, and preferably not by the pupils so that they are not disturbing others. It *must only* be for a few minutes. If the situation does not improve after this time the pupil should be referred to another colleague (see buddy system below) or sent to the quiet room.

The buddy system: all faculties have a system where classroom teachers know who can be used in support if a pupil needs to be sent out. It is sometimes appropriate to ask a teacher in close proximity to accommodate a pupil in the back of their class. This system may precede a referral to the quiet room.

Heads of faculty: it is primarily the responsibility of each member of staff to deal with discipline within their classroom. Heads of faculty are responsible for the work and progress achieved by members of their faculty, so that faculty-based support is available in any incidents of indiscipline in the classroom. Matters relating to the behaviour of individual pupils should be discussed at the earliest opportunity with the head of faculty. Details should be written on an information sheet if appropriate. Heads of faculty are responsible for organising quiet room follow-up.

Duty teacher system: the duty teacher system should be used for incidents deemed to be serious. Responsibility for classroom management in the first instance must be with the class teacher. However, if staged classroom management strategies once having failed to work and a pupil refuses to cooperate to such a degree that that pupil disrupts the learning of others and refuses to go to the quiet room, it is appropriate to call for the duty teacher to remove that pupil.

The system can also be adopted if the pupil refuses to cooperate and the member of staff is subjected to verbal abuse, or the health and safety of others are at risk. A duty teacher referral form will then be filled out by the duty teacher and appropriate action taken, for example, warning, contacting parents, fixed-term exclusion (headteacher/deputy headteacher only). A follow-up meeting will be arranged to negotiate the pupil's re-entry to class.

Detentions: if a pupil persistently breaches the pupil code of practice, a detention may be an appropriate action to take. This may involve pupils being detained at breaktimes, lunchtimes and after school for a maximum of twenty minutes. If it is deemed necessary to detain pupils for a longer time to a maximum of one hour:

- pupils must be given at least twenty four hours' notice that they will be kept in after school
- a written record of detention must be given to pupils – use the green detention card. This must be signed and returned
- pupils must be given a clear explanation of why the detention has been given
- if a pupil fails to complete a detention the responsibility for following this through, in the first instance, rests with the staff who have set the detention
- if a pupil persistently fails to attend, he/she should be referred to the head of detention.

Pupils with emotional and behavioural difficulties are those who exhibit a pattern of inappropriate behaviour over a significant period of time that it impedes their own learning or that of other children, regardless of their class or teacher. Such pupils are unlikely to respond to normal classroom/school behavioural support or disciplinary interventions. They are likely to be on the school's Special Needs Register on a Stage 1–5. Each September, all teachers will have a copy of the Register for the classes they teach. The Special Needs Register names the key-person for each child to whom staff should go with concerns.

Pupils on Stages 2–5 of the Register will have an Individual Education Plan (IEP), which is reviewed regularly by their key-person. Copies of IEPs are sent to relevant teachers. The IEP will not usually prescribe classroom responses, which are considered to be the responsibility of the individual teacher or faculty and may well be logged in lesson planning. It is advised, however, that classroom support/sanctions should take into account information on the IEP.

Role of support staff: special support staff are employed to work with statemented pupils but also may be named on IEPs as having some responsibilities for other children. Each member of staff needs to clearly tell special support staff how they wish them to work with the children to manage behaviour at either class, group or individual level.

Pastoral support group: the pastoral support group meets weekly to discuss pupils referred by head of year. Staff present at these meetings include deputy headteacher, SENCO, assistant SENCO, education welfare officer, educational psychologist, school nurse and staff from behaviour support groups. Action minutes are circulated to head of year, head of faculty, SENCO, special needs, as well as senior management team. It is important that all staff read these minutes.

Case studies A and B are both examples of good practice. As the government has stated, schools should take responsibility for the development of their own discipline policy within legislative guidelines. In addition to a discipline policy schools must also consider developing and implementing an anti-bullying policy.

MONITORING AND EVALUATION

Monitoring and evaluation by members of the school community are critical to the successful implementation of a discipline policy. This will involve the school council, parent-teacher association, teachers, senior management and governors. If a policy is not monitored it will not be possible to determine whether objectives have been achieved. The process of monitoring will also enable members of the school community to move further towards agreed objectives. Having adopted a collegial approach to the development of a discipline policy, the school can move forward with confidence. Monitoring must be based on practice and outcomes, and related to agreed criteria/set targets. Monitoring should provide a framework in which teachers can reflect on their own practice (see Chapter 12).

In contrast to monitoring, evaluation encompasses reviewing the status of the policy aims. Through the evaluation process the school community will be able to determine the need to change. Evaluation is a collaborative exercise involving:

- asking questions
- gathering information
- forming conclusions.

in order to:

- make recommendations.

(Hall and Oldroyd 1990b: 34)

When evaluating the discipline policy, the school community must reconsider its purpose, content, procedures, context and outcomes. If there is a recognised need to change the purpose of the policy, for example, to focus on attendance not classroom management, the policy must be rewritten. Should the content, for example, rewards and sanctions be deemed to be inappropriate, these too may be revised. The procedures to support the policy will need to be considered in the light of any changes. The context in which the school may also be adapting to changing circumstances, for example, new staff, new buildings or increased numbers will also be considered. The discipline policy must reflect such changes. The policy must be current and effective in order to be valued by the school community. A school discipline policy must build on a system of positives if it is to succeed.

School discipline policies do not 'stand alone': they inter-relate with LEA policies concerning education welfare, emotional and behavioural difficulty support, special educational needs, social services and health. The multi-agency approach to managing behaviour will also require a multi-agency approach to developing, implementing and evaluating related policies. A discipline policy written without consultation with internal and external agencies will fail to benefit from the professional support that exists within the education service. Such a policy would also be difficult to manage, as all support agencies impact on the management of discipline in schools. The review process may focus on how to evaluate the effectiveness of our practice. Policy statements should be turned into a series of evaluation questions and applied regularly to the developing practices. The timetable for monitoring and evaluating a policy should be:

Term 1:

- identify focus area
- identify personnel and roles in the review process
- discuss timescale
- set up performance indicators

Term 2:

- formative review process that may involve classroom observation, discussion groups, interest groups, head of department, head of year or coordinators' groups, staff meetings or governor groups
- informal feedback to appropriate staff and action taken where necessary

Term 3:

- final feedback to all teaching and non-teaching staff and governors

- summative document/statement produced with agreed recommendations and action plan
- validation
- feedback into school development plan

End of Term 3:

- back to review cycle for following year.

11

PROFESSIONAL DEVELOPMENT

If the development, implementation and monitoring and evaluation of discipline policies are to be successful, staff need to be trained. In-service training for teachers (INSET) should link professional development and school development. Senior managers have become increasingly aware of the tensions that exist between the individual and whole-school needs. Continuing professional development for teachers has, until recently, been ignored in the context of practitioner development.

The work of the School Management Task Force and the emergence of the Teacher Training Agency have led to a more structured approach to the issue of continuing professional development. In 1995, the Agency commissioned MORI to survey teachers on the value and effectiveness of INSET programmes. The results were disappointing. While INSET represented a huge investment nationally of around £400 million per annum, teachers were less than enthusiastic about the impact of existing programmes on improving their practice. 'In response, the Teacher Training Agency is in the process of developing a structure of national standards for teachers in order to promote well-targeted, effective and coordinated continuing professional development' (TTA 1995: 12).

National standards will provide a focus for professional development for:

- Newly Qualified Teachers (NQT)
- Expert Teachers
- National Professional Qualification for Subject Leaders (NPQSL)
- National Professional Qualification for Special Educational Needs Coordinators (NPQSENCO)
- National Professional Qualification for Headship (NPQH)
- National Professional Qualification for Serving Headteachers (NPQSH).

The development of national standards is in its infancy and the Agency is currently focusing on the National Professional Qualification for Headship (NPQH) which sets out five areas in which expertise is required:

- strategic direction and development of the school

- learning and teaching in the school
- people and relationships
- human and material resources and their development and deployment
- accountability for the efficiency and effectiveness of the school.

The management of discipline would appear to relate directly to all areas of expertise. Given that the Agency is committed to raising standards in schools, it is obvious that quality training focusing on discipline-related issues is required for all teaching and non-teaching staff.

The majority of schools currently allocate the management of INSET programmes and funds to either a deputy headteacher or aspiring deputy headteacher. In small primary schools it is the responsibility of an already over-committed headteacher. Evidence from a review of OFSTED reports (Levačić and Glover 1995) suggested that those responsible for planning professional development in schools need to follow a rational planning approach, linking priorities for expenditure more closely to school aims. This should be followed by an assessment of providers based on their potential to offer value for money. In practice, the effectiveness of continuing professional development in schools will be dependent on the management of:

- information – available for all staff concerning continuing professional development programmes, INSET and grants for education support and training
- planning – collaboration between multi-agencies in consultation with their teams
- evaluation – of all courses, teachers' needs in relation to pupils' needs and the school
- resources – utilisation of experts from LEA agencies, school, higher education institutions, Agency and other consultancies
- networking – the need for management and teachers to consult with teams and INSET providers.

When planning, implementing and reviewing INSET programmes, the focus should be on the relevance of the programme to enhancing pupils' self-esteem and self-confidence in the management of discipline in schools and the teachers' ability to teach. Critically, INSET evaluations should reflect, inform and review policy; the process should involve:

- an evaluation brief that will inform policy
- a statement of aims
- a list of performance indicators relating to targets or outcomes that are specific, measurable, attainable, relevant and time-limited
- detailed questions related to the above
- information arising from the evaluation process that is related to practice
- outcomes that are accessible to all staff

- conclusions that will inform policy.

In order for INSET to be effective, it has to relate theory to practice and provide a framework for action that will improve and develop the management of discipline in the school. The school as a whole has a responsibility to develop policies and provide resources for staff development. Development experiences perform four major functions. They are:

- to enhance the personal and professional lives of teachers
- remedial
- to set the groundwork for implementing school aims
- to introduce changes.

In general, senior managers have a responsibility to see that individuals develop new skills. Staff development should not necessarily mean an additional activity; often development activities will happen as a matter of course. Staff development includes personal development, team development and school development. Staff development has a wider importance in:

- promoting shared values
- implementing change
- promoting equal opportunities.

The National Policy Board for Educational Administration (NPBEA 1993: 11–6) advised that 'to be implemented successfully, staff development programmes must have an operational plan headed by the senior management team'. Good operational plans set clear and specific objectives for each development activity and assign responsibility to those involved. Participation in staff development is critical to success. Appraisal is a means to assess staff needs and to measure short-, medium- and long-term results. An operational plan for staff development should also reflect the aims of both the school development plan and the department development plan.

Once targets have been set, there must be adequate time, resources and follow-up support for development. The following model (Figure 11.1) based on American practice (NPBEA 1993) illustrates the process of school development planning.

Further models of staff development include:

- self-development/team-development – a sharing of expertise
- action learning – identifying an area of development, sharing learning directed towards solving problems
- 'in-house' course – sharing expertise within the school
- job exchange – working in a different environment
- distance learning
- job-rotation – encouraging your team to share classes.

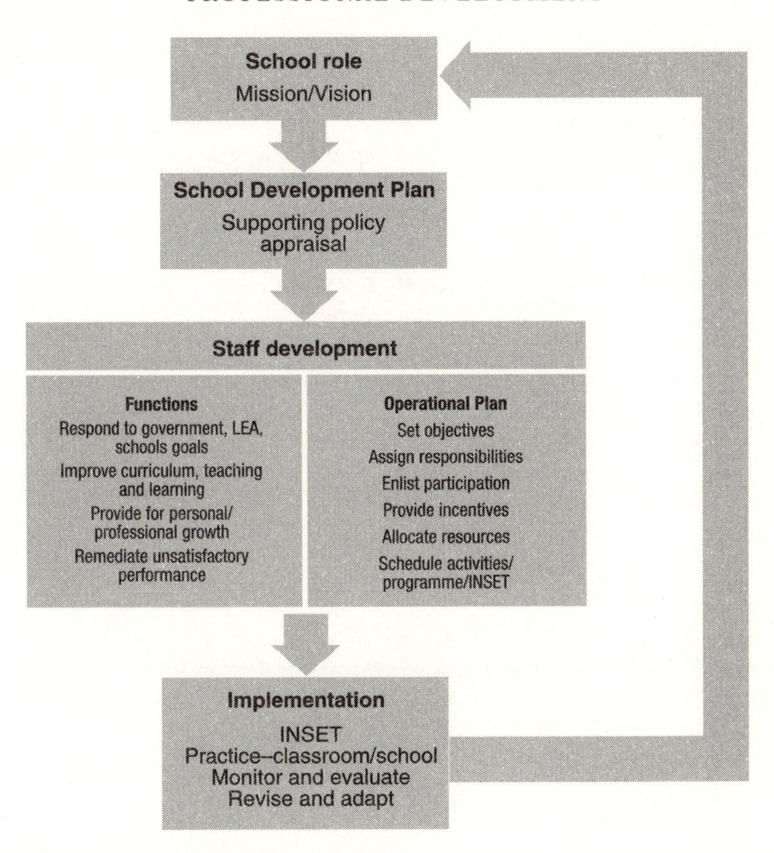

Figure 11.1 Staff development model

Source: Blandford 1997a: Figure 10.1

Within education, the market-place is saturated with providers of training and education for teachers, for example, consultants who are experts in the field. When considering how to identify suitable training, it would be useful to establish the areas of expertise available within the school, LEA or partner Higher Education Institutions.

INITIAL TEACHER TRAINING

Within the national standards framework for teachers, the Teacher Training Agency has produced regulations for all newly-qualified teachers; the main focus of which is knowledge of, and ability to teach, the national curriculum. In addition, newly qualified teachers need to have planning, teaching and class management skills. The criteria developed by the Agency relate, in part, to the management of discipline in schools.

Inevitably, teacher educators will need to consider this aspect of their courses and assessment procedures. Newly qualified teachers will need to demonstrate the ability to plan their teaching to achieve progression in pupils' learning through:

- identifying clear teaching objectives and content
- setting tasks which challenge and interest pupils
- setting appropriate and demanding expectations
- setting clear targets for pupils' learning, building on prior attainment
- identifying pupils' needs
- making effective use of assessment information
- planning opportunities to contribute to pupils' personal, spiritual, moral, social and cultural development.

In the context of teaching and class management the Agency requires newly qualified teachers to be able to:

- ensure effective teaching of whole classes, groups and individuals
- monitor and intervene when teaching to ensure sound learning and discipline
- establish a safe environment
- use teaching methods which sustain the momentum of pupils' work and engage all pupils
- be familiar with the code of practice on special educational needs
- ensure that pupils acquire and consolidate knowledge, skills and understanding in the subject.

The professional development of student teachers is now firmly rooted in partnerships between local schools and higher education institutions (HEI). Initial teacher training programmes are now set within a framework of shared practice that is dependent upon mutual respect and understanding. A more detailed discussion of these issues may be found in *Managing Partnership in Teacher Training and Development* (Bines and Welton 1995). Critically, school and HEI partnerships need to consider the management of discipline as a key factor in training programmes and the assessment of students. It is fundamental that teacher training institutions should focus on discipline and organisational issues when they prepare student teachers for professional practice in education. It is beneficial for teacher educators to work in schools in order to experience the problems encountered by students and newly qualified teachers.

INDUCTION PROGRAMMES

Teaching is an increasingly challenging career, and induction for newly qualified teachers or newly appointed staff is vital if teachers are to fulfil their roles professionally (Shaw *et al.* 1995: 107). In any profession, the transition from training into the workplace generates certain tensions; employees need to know that the contributions they make are valued, and employers need to ensure that their staff have the appropriate training.

The classroom is the most important place in school education. Pupils need a calm and purposeful classroom atmosphere. If teachers do not keep order, pupils will not learn. Government requirements for initial teacher training courses make it clear that all successful students must have demonstrated, in the classroom, their ability to manage pupil behaviour. Newly qualified teachers should be able to establish clear expectations of pupil behaviour and secure appropriate standards of discipline, so as to create and maintain an orderly classroom environment. To achieve this, all teachers need to recognise, and respond to, pupils' needs as required. Newly qualified teachers and new staff will require guidance in policies, procedures and practice and support from colleagues. There should be a clear policy on discipline available for newly appointed teachers. An effective method of professional induction and development for newly appointed teachers is mentoring (Shaw *et al.* 1995: 115).

Mentoring

Mentoring is a term which is used in several different contexts in education (Ormston and Shaw 1993). It generally means the positive support offered by staff with some experience, to staff with less experience of the school. This experience can extend over a wide range of activities, or be specific to one activity, for example, discipline. Teachers may engage in a number of mentoring relationships:

- mentoring of newly qualified teachers joining their teams
- mentoring of colleagues to support them in their new role
- as a mentee, either of a middle manager or senior manager in preparation for current or future post.

It is important to understand that mentoring is a continuous staff development activity which, once the system is in place, happens during normal school life. Mentors need to know and understand the essential elements of a mentoring relationship. These are:

- a recognised procedure, formal or informal
- a clear understanding of the procedure and the roles of mentor and mentee
- trust and a rapport between both parties
- the credibility and genuineness of the mentor as perceived by the mentee

- confidentiality and discretion
- the relationship is based on the mentee's perception of his/her own needs
- a suitable range of skills used by the mentor: counselling, listening, sensitive questioning, analysis and handing back responsibilities
- an appropriate attitude by both parties, for example the ability of the mentor to challenge the mentee, and the self-motivation of the mentee to take action when necessary.

In addition, teachers need to be aware of equal opportunity issues that need to be addressed in the selection and training of mentors. The roles fulfilled by mentors can be categorised into:

- Vocational: these roles help the newly qualified teacher, middle manager or new headteacher to adjust to changes in his/her career pattern and in advancing within the profession.
- Interpersonal: these roles enable the mentee to clarify a sense of identity and to develop a greater sense of competence and self-esteem.

Vocational roles include: educating through enhancing the mentee's skills and intellectual development, helping to develop a set of educational values, consulting to help the mentee to clarify goals and ways of implementing them, helping to establish a set of personal and professional standards, and networking and sponsoring by providing opportunities for the mentee to meet other professionals.

Interpersonal roles include: sharing and role modelling, and allowing the mentee to gain an insight into how the mentor works in a professional capacity. A mentor should also encourage a mentee in order to build his/her self-confidence, recognising success. A mentor is also a counsellor who listens but does not tell the mentee what to do. Not all mentors will fulfil all the roles above, but the greater number of roles, the richer the relationship.

Mentors are likely to have a number of roles within the school and they need to decide who to mentor in the context of their other tasks and responsibilities. Mentoring is time consuming. Mentees should select their mentor on the basis of professional needs, present and/or future.

Mentoring is a positive mechanism for developing management skills for both the mentor and mentee. As a process, mentoring should move through the following stages shown in Figure 11.2.

The National Foundation for Education Research (NFER) found that only one-third of the schools surveyed had policies for the induction of newly appointed staff (Earley and Kinder 1994). There is a need for all teachers to feel confident with their environment; induction is a whole-school issue. Mentoring is only a part of the induction and training process of the professional development of teachers. Good induction has to be planned and resourced, it is an investment in teachers impacting on the quality of the education they will provide for pupils. It is a clear

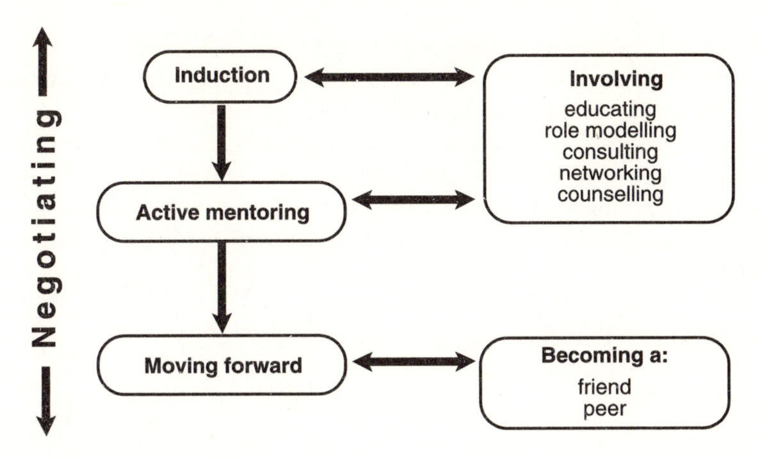

Figure 11.2 A model of mentoring

statement to teachers that their needs are important. It is also a mechanism for identifying and focusing on pupils' needs within each school.

CONTINUING PROFESSIONAL DEVELOPMENT

Until 1987, the professional development of teachers focused on award-bearing courses together with some provision for shorter, specific training (Gaunt 1995: 117). The White Paper *Better Schools* (DES 1985) asserted that INSET resources were not effective and that shorter, less traditional activities would be more appropriate. Teachers would be able to access such courses from several sources including LEA, HEI and consultants. Professional development was to relate directly to practice, the improvement of teaching and learning, classroom management and assessment. Funding is available for teachers to be trained in matters specific to practice.

An example of good practice is a course that emanated from a collaborative approach to INSET in a large suburban coeducational primary school. Teachers had expressed concern over increasing problems with individual pupil and classroom management. They felt that the existing discipline policy and procedures did not meet pupil needs. As a consequence teachers were highly stressed, and staff and pupil absenteeism was prevalent. The headteacher, in consultation with LEA support agencies and his staff, devised a course that focused on managing behaviour. The course programme was based on a series of case studies on video and covered:

- positive correction
- consequences
- prevention
- repair and build.

The course ran during twilight sessions over a six-week period. The following statement introduced the courses: 'Behaviour management is an important area when considering raising expectations. Issues about behaviour and discipline are in the frame each and every working day and new and proven strategies are surely welcome to [all teachers]' (Priest 1997: 1).

The value of this course lies in its common sense, jargon-free strategies of helping teachers prepare for dealing with the situations which are likely to occur in the classroom:

- the child who refuses to leave the room
- the child who answers back
- the noisy classroom.

The case studies are all the more convincing and absorbing because the presenter comes across as a colleague, speaking from experience and explaining strategies which clearly work in the classroom.

In the first of the case studies, *positive correction*, the presenter states the painfully obvious truth that most teachers under stress will correct a pupil from feelings of anger rather than in a reasoned, calm and rational way. It is explained that behaviour management is an emotional issue, but that there are more efficient and successful methods of correction than resorting to intrusive and confrontational ways. Amongst the strategies discussed and demonstrated in classroom settings are the following:

- tactical ignoring by teachers
- distraction and diversion
- cool-off time and rule reminders.

'Take-up-time' is also defined; this gives pupils enough time to do what the teacher asks them and enough time to allow both of them to save face.

The second case study, *consequences*, deals with the emotive issue of bullying and how to deal with a pupil who rushes out of the classroom. It highlights the importance of children being helped to make connections between their behaviour and the result which has come about. It also emphasises the importance of 'certainty' rather than 'severity', and by this stresses crucially that there is always follow-up by the teacher after an incident, even if it is not possible at the end of the lesson or day.

The third case study, *prevention*, looks at how schools can maximise positive behaviour by way of a structured framework and approach, used and agreed by all staff.

The final case study, *repair and rebuild*, explores skills and strategies to encourage pupils to respect the rights of others and to take responsibility for their own behaviour. This could be linked with the Code of Practice (DfEE 1994a). It also deals with how teachers can restore strained relationships and break the cycle of attention-seeking and power games.

The case studies are eminently suitable for staff discussion on behaviour management. If staff could be encouraged to attend more INSET training in this area, the headteacher was confident that the case studies videos would form the basis for very worthwhile discussion as they provide a visual, rather than written, stimulus that is a welcome and accessible source on the subject.

There are several important features of the approach adopted by this headteacher and his staff when implementing the behaviour management course. The programme was an outcome of discussions that focused on teacher and pupil needs; something needed to happen. The programme involved case studies that were real and related directly to the teachers' practice. Teachers were able to reflect individually (blank paper was provided) and to discuss with colleagues in small groups their thoughts and feelings emanating from behaviour management issues. No judgements were made and teachers felt confident with the process and the outcomes of each session. The atmosphere was collegial, supportive and directed to meeting the challenge of the escalating problems in their school.

The course provided strategies for resolving these problems. The strategies were not solutions in themselves, but were a focus for teachers to reflect on their own practice. The course culminated in a review of the existing discipline policy and procedures. Teachers felt confident in expressing the view that there needed to be a period of review, that changes were necessary, but that these had to be planned. The initial impetus for the course was based on fear, confusion and stress; the outcome was an emphatic celebration of good practice. Teachers were able to share their strengths in preparing a programme of change. A key factor was the collegial approach and collective response to the difficult, multi-faceted issue of managing discipline in schools.

EXPERT ADVICE

Since 1992 the DfE has funded Grants for Education Support and Training (GEST) that enabled LEAs, either to provide training using their own staff, or to buy in expertise from higher education or the growing number of private trainers. GEST funds also provided the means for purchasing materials and equipment, the employment of advisory teachers and the training of non-teaching staff and governors (Gaunt 1995: 118). This change in the funding process presented headteachers with the opportunity to collaborate with LEA support staff on the development of INSET programmes. With the emphasis on practitioner training, the GEST initiative provided a framework for whole-school staff development. The broad scope of GEST funding accommodated INSET programmes that focus on discipline and related issues.

LEA support teams have the specific discipline-related expertise to help mainstream teachers to improve their skills in dealing with pupils who present them with difficulties. Such help may be through individual discussions with teachers and pupils in order to provide a solution to a particular problem. Support staff, education welfare officers, educational psychologists and advisory teachers may also work with teachers on case conferences, facilitating peer support groups or specific approaches to discipline. They may also provide training in developing teachers' group management skills, or act as consultants on matters related to behaviour and discipline (DES 1989: 155). LEA support and advisory teams are able to develop whole-school training programmes covering:

- discipline policies and procedures
- team-work and communication
- effective partnerships with parents in supporting the education of pupils
- initiatives, such as peer mediation, assertive discipline, circle time, 'no-blame' approach and peer counselling
- working with multi-disciplinary teams
- implementing the code of practice at whole-school level
- pre- and post-OFSTED action planning to meet behavioural needs
- defusing violence in the classroom
- improving break and lunchtimes through cooperative activities
- developing action plans/individual education plans
- lunchtime supervisor training.

A specific example of an INSET course developed for schools by LEA experts illustrates the flexibility of the GEST framework. Half-day courses were aimed at support teachers and lunchtime supervisors working in primary schools, focusing on behaviour management. Participants were able to explore some of the reasons why inappropriate behaviour may occur and consider strategies that would be effective in defusing difficult situations. The child-centred course explored an accepting, non-judgemental, active-listening approach to behaviour management, where appropriate boundaries are enforced to provide a sense of safety and security for the child (Avon EBD Special Needs Support Team 1996: 12). The more recent standards initiative introduced by the government (DfEE 1997e) encompasses implementation and management of discipline policies. Training will now be dependent on LEAs gaining funds through a process of bidding..

MANAGEMENT OF INSET PROGRAMMES

Teachers and support staff should be trained in a professional manner. The style, content and relevance of INSET should be complemented by appropriate management. The exemplars of good practice have shown the importance of teaching and learning styles in training programmes. A headteacher who considers that a 'stand and deliver' approach to training will encourage staff participation could be considered naive. Teachers need an approach that is supportive in order to feel confident that their contribution will be respected and valued. Staff should be given the opportunity to reflect individually and in groups on the material presented during training. Relevant information should be circulated in advance to enable staff to consider their position in relation to important policies, procedures and practice.

The presentation of the material should be varied and interesting. A lot of printed words will generate little response from staff with busy professional lives. Relevant information should be presented in a succinct, accessible style. Long lists or meaningless prose will not be appreciated. Teachers need to engage with key issues in an informed way. Teachers need to know and understand the essential points that relate to their practice in order to make a judgement.

INSET should focus on issues that are relevant to the individual school and which will lead to a confirmation or change of practice. Discipline is a difficult area to debate in an open forum. Teachers need to feel confident that they are working with colleagues they trust, if they are to be open about such an emotive subject. INSET coordinators need to plan their groups with care, not allowing dominant individuals who do not 'have a problem' to lead or intimidate others. All teachers should be committed to an open, honest approach to discussing individual and whole-school problems. The use of case studies will enable staff to share concern about a particular disruptive pupil or class. All discussions should be solution-orientated.

The frequency of INSET days, half-days or twilight sessions will also impact on the quality of the programme and subsequent outcomes. Isolated days that are scheduled in a random manner throughout the year will not promote an active, all-inclusive debate on discipline. Time needs to be invested in building a positive, supportive atmosphere among staff. Given the restrictions of the school day, whole days of training followed by twilight sessions may provide the most appropriate structure. Senior managers and INSET teams would have to consider this aspect of organisation in their planning. The venue is also important. It is sometimes beneficial to have an off-site venue to generate the right atmosphere for teachers to feel confident. When INSET is school-based, the careful selection of rooms, chairs, tables and display equipment is important. The room should be large enough to accommodate the group, without being too large. Chairs should be comfortable: not at varying heights, or in rows. Tables should be provided if staff are expected to write. Display equipment (video, overhead projector and flip-charts) should be visible to all. Technical equipment should be checked before the session. If staff require pens/pencils and paper, these should be available.

INSET programmes should be planned by a team representing the views of all staff. Once planned, the programme should be circulated and views sought from colleagues on appropriate approaches to each element. The final details should reflect staff needs and concerns. These should relate directly to pupil needs. INSET is only part of the process of developing, implementing and reviewing change (see Chapter 4). It is not a panacea of all ills but should be placed in the context of practice. If change is needed, it should be considered within the priorities of the school development plan and discipline policy (see Chapters 4 and 10). Planning for INSET will require several months of review and consultation. Staff should not be expected to accommodate suggestions immediately.

As professionals, teachers should view the place in which they work as a place of learning. Within the framework of continuing professional development, self-development and staff development are essential pre-requisites to effective management and effective schools. Equally, a precondition and an outcome of effective continuing professional development policies is a culture that encourages reflection and development. This is often the antithesis of the teachers' experience of classroom and staff room isolation (Ingvarson 1990: 165). The management of discipline is complex and the management of changes to policy, procedure and practice, as has been emphasised throughout this chapter, requires time for consultation and reflection.

12

SELF-EVALUATION

The culture of the teaching profession is changing, reflecting the changing society in which we live with its proliferation of cultures, beliefs and values. Effective discipline in schools is based on shared beliefs and values. The school community works towards a common goal, reaching for and achieving targets. In practice, teachers need to relate their actions to their beliefs and values. If the two do not equate, teachers should consider their position in the school in relation to pupils' needs. Schools should be places in which success is celebrated, the 'blame culture' prevalent in the 1980s replaced by the 'caring culture' of the 1990s. How does this happen? Do teachers willingly participate in the change process, or are they passive in their response to the dominant ideology of the day? These are matters of sociological debate.

Self-evaluation of professional competence is more than an assessment of traditional conformity or technical accountability. It is assessed in terms of moral and prudent answerability for practical judgements actually made within the context of existing educational institutions (Carr and Kemmis 1986: 31).

A means of developing the skills required for self-evaluation is to consider the range of knowledge that exists regarding educational practice:

- common-sense knowledge about practice that is simply assumption or opinion, for example, the view that students need discipline
- folk-wisdom of teachers, like the view that pupils get restless on windy days
- skill knowledge [used by] teachers: [how to line pupils up], or how to prevent [pupils] speaking while instructions about a task are being given
- contextual knowledge: [the background] knowledge about this class, this community or [pupil,] against which . . . aspirations [are measured]
- professional knowledge about teaching strategies and curriculum
- educational theory: ideas about the development of individuals, or about the role of education in society

- social and moral theories and general philosophical outlooks: about how people can and should interact, . . . the uses of knowledge in society, or about truth and justice.

(Carr and Kemmis 1986: 42)

Theory and knowledge can, therefore, transform a teacher's beliefs and values. In the process of self-reflection, interaction with educational theory may not dictate practice, but it may transform the outlook of the practitioner. Providing individuals with new concepts is a means not merely to offer them a new way of thinking, but also to offer them the possibility of becoming more self-aware of their thoughts and actions (Carr and Kemmis 1986: 91). The full task of self-reflection and evaluation requires teachers to collaborate in decision-making that will transform their situation. The process of self-evaluation encompasses the interaction of the teacher with the school. Teachers should consider whether they are in the right school for them.

PRACTICE

The case for teachers to work on their own development was made in a study by Constable and McCormack (1987) quoted in Isaac (1995: 128). The report suggested that teachers should:

- own their own career, and positively seek out continuous training and development
- acquire the learning habit early in their career
- recognise when new knowledge and skills are required and seek them out.

Self-evaluation involves learning and understanding where you are within your job and career. Many teachers have recently been involved in the Investors in People programme which supports personal development. In schools where time and funds have been given to the programme, teachers have been encouraged to reflect on their own development.

Teachers should have a clear view of what their job is about; the relationship between teaching and management, and so on. Teachers should also have an understanding of their position in relation to the members of the school community. For a teacher, the process of self-evaluation is difficult. Teachers face many demands including:

- government demands: deliver the curriculum, register pupils, parents' evenings
- senior management demands: implementation of school policy
- colleague demands: requests for assistance, information or help from others at a similar level or within the team

- pupil demands: to inform and liaise
- externally-imposed demands: social services, police, agencies which work for and with young people
- system-imposed demands: LEA, budgets, meeting, social functions which cannot be ignored.

In addition there are other demands such as family, friends, hobbies and social commitments. This affects our self-perception and self-esteem and therefore how we evaluate ourselves. Self-development is systematic; we never stop learning and developing. The art of self-evaluation is to be continually learning:

> People with a high level of personal mastery live in a continual learning mode. They never 'arrive'. People with a high level of personal mastery are acutely aware of their ignorance, their incompetence, their growth areas. And they are deeply self-confident. Paradoxical? Only for those who do not see that the journey is the reward.
>
> (Senge 1990: 142)

Specifically, teachers should reflect on which choices are available within the context of self-development, identifying:

- what is required to improve performance
- how this will be done
- when this will be done.

PROCESS

In the process of evaluating their practice, teachers need to consider the purpose of the exercise. In the context of the management of discipline, what do teachers need to ask? Teachers may consider their role in terms of pupils, parents, school and community. Questions relating to discipline could be structured in an objective way as shown in the following (Brighouse 1978):

Teacher with pupils

- to what extent am I aware of, and do I take account of, individual needs?
- am I aware of pupils with particular problems?
- how do I deal with them?
- how do I respond to poor attendance?
- how do I respond to behavioural problems?
- how well do I know my pupils?

Teacher with parents

- do I know the parents?
- how effectively do I communicate with parents?
- is there a shared understanding of how their child should behave, and about attendance?
- is the home situation stable or changing?
- how well do I know the family?

Self-evaluation relates directly to how the school, and as a member of its teaching staff, a teacher evaluates whole-school issues including:

School and its environment

- what is the general appearance of the school like – playground, corridor, classroom, lavatories, playing fields?
- who ensures that displays are of quality and reflect all pupils' work?
- what is the manner in which pupils move around the school between lessons, during breaks and at the start and end of the day?
- how would the noise level be described?

School and its practice

- what is the provision for pupils with behaviour problems?
- how are teaching and non-teaching staff supported when dealing with discipline-related matters?
- what staff training opportunities are there?
- how well does the school communicate with LEA support agencies and advisors?
- how effective is the discipline policy?
- does policy reflect practice?
- are there sufficient discipline procedures and practices to support staff and pupils?
- praise, rewards and sanctions – what are used and why?
- what opportunities are given for the development of initiative and responsibility?
- what is the procedure for checking lateness and absence?

School and communication

- how does the school communicate with members of the wider community?
- are there adequate opportunities for all members of the school community to express their views?

- what consultative process is used to help arrive at policy decisions related to discipline?
- what are the links with the EWO, educational psychologist and schools' advisory service?

School and parents

- how is a parent first introduced to the school?
- how do parents personally meet members of staff?
- are there opportunities for parents to meet staff
  - as a matter of routine?
  - at their own or the school's request?
- is there a parents' association? What are its functions? Is it effective?
- what are the various kinds of meetings held for parents? What proportion of parents attend meetings and how is information communicated to those who do not attend?
- do parents know and understand the school's discipline policy, procedures and practices?
- how are parents aided and encouraged to be interested in helping their children to achieve their potential?
- is there a home-school contract?
- how does the school meet family needs?
- is information to parents communicated appropriately, in a language and style that is understood by members of the family for ethnic groups, translated into their own language?

School and community

- does the school see itself as a focus of the community? How does it promote such an image?
- how does the school ensure good relationships with the local community?
- what is the relationship between the school and community?
- are pupils involved in any way with local community service?
- does the school have regular contact with the local family centre?
- how closely does the school work with social services in order to meet community needs?
- how well does the school relate to the cultural aspirations of the community in terms of behaviour, respect and family values?

The list of points to be considered in the evaluation is by no means conclusive. All schools have their own needs that should be identified and the school's response to each evaluated. Much of the above is objective and school-orientated however, teachers will have their own belief and value systems that also need to be evaluated.

The challenge of teaching is to enable pupils to become autonomous, valued, human beings within the culture and society in which they live. If school, culture and societal values clash, tensions are created that need to be resolved in a way that remains true to each. As an example, pupils from many multi-ethnic backgrounds appear to have a facility for reconciling their family's cultural values with those they experience in society and school. Teachers must also reflect on their beliefs and values and reconcile these with the philosophy of the school in which they work. If there are tensions, pupils' needs will not be met. The practice of moaning about management, professional status, pay, pupil behaviour and lack of support that prevail in some staff rooms will achieve very little. Staff need to direct their energies towards providing an experience for pupils and themselves that is positive and worthwhile.

The process of self-evaluation should allow teachers to consider whether they are suited to the age-group, subject, school and community where they work. There should be a sense of 'fitness for purpose' in the lives of teachers. This does not mean that every day will be perfect as pupils do not always behave rationally (OFSTED 1994). The issue is the teacher's capacity to deal with irrational acts and the frequency with which they occur. There are so many variables that affect a teacher's practice that it would be almost impossible to provide a solution to each problem before it arises.

If, on reflection, teachers feel that their beliefs and values cannot be reconciled with those of their colleagues and the behaviour of their pupils, perhaps it is time to move on. In relation to the management of discipline, there should be mutual agreement on:

- identifying and meeting pupils' needs
- developing a supportive environment for all members of the school community
- discipline policy, procedures and practice
- providing opportunities for initiative and responsibility
- staff development and decision-making procedures
- the interaction between school vision, its development plan and discipline
- communication.

In 1986 the DES proposed a means of structuring self-evaluation through appraisal. This provides an opportunity for teachers to discuss with colleagues matters relating to their practice within the context of the school development plan.

APPRAISAL

Appraisal has been a contentious issue in schools since it was first legislated in 1991. This followed a lengthy period of arbitration between the government and teaching unions from 1982–86. Statutory regulations (National Steering Group 1991) state that the aims of teacher appraisal are to:

- improve skills and performance
- improve careers through appropriate in-service training (INSET)
- help teachers having difficulties with their performance
- provide references
- improve the management of schools.

The primary purpose of appraisal is performance enhancement. An outcome of the appraisal process should be an action plan which identifies specific targets and training needs. Appraisal is developmental.

Ultimately the outcome of a staff appraisal scheme should be to the benefit of both staff and school. Members of staff should gain better understanding of the job, improved feedback and recognition, opportunity to regularly consider professional development needs, increased accuracy of references, greater awareness of career development factors and opportunities, support for work-related issues and greater job satisfaction. The school should profit from the coordination of school aims and staff aims, priorities clarified and determined, staff clarity about roles and responsibilities, professional development of management, school needs met through target setting, improved communication, greater exchange of ideas and a more supportive environment.

As a formal means of evaluating practice, appraisal has its place. The need to include discipline-related issues in the process is critical to the development of effective strategies in schools.

TEACHERS

Central to the management of discipline in schools is the level of self-esteem that emanates from the teacher. Teachers with a low self-esteem will be unable to participate. Teachers can gain confidence by adopting a few straightforward procedures to meet their needs (Haigh 1997: 20–1):

- Preparation: reflect on the successes of the previous lesson, repeat these strategies, prepare lesson content around available resources, note any particular problems with pupils or class.
- Starting the day: arrive early and take time to check whether everything that is required is at hand, rehearse lessons mentally and aim to make a good, confident start to each lesson; allow time to consult with colleagues about individual pupil and class needs.
- Colleagues: be a good team player by making well-researched suggestions on strategies to overcome difficulties with disruptive pupils, listen to advice when

offered, collaborate with all agencies to gain support, be assertive when appropriate.

- Senior managers: do not waste time discussing their failings as managers or your own perception of their attitude towards your work, but find ways of working with them. They are busy people who may not feel that it is appropriate for them to deal with every discipline-related incident that occurs in their school. Be pleasantly assertive when you feel that your needs are not being met.
- Keep things under control: teaching is filled with false starts, incomplete conversations, classes that arrive at the wrong time, pupils that behave in an irrational manner. Do not strive for all-round perfection, make priorities and be ready to say no, work within your limits.
- Pupils: if discipline is a problem it must also be made a priority before it starts to cause unacceptable stress. Do not cover it up; seek support from a mentor or understanding colleague and from sympathetic senior managers. A major difficulty with a particular pupil or class should be a whole-school issue and not a private problem. Be assertive, ask for time to talk about the problem, and make it clear that you need support. Try hard not to take a pupil's misbehaviour as directed personally to you. Take opportunities to discuss discipline problems with colleagues, senior managers and support agencies.
- Colleagues: give feedback to them when you have received help, this will make both of you feel better and encourage others to support you.
- Get a life: not participating in anything other than school is a downhill step and bad for self-esteem, for mental-health and for the ultimate well-being of pupils.
- Keep fit: feeling fit is good for self-esteem and helps to get you through a tiring week.
- Focus on the manageable: move the focus from teaching to particular teaching tasks. An alternative approach to thinking a class is difficult and beyond your ability to cope, is to start thinking what, and who, makes the class difficult, then devise ways of dealing with these individual issues.
- Change direction: if a school or area is not suited to you, move.
- Celebrate success: it is in the nature of conscientious people that they dwell on things that go wrong. Try to think what has gone well; this will give you the energy to deal with problems as they arise.

Remember, a teacher's perception of themselves will impact on the self-esteem and confidence of their pupils. Be confident, assertive, realistic and get expert advice when needed. You will succeed in managing discipline in schools.

WHERE NEXT?

When evaluating your own position in relation to the management of discipline in school, it is important to consider what can be done to sustain or improve current practice. Schools need to have a code by which members of their community can monitor their behaviour and attitude towards each other and their environment. Self-esteem and self-confidence are to be nurtured, schools should allow individuals to develop and grow. This should happen within a collective framework based on shared beliefs and values.

Schools should provide equality of opportunity for all, expectations should apply to the community as a whole. Teachers and pupils need to consider how their management of discipline affects others. Schools should be places where all teachers can teach, and all pupils can learn.

Classrooms should not be battlegrounds for pupils or teachers. Teachers and pupils should respect their environment and demonstrate respect for others. This can be achieved by listening and supporting each other. Expectations of ourselves and others will determine behaviour in school. The school environment will reflect the accepted standard in the school. They should be professional at all times. Teachers should be consistent, listen to pupils and record incidents of bad behaviour. They should also be honest, to themselves and others, when a problem occurs. Critically teachers must have the support of their managers if they are to manage discipline effectively.

Teachers can create a positive environment by nurturing their pupils' self-esteem. Encouragement and support are effective tools in the management of discipline. Pupils will respect boundaries that are understood and practised by all. Rewards and sanctions should only be used when appropriate. The positive aspects of rewards far outweigh the negative effects of sanctions. Sanctions need to be managed. Acceptable standards of behaviour and work should reflect respect for each other and the school environment. Codes of conduct need to be based on high standards and rules applied firmly and fairly.

Detentions should not happen without notification to parents/carers. Parents/carers need to know if their child's behaviour is inappropriate. It is only through partnership with parents and other members of the community that sanctions will be effective.

School managers need to establish a regime that is firm and fair. The need for praise is as appropriate for teachers as it is for pupils. Praise and encouragement should be used as much as possible. Home-school contracts can be a useful mechanism if approached in a reasonable and consistent manner. Expectations must be achievable. Collaboration with members of the school community and support agencies is essential to good practice.

Multi-agency approaches to managing individual, group, class or whole-school discipline issues should be adopted. Research has shown that the expertise of education welfare officers, educational psychologists and support teachers for pupils with emotional and behavioural difficulties should be utilised in the development and implementation of behaviour management policies and strategies.

Exclusion, temporary or permanent, is a mechanism that should only be used when all else has failed. Many pupils who are excluded from school find involvement in criminal activities as an alternative to school. Local education authority officers need to work with support teams, headteachers and their staff (teaching and non-teaching) to avoid reaching the point where a pupil is excluded from school.

Communication is essential in the development and implementation of an effective discipline policy. Teachers and pupils should have a voice in the development of policy, procedures and practices. Relationships with everyone are critical, teachers, managers and pupils need to relate to each other positively. Negative reactions to difficult situations will not lead to an early resolution. Anger and confrontations should be avoided. Teachers need to monitor the levels of stress created in their classrooms.

Central to the management of discipline in schools is the recognition that individual self-confidence and self-esteem should be nurtured and maintained. Members of the school community need to be known as individuals and their needs met. When problems occur they should be acknowledged and resolved. Success can only be achieved through the identification and meeting of needs. All success, great and small should be celebrated.

There is much to be celebrated in schools; teachers need to know when they are effective. They also need to know that they can be honest, and that support will be given when needed. Managing discipline in schools is a whole-school responsibility based on shared beliefs and values, clear expectations and boundaries, and consistency as reflected in collaborative policies, procedures and practices.

APPENDIX A

Home-School Contract

THE PARENT PROMISES:

To have high expectations of their children and work with the school to ensure they fulfil potential.

To monitor homework and encourage child to complete it to the best of his/her ability.

To encourage full attendance and punctuality and notify school in writing of any genuine absence.

That their child will wear full school uniform and carry correct equipment and books in a bag.

To support the school in reinforcing high standards of behaviour.

To read newsletters and note the dates and contents.

To attend Parents' Evenings and any other requested meetings.

To work with the school in partnership for the benefit of the child.

Signed:

Date: Parent

THE SCHOOL PROMISES:

That it will have high expectations of all students and endeavour to help them reach their full potential.

To set and mark homework on a regular basis.

To encourage and acknowledge good attendance and punctuality.

To encourage a high standard of dress with a strong uniform policy.

To encourage high standards of behaviour at all times.

To keep parents regularly informed of developments in school.

That, in addition to Parents' Evenings, an opportunity will always be made available to discuss students' progress.

To support the child socially and academically.

To provide a broad and balanced curriculum which caters for individual needs and abilities.

Signed:

Date: For the school

THE STUDENT PROMISES:

To always work to the best of his/her ability.

To complete and meet deadlines for any homework set.

To be punctual and attend regularly.

To always wear full school uniform and have appropriate books and equipment in a bag.

To behave in an acceptable manner and agree not to chew in class, use abusive language or run in corridors.

To be responsible for taking home all communications from school.

To discuss work and any problems with parents and staff.

To treat other students and staff with respect.

To treat school buildings/property and local environment with care.

Signed:

Date: Student

APPENDIX B

School Development Plan 1996/8

This is a two-year rolling plan which focuses the aims and objectives of the school following the completion of the five-year plan which preceded it. In this version of the plan, there is a deliberate concentration on short-term aims to achieve clarity on the immediate objectives of the school.

The plan will be monitored continuously and reviewed annually through the school's Annual Review process. External evaluation will be provided by the governing body, OFSTED inspection and monitoring by the LEA inspectorate.

AIM-RAISING ACHIEVEMENT: IMPROVING STANDARDS OF TEACHING AND LEARNING

OBJECTIVES:

- by the end of 1997, all subject departments will have placed differentiation at the head of their priorities, and plans for developing differentiation will have been fully funded as priorities in the budget
- the organisation of teaching groups in Year 8 will have been discussed and any changes implemented in the school timetable 1997/8
- a policy statement on Equal Opportunities will have been written, disseminated and be reflected in practice
- assessment and reporting will have been reviewed to establish a system which shows progress, incorporates target setting and is motivating for pupils of all abilities
- a whole-school policy on language across the curriculum will be developed in 1996/7, tied in with the partnership project to raise reading standards at all ages and levels of ability
- the curriculum at Key Stage 4 will have to be reviewed and any plans to introduce vocational courses implemented by 1997

- the curriculum in the sixth-form will have been reviewed and any plans to extend GNVQ work to advanced level implemented by 1998
- IT facilities in the school will be upgraded in the library in 1997, and made more accessible to pupils by extending opening hours by 1998
- a rolling programme of updating and extending the book stock of the library will begin in 1997

AIM-RAISING ACHIEVEMENT: IMPROVING STANDARDS OF BEHAVIOUR

Objectives:

- the Good Behaviour Policy will be published and become the basis of practice for all staff
- training in positive discipline strategies will be made available to a range of staff and disseminated
- Anti-Bullying work will continue, advised by a group of parents, pupils and staff established in 1996
- display areas will be created throughout the school and pupils' work and records of activities put on exhibition to make corridors reflect the life and ethos of the school
- building and redecoration work will focus on improving the physical conditions for pupils in the school: cloakroom spaces converted into attractive social areas, lavatories and changing rooms refurbished and redecorated. The School Council will be able to recommend spending up to £1,000 on the fabric of the building
- arrangements for home/school transport will be overhauled, with the emphasis on higher standards of behaviour on the buses and in the bus park
- a professional counselling service will be made available to pupils in 1997

AIM-RAISING ACHIEVEMENT: IMPROVING SCHOOL MANAGEMENT AND CONTINUING STAFF DEVELOPMENT

Objectives:

- a new and wider forum for discussion of the curriculum will have been established by September 1997
- opportunities for new responsibilities will have been offered at middle management level within the school for fixed periods, to retain flexibility

- members of the Senior Management Team will have been linked to all subjects to provide a clear line of communication, monitor standards and offer support
- all staff will have completed their first cycle of appraisal by July 1997, and meeting time will have been made available
- a revised pattern of meetings will be introduced from September 1997, increasing the number of 'task groups' and increasing the number of whole staff, subject and year team meetings
- management training courses for all interested teaching and support staff will have been arranged in 1997/8
- the standards set by Investors in People will be used as a benchmark for the development of in-service training, planning and communication: the school should be ready for IIP assessment by the end of 1997.

APPENDIX C

Contacts for alternative models

Peer Mediation
Christine Stockwell
Schools Project Coordinator
British Mediation
Alexander House
Telephone Avenue
Bristol
BS1 4BS

Coping with Kids
Tonia Robinson
Educational Psychologist
Psychology Service
Advice and Development Centre
Sheridan Road
Horfield
Bristol
BS7 0PU

Lunchtime Supervisor – City and Guilds
Anne Gurner
Bristol Special Needs Service (EBD Team)
British Road
Bedminster
Bristol
BS3 3AU

Behaviour Management Plan
Christopher Wardle
Behaviour Coordinator
Pen Park School
Southmead
Bristol
BS10 6BP

Schools Outreach
Gordon Bailey
10 High Street
Bromsgrove
Worcestershire
B61 8HQ

Family Connections
Kate Schnelling
Family Services
Oxford County Council Education Department
West Oxford School
Ferry Hinksey Road
Oxford
OX2 OBY

APPENDIX D
Target book

TARGET BOOK

Name:
Tutor group:

YOU

TARGETS

SUCCESS

[Front Cover]

HOW TO USE THIS BOOK

You will negotiate a target to be completed by the date agreed by you, your teacher(s) and parent/guardian.

1 YOU MUST

- Remember to bring your book to school *every* day and show your tutor.
- Remember to show your book to your class teachers at the start of every lesson, they will then write a comment.
- Remember to show your book to your parent/guardian *every* day.

2 TARGETS
These will be:

- Negotiated: between subject teachers and/or tutor and pupil
- Clear: understood and workable
- Goal orientated: with achievable aims and measurable success
- Possible!: can be achieved by the pupil at home or at school
- Positive: pupils and teachers must be able to identify with any progress made
- Active: doable!
- Time-limited: a time must be set and kept to

3 SUCCESS

- you and your teachers will know when you have reached your target
- when you have reached your target you can then move on to another one
- if you cannot reach your target you must negotiate a new target with your teachers

THIS BOOK *IS NOT* A PUNISHMENT: IF USED PROPERLY IT WILL HELP YOU TO LEARN

[Page 2]

TARGET PAGE

TARGET 1:	
TO BE REACHED BY:	COMPLETED:
TARGET 2:	
TO BE REACHED BY:	COMPLETED:
TARGET 3:	
TO BE REACHED BY:	COMPLETED:

[Page 3]

TARGET BOOK : GUIDELINES FOR STAFF

WHO WILL USE THE TARGET BOOK?

- pupils who are statemented
- pupils who have particular behavioural and/or learning difficulties
- pupils who have a specific difficulty in any subject.

HOW WILL THE TARGET BOOK OPERATE

- identify pupil – by subject teacher/tutor/parent/special needs/pupil?
- notify Head of Year
- Head of Year will contact parents
- targets will then be negotiated by pupil/parent/tutor/(Head of Year/Head of Faculty) Special Needs coordinator, as appropriate
- Target Book will be monitored according to need
- parents will be consulted prior to the end of the target date.

WHAT WILL THE TARGETS BE?

- These will vary according to the nature and scope of the problem.

Examples

A Special needs/cross-curricular

- self-organisation
- independent work
- reading – corrective reading
- spelling – spelling programme
- literacy tasks

Monitored by: Learning Support Coordinator

B Behavioural/Organisational

- lateness
- equipment
- relationships with peers
- bullying
- uniform

Monitored by: Tutor/Heads of Year

C Subject-based

- concepts, understanding

[Page 4]

- skills
- homework
- spelling of subject specific words

Monitored by : Head of Faculty

WHERE WILL INFORMATION BE RECORDED?

- information/negotiations will be recorded on the action plan
- action plans will be retained by the deputy headteacher in consultation with external agencies
- Target Books and duplicate copies of Action Plans will be retained on pupil's file in Head of Year's office

TARGETS: EXAMPLES

A SPECIAL NEEDS
'Will set out work correctly in each subject by ________________ '

B BEHAVIOURAL/ORGANISATIONAL
'Will arrive on time at school and to each lesson by ________________ '

C CURRICULUM
'produces half a page of homework (written or word processed) in each subject on a regular basis by ________________ '

USE OF DIARY

- one page for each day
- target clearly stated
- teacher comment at the end of each lesson
- pupil comment realistic/positive
- homework section, date to be completed

SIZE OF BOOK

- exercise book, giving ample space to record *all* information

TIMETABLE

- printed on the back of the book

[Page 5]

BIBLIOGRAPHY

Advisory Centre for Education (ACE) (1994) 'Discipline – how schools consult pupils', *ACE Bulletin 61*, September/October 1994, 7–9, London: ACE.

—— (1995) 'Prompt response aims to prevent exclusions', *ACE Bulletin 68*, November/December 1995, 8–9, London: ACE.

Avon Education Department (1993) *Children with Special Educational Needs: Targeting Special Educational Needs within Mainstream Schools*, Bristol: Avon Education Department.

—— (1995) *A Report on the Work of the Child and Family Support Centre Teachers 1994/5*, Bristol: Avon Education Department.

Avon Education Welfare Service (1996) *Education Supervision Orders: Summary of Cases 1992–1996*, Bristol: Avon Education Department.

Avon Emotional and Behavioural Difficulties Special Needs Support Team (1996) *Service for Special Educational Needs: Information Pack for Schools*, Bristol: Avon Education Department.

Badger, B. (1992) 'Changing a Disruptive School' in Reynolds, D. and Cuttance, P. (eds) (1992) *School Effectiveness: Research, Policy and Practice*, London: Cassell.

Bailey, G. (1997) *Schools Outreach: Introductory Pack*, Bromsgrove: Schools Outreach.

Bines, H. and Welton, J. (eds) (1995) *Managing Partnership in Teacher Training and Development*, London: Routledge.

Blandford, S. (1997a) *Middle Management in Schools*, London: Pitman.

—— (1997b) *Resource Management in Schools*, London: Pitman.

Blandford, S., Wright, G. and Senior, J. (1991) *Modular Curriculum*, London: Centre for the Study of Comprehensive Schools.

Brighouse, T. (1978) *Starting Points in Self-Evaluation*, Oxford: Oxfordshire Education Department.

Bristol City Council Education Directorate (1997a) *Education Welfare Service: Mission Statement*, Bristol: Bristol City Council.

—— (1997b) *Education Welfare Service: Policy and Practice*, Bristol: Bristol City Council.

Bristol Special Needs Support Service (1996) *A Report on the Work of the EBD Support Service 1995/96*, Bristol: Bristol City Council.

Brown, M. and Ralph, S. (1995) 'The Identification and Management of Teacher Stress' in Bell, J. and Harrison, B.T. (eds) (1995) *Vision and Values in Managing Education*, London: David Fulton.

Burstall, E. (1996) 'What Really Stresses Teachers', *Times Educational Supplement*, 16 February 1996, 4.

Caldwell, B. J. (1996) 'Beyond the Self-Managing School', *Paper presented at the BEMAS Conference*, Cambridge, March 1996.

Calvert, M. and Henderson, J. (1995) 'Leading the Team: Managing Pastoral Care in a Secondary Setting' in Bell, J. and Harrison, B.T. (eds) *Vision and Values in Managing Education*, London: David Fulton.

Canter, L. and Canter, M. (1976) *Assertive Discipline*, Santa Monica: Lee Canter and Associates.

—— (1992) *Assertive Discipline: Positive Behaviour Management for Today's Classroom*, Santa Monica: Lee Canter and Associates.

Carlton, E. (1997) 'It's Cool to be Bright', *Times Educational Supplement* 2, 20 June 1997, 17.

Carr, W. and Kemmis, S. (1986) *Becoming Critical: Education, Knowledge and Action Research*, Lewes: Falmer Press.

Claxton, G. (1990) *Teaching to Learn*, London: Cassell.

Cleugh, M.F. (1971) *Discipline and Morale in School and College*, London: Tavistock Publications.

Coleman, M. and Bush, T. (1994) 'Managing with Teams' in Bush, T. and West-Burnham, J. (eds) *The Principles of Educational Management*, Harlow: Longman.

Comber, L.C. and Whitfield, R.C. (1978) *Action on Indiscipline*, Birmingham: NAS/UWT in association with the University of Aston, Birmingham.

Commission for Racial Equality (1997) *Equality in Education (Draft Paper)*, London: Commission for Racial Equality.

Constable, J. and McCormack, R. (1987) *The Making of British Managers*, London: BIME, CBI.

Coulby, D. and Harper, T. (1985) *Preventing Classroom Disruption*, London: Croom Helm.

Cutts, N.E. and Moseley, N. (1957) *Teaching the Disorderly Pupil*, New York: Longmans.

Department for Education (DfE) (1993) *Education Act*, London: DfE.

—— (1994a) *Code of Practice on the Identification and Assessment of Children with SEN*, London: DfE.

—— (1994b) *Circular 8/94, Pupil Behaviour and Discipline*, London: DfE.

—— (1994c) *Circular 9/94 – The Education of Children with Emotional and Behavioural Difficulties*, London: DfE.

—— (1994d) *Circular 10/94 – Exclusions from School*, London: DfE.

—— (1994e) *Circular 11/94 – The Education by LEAs of Children Otherwise Than at School*, London: DfE.

—— (1994f) *Circular 12/94 – The Education of Sick Children*, London: DfE.

—— (1994g) *Circular 13/94 – The Education of Children Being Looked After by Local Authorities*, London: DfE.

—— (1994h) *School Attendance: Policy and Practice on Categories of Absence*, London: DfE.

—— (1994i) *Circular 17/94 – Arrangements for Money to Follow Pupils Who Have Been Permanently Excluded From School*, London: DfE.

Department for Education and Employment (1997a) *Excellence in Schools*, London: DfEE.

—— (1997b) *Framework for the Organisation of Schools*, London: DfEE.

—— (1997c) *Education Act*, London: DfEE.

—— (1997d) *News 77/97*, 21 March 1997, London: DfEE.

—— (1997e) *Circular 13/97 – The Standards Fund 1998/1999*, London: DfEE.

Department of Education and Science (DES) (1985) *Better Schools*, London: HMSO.

—— (1988) *Education Reform Act*, London: HMSO.

—— (1989) *Discipline in Schools: Report of the Committee of Enquiry*, London: DES and Welsh Office.

DeVeer, A.J.E. and Janssens, J.M.A.M. (1994) 'Victim-orientated Discipline, Interpersonal Understanding and Guilt', *Journal of Moral Education*, 23(2), 165–82.

Dew-Hughes, D. (1997) 'Children with Emotional and Behavioural Difficulties', unpublished research paper.

Docking, J.W. (1980) *Control and Discipline in Schools*, London: Harper & Row.

Drucker, P.F. (1980) *Managing in Turbulent Times*, London: Heinemann.

Dunham, J. (1992) *Stress in Teaching*, London: Routledge.

Earley, P. and Kinder, K. (1994) *Initiation Rights*, Slough: NFER.

Evans, J. (1994) 'Problems in the Playground', *Education*, 3–13 June 1994, 34–40.

Everard, K.B. (1986) *Developing Management in Schools*, Oxford: Blackwell.

Everard, K.B. and Morris, G. (1990) *Effective School Management*, London: Paul Chapman Publishing.

Fidler, B., Bowles, G. and Hart, J. (1991) *Planning Your School's Strategy: ELMS Workbook*, Harlow: Longman.

Fish, J. and Evans, J. (1995) *Managing Special Education*, Buckingham: Open University Press.

Fontana, D. (1994) *Managing Classroom Behaviour*, Leicester: BPS Books.

Galloway, D., Ball, T., Blomfield, D. and Seyd, R. (1982) *Schools and Disruptive Pupils*, London: Longman.

Garforth, D. (1991) *Developing Whole School Policies for Assessment, Recording and Reporting*, Bristol: University of Bristol.

Garner, N., Fenwick, G., Garner, J., Harman, P., Harris, F., Martlew, J., Martlew, M., Midwinter, E., Parton, J., Rennie, J. and Reynard, J. (1973) *Teaching in the Urban Community School*, London: Ward Lock Educational.

Gaunt, D. (1995) 'Supporting continuing professional development' in Bines, H. and Welton, J. (eds) (1995) *Managing Partnership in Teacher Training and Development*, London: Routledge.

Glenny, G. and Hickling, E. (1995) 'A developmental model of partnership between primary schools and higher education' in Bines, H. and Welton, J. (eds) (1995) *Managing Partnership in Teacher Training and Development*, London: Routledge.

Graham, J. (1988) *Schools, Disruptive Behaviour and Delinquency: A Review of Research*, London: HMSO.

Haigh, G. (1997) 'Don't Worry, be Happy', *Times Educational Supplement* (First Appointments), 10 January 1997, 20–1.

Hall, V. and Oldroyd, D. (1990a) *Management Self-Development for Staff in Secondary Schools, Unit 2: Policy, Planning and Change*, Bristol: NDCEMP.

—— (1990b) *Management Self-Development for Staff in Secondary Schools, Unit 4: Implementing and Evaluating*, Bristol: NDCEMP.

Hargreaves, D.H. (1984) *Improving Secondary Schools*, London: ILEA.

Hargreaves, D.H., Hopkins, D., Leask, M., Connolly, M. and Robinson, P. (1989) *Planning for School Development*, London: DES.

Harrison, B.T. (1995) 'Revaluing leadership and service in educational management' in Bell, J. and Harrison, B.T. (eds) *Vision and Values in Managing Education*, London: David Fulton.

Hart, P.M., Wearing, A.J. and Conn, M. (1995) 'Conventional wisdom is a poor predictor of the relationship between discipline policy, student misbehaviour and teacher stress', *British Journal of Educational Psychology*, 65, 27–48.

Hart, S. (1996) *Beyond Special Needs,* London: Paul Chapman.

Hinds, C. (1997) 'Children Behaving Better', *Times Educational Supplement 2*, 16 May 1997, 13.

Holmes, G. (1993) *Essential School Leadership*, London: Kogan Page.

Houghton, S., Wheldall, K., Jukes, R. and Sharpe, A. (1990) 'The Effects of Limited Private Reprimands and Increased Private Praise on Classroom Behaviour in Four Secondary School Classes', *British Journal of Educational Psychology*, 60, 255–65.

Hoyle, E. (1986) *The Politics of School Management*, London: Hodder and Stoughton

Ingvarson, L. (1990) 'Schools: Places where teachers learn' in Chapman, J. (ed.) *School-based Decision-making and Management*, Basingstoke: Falmer Press.

Isaac, J. (1995) 'Self-management and development' in Bell, J. and Harrison, B.T. (eds) *Vision and Values in Managing Education,* London: David Fulton.

Johnson, B., Whitington, V. and Oswald, M. (1994) 'Teachers' Views on School Discipline: a theoretical framework', *Cambridge Journal of Education*, 24(2), 261–276.

Jones, N. (ed.) (1989) *School Management and Pupil Behaviour*, Lewes: Falmer Press.

Joyce, B. and Showers, B. (1982) 'The Coaching of Teaching', *Educational Leadership*, 40, 4–8,10.

Kyriacou, C. (1981) 'Social support and occupational stress among school teachers', *Educational Studies*, 7, 55–60.

—— (1986) *Effective teaching in Schools,* Oxford: Blackwell.

Levačić R. and Glover, D. (1995) 'The Relationship between Efficient Resource Management and School Effectiveness, and School Effectiveness', *Paper presented at the European Conference on Educational Research*, University of Bath, September 1995.

Lifeskills Associates Limited (1995) *Stress Levels*, London: Lifeskills Associates Limited.

Lloyd-Smith, M. (1993) 'Problem Behaviour, Exclusions and the Policy Vacuum', *Pastoral Care*, December 1993, 19–24.

Lowe, J. and Stance, D. (1989) *Schools and Quality*, Paris: OECD.

Maines, B. and Robinson, G. (1994) *The No Blame Approach*, Bristol: Avon Education Department.

Martin, S.C. (1994) 'A Preliminary Evaluation of the Adoption and Implementation of Assertive Discipline at Robinton High School', *School Organisation*, 14(3), 321–30.

Mediation UK Education Network (1996) *What's Peer Mediation?*, London: Mediation UK.

Merrett, F. and Jones, L. (1994) 'Rules, Sanctions and Rewards in Primary Schools', *Educational Studies*, 20(3), 345–55.

Midwinter, E. (ed.) (1972) *Projections*, London: Ward Lock Educational.

—— (1975) *Education and the Community*, London: George Allen and Unwin.

Mortimore, P., Sammons, P., Stoll, L., Lewis, D. and Ecob, R. (1988) *School Matters: The Junior Years*, Salisbury: Open Books.

Moss, G. (1995) 'Making assertions about discipline', *Managing Schools Today*, October 1995, 10–13.

National Commission on Education (NCE) (1996) *Success Against the Odds*, London: Routledge.

National Policy Board for Educational Administration (NPBEA) (1993) *Principals for our Changing Schools: Knowledge and Skill Base*, Virginia: NPBEA.

National Steering Group (1991) *School Teacher Appraisal: A National Framework*, London: HMSO.

National Union of Teachers (NUT) (1996a) *Discipline in Schools – Advice to NUT Members*, London: NUT.

—— (1996b) *Discipline in Schools – The Real Issues*, London: NUT.

Newmark, V. (1997) 'Parents as friends in waiting', *Times Educational Supplement*, 10 January 1997, 17.

Office for Standards in Education (OFSTED) (1993) *Section 5: Pupils' personal development and behaviour, OFSTED Handbook, Part 2 – The Framework*, London: HMSO.

—— (1994) *Spiritual, Moral, Social and Cultural*, London: HMSO.

—— (1995) *The Challenge for Education Welfare*, London: OFSTED.

—— (1996) *Exclusions from Secondary Schools 1995/6*, London: HMSO.

Ormston, M. and Shaw, M. (1993) *Mentoring*, Oxford Brookes University: School of Education.

Oswald, M. (1995) 'Difficult-to-manage Students: a survey of children who fail to respond to student discipline strategies in government schools', *Educational Studies*, 21(2), 265–76.

Oxford County Council Education Department (1997) *Family Connections Annual Report 1997*, Oxford: Oxford Education Department.

Parsons, C. (1975) *Exclusions: Research Project*, Canterbury: Christchurch College, University of Kent.

Parsons, C. and Howlett, K. (1995) 'Difficult Dilemmas', *Education*, 22/29 December 1995, 14.

Perfect, M. and Renshaw, J. (1997) *Misspent Youth: Young People and Crime*, London: HMSO.

Poster, C. (1982) *Community Education*, London: Heinemann.

Priest, R. (1997) *Discipline Policy*, Bristol: St George's Community School.

Reid, K. (1989) 'Discipline: The Teacher's Dilemma' in Jones, N. (ed.) (1989) *School Management and Pupil Behaviour*, Lewes: Falmer Press.

Rennie, J. (ed.) (1985) *British Community Primary Schools*, Lewes: Falmer Press.

Reynolds, D. and Cuttance, P. (eds) (1992) *School Effectiveness*, London: Cassell.

Robinson, G. and Maines, B. (1994) 'Who Manages Pupil Behaviour? Assertive Discipline – A Blunt Instrument for a Fine Task', *Pastoral Care*, September 1994, 30–5.

Robinson, T. (1997a) *Bristol Primary Exclusion Project: Annual Report*, Bristol: Bristol County Council.

—— (1997b) *Coping with Kids: Assertive Discipline for Parents, UK Leader's Manual*, Bristol: Behaviour Management.

—— (1997c) *Coping with Kids: Annual Report 1996–97*, Bristol: Educational Psychology Team, Bristol City Council.

Rogers, W.A. (1996) *Managing Teacher Stress*, London: Pitman.

Rutter, M., Maughan, B., Mortimore, P. and Ouston, J. (1979) *Fifteen Thousand Hours: Secondary Schools and Their Effects on Children*, London: Open Books.

Sarason, I.G., Glaser, E.M. and Fargo, G.A. (1972) *Reinforcing Productive Classroom Behaviour*, New York: Behavioural Publications.

Senge, P.M. (1990) *The Fifth Discipline – The Art and Practice of the Learning Organisation*, New York: Doubleday.

Sharp, S. and Smith, P.K. (eds) (1994) *Tackling Bullying in Your School*, London: Routledge.

Shaw, M., Boydell, D. and Warner, F. (1995) 'Developing induction in schools: managing the transition from training to employment' in Bines, H. and Welton, J. (eds) (1995) *Managing partnership in teacher training and development*, London: Routledge.

Skelton, M., Reeves, G. and Playfoot, D. (1991) *Development Planning for Primary Schools*, Windsor: NFER/Nelson.

Smith, P.K. and Sharp, S. (eds) (1994) *School Bullying*, London: Routledge.

Spinks, J. M. (1990) 'Collaborative decision-making at the school level' in Chapman, J. (ed.) (1990) *School-based Decision-making and Management*, Basingstoke: Falmer Press.

Stockwell, C. (1996) *Bristol Mediation Schools Project*, Bristol: Bristol Mediation.

—— (1997) *Bristol Mediation: Annual Review 1996–7*, Bristol: Bristol Mediation.

Tannenbaum, R. and Schmidt, W.H. (1973) 'How to choose a leadership pattern', *Harvard Business Review*, 36(2), 95–101.

Tattum, D. (1989) 'Alternative Approaches to Disruptive Behaviour' in Jones, N. (ed.) (1989) *School Management and Pupil Behaviour*, Lewes: Falmer Press.

Teacher Training Agency (TTA) (1995) *Annual Report 1995*, London: TTA.

—— (1997) *General Standards for the Award of Qualified Teacher Status in Secondary and Primary Schools in National Curriculum for Teacher Education*, London: TTA.

Tuckman, B.W. (1965) 'Development sequence in small groups', *Psychological Bulletin*, 63(6), 384–99.

United Nations (1989) *The Convention on the Rights of the Child*. Adopted by the General Assembly of the United Nations, 20 November 1989.

Walker, L. (1989) 'TVEI: All Change or Small Change', in Jones, N. (ed.) (1989) *School Management and Pupil Behaviour*, Lewes: Falmer Press.

Wallace, M., Hall, V. and Huckman, L. (1996) 'Senior Management Teams in Primary and Secondary Schools', *British Education Management and Administration Society (BEMAS) Partners in Change Conference (Cambridge)*, March 22–7, 1996.

Wardle, C. (1997) *Behaviour Management*, Bristol: Pen Park School.

Watkins, C. and Wagner, P. (1987) *School Discipline*, Oxford: Blackwell.

Wedge, P. and Prosser, H. (1973) *Born to Fail?*, London: Arrow Books.

West-Burnham, J. (1992) *Managing Quality in Schools*, Harlow: Longman.

White, P. and Poster, C. (eds) (1997) *The Self-Monitoring Primary School*, London: Routledge.

Whitehead, M. (1997) 'Bad Behaviour: Now', *Times Educational Supplement*, 6 June 1997, 2.

Willower, D.J. (1986) 'Organisational Culture in Schools', *Paper presented at the Annual Meeting of the American Educational Research Association*, San Francisco, April 16–20.

Wilson, J. and Cowell, B. (1990) *Children and Discipline*, London: Cassell Educational.

INDEX

absence, unauthorised *see* attendance
absenteeism: pupil *see* attendance; staff 62, 151
abuse: avoiding 58; child 80; protection from 80–2; substance 56; verbal 55, 61–2, 135, 140
academic: emphasis 42, 57; monitoring 108, 175, 176; support 99
accelerated learning 108
acceptable behaviour 2, 3, 9, 12, 13, 25, 93, 127
accountability *see* responsibility
achievements *see* success
action learning 146
action planning 9, 45, 66, 86, 90–2, 99, 154; primary schools 115, 116; secondary schools 116; *see also* individual education plan *and* home-school contracts
active listening 154
administration: effective 38, 114; overload 65
admissions 84
advice, expert 153–4
after school groups 85; *see also* lunchtime clubs
aggressive behaviour 13, 14; defusing 154; physical 1, 8, 14, 40, 56, 61–2, 94, 135, 139; *see also* fighting
agreement: home-school 12, 13, 167; on rules 58
aided schools 26
aims, school *see* goals; *see also* vision
alertness, staff 64, 73
alternative provision 11, 22–3, 78, 79, 84, 85
anger 2; controlling 68, 87, 152, 166; expressing 67–8; managing 97, 102; as secondary emotion 117; using 67, 68
answering back *see* argumentativeness; *see also* cheekiness
anti-social behaviour 1, 7, 8, 103, 104
anxiety 14, 65
appeals committees 22
appearance, teacher 4, 70
appointments policy 10, 79
appraisal: school 79, 162, 163; self- 129; staff 79, 146, 163; *see also* assessment
argumentativeness 4, 14, 61, 152
art therapy 87
assembly 107, 117
assertive discipline 22, 25, 36, 90, 100–3, 106, 133, 136, 154
assertiveness 65
assessment: progress 45; pupil 86, 107, 148; special educational needs 10, 13, 89, 133; *see also* appraisal
atmosphere, school *see* ethos
attainment, school *see* School Attainment Tests (SATs)
attendance 10–14, 22, 32, 59, 60, 78, 81, 82, 83, 113–15, 131–2, 151, 167; improvements in 82, 97; monitoring 13, 132; policy 132; rates 10; responsibility for 55; *see also* absenteeism
attention: difficulties 14, 61, 102; seeking 102, 153
attitudes: authoritarian 30, 124; boundaries 2; disruptive 1; staff 40
authoritarian attitudes 30, 124
authority, challenging 9
Avon Education Department 88–9

Badger, B. 52

balance, curricular 76, 77, 133, 167
behaviour: acceptable 2, 3, 9, 12, 13, 25, 93, 127; aggressive 1, 8, 13–14, 40, 56, 61–2, 94, 135, 139, 154; analysing 19; anti-social 1, 7, 8, 103, 104; boundaries 2, 3, 9, 12, 98, 116; and class size 10; classroom 107; clinging 14; codes 30, 35; constructive 102; continuum 3; coordinator 106, 108; DfE Circular 8/94 (1994b) 11–13; courteous 31; difficulties 89; at home 99; improving 100, 169; influences on 5, 53; lunchtime 107; management 80, 85, 99, 105–8, 121, 152, 171; modification *see* reward systems; normal 3; orderly 4, 30, 136–8; and organisation 29; out-of-seat 62; plans 56, 78, 105–8; policy 2, 5, 10, 22, 30, 58, 69, 72, 89, 125–43, 154, 156; and supply teachers 10; on task 103, 138; policies 30, 89; problems 89; severity 19; and staff morale 62; standards 6, 133; and timetables 105, 108–12, 176; variables 3; withdrawn 13; *see also* disruptiveness
beliefs *see* values
Better Schools, White Paper (DES 1985) 151
Bines, H. 148
blame: attributing 72; culture 157; *see also* no-blame approach
Blandford, S. 41, 46, 63, 92, 110, 147
boredom, staff 65, 77
Born to Fail?, National Children's Bureau 27
boundaries: accepting 2, 165; attitude 2; behavioural 2, 3, 9, 12, 98, 116; enforcing 154; maintaining 3; setting 2, 9, 25, 58, 71, 102, 106, 123; testing 9
breaktime: groups 85, 154; observation 87; supervision 105
Brighouse, T. 159
Bristol City Council Education Directorate (1997a) 81
Bristol Mediation Schools Project (BMSP) 94, 95
Bristol Primary Exclusion Project (BPEP) 97–100
Bristol Special Needs Support Service 85, 116
Brown, M. 65, 66
buddy system 139; *see also* sanctions
buildings repairs 79
bullying 11, 12, 13, 22, 58, 80, 83, 85, 97, 107, 112–13, 132–3, 134, 175; approach to 103, 104; rejecting 125; by teachers 71
Burstall, E. 65
Bush, T. 44

Callaghan, J. 7
calling out *see* shouting
calm, staying 102
calming down 99
Calvert, M. 57
Canter, L. and M. 100, 101, 102
care: education of children in, Circular 13/94 (DfE 1994g) 33, 34; pastoral 57, 96, 97, 141
career services 79
caring: culture 157; environment 8, 43, 60, 134
Carr, R. 157, 158
case studies 133–41, 155
certainty 152
certificates, reward 139; *see also* merit marks
challenges, in teaching 63
change: management of 37, 38, 46–8, 156; resistance to 47; and stress 65, 66; support for 47; training for 146
cheating, rejecting 125
cheekiness 4, 62; *see also* answering back
child abuse *see* abuse
child-centred approaches 52, 154
Child and Family Support Centres 87, 88
Children Act (1989) 81
children in care, education of, DfE Circular (1994) 11
children with emotional and behavioural difficulties, education of, Circular 9/94 (DfE 1994c) 13–18
children, sick, education of, DfE Circular (1994) 11
Children and Young Persons' Acts (1933–69) 81, 131
circle time 154
Circulars, DfE (1994) 11–21, 33
class size, and behaviour 10
classroom: behaviour 107; control 67; environment 74–6, 131; evaluation 73; monitoring 71, 73, 116, 148; observation 87; support 87; work 86
Cleugh, M.F. 62
clinging behaviour 14
Code for Success 106–7
codes of practice 58; DfE 1994a 6, 15, 16,

19, 21, 85, 89, 90, 136, 148, 152; implementation of 90, 154
Coleman, M. 44
collaboration 45, 54, 54, 58, 77, 86, 88, 141, 165, 166; community 32–6; *see also* consultation *and* decision-making processes
Comber, L.C. 67
commitment 43, 44; engendering 9, 39; pupil 58
common-sense knowledge 157
communication 37, 48–9, 60, 86, 93, 154, 166; development 123; evaluation 160; home-school 10, 25, 29; skills 4, 48, 65, 95; support agencies 78; systems 5, 6, 29, 43, 53
community: collaboration with 32–6; collective 24; cultural interaction 26; definition 27; developing sense of 31, 34–6, 37, 55; governors representing 55; individual 24; provision 26; reflective 24; school as 7, 24–36, 38, 126, 161; school within 26, 27; schools 26, 94; service 130
concentration, lack of 14
concluding lessons 74
conditions, of work 51, 74, 75
conflict 57; mediation 94, 95; resolution 65, 68, 80, 85, 87, 94, 123
confrontation, avoiding 117, 166
confusion, mental 65; *see also* stress
consensus 39; lacking 57
consent, team 39
consequences, behavioural 151–2
consideration for others 125, 126, 127, 134
consistency 1, 13, 25, 30, 40, 50, 58, 70–72, 74, 86, 101–2, 104, 116, 130, 135–6, 166; lacking 123
Constable, J. 158
constructive behaviour 102
consultancy 10, 56; *see also* support
consultation 39, 43, 58, 107, 156; parent 53; staff 53; student 53; *see also* collaboration *and* decision-making processes
contextual knowledge 157
contracts: home-school 105, 107, 115–16, 165
control 2; of anger 68, 87, 152, 166; classroom 67; external 66; feelings of 92, 164; internal 66; negotiated 66, 67; self 2, 5, 12, 70, 106, 118, 121; and stress 64, 66
cooling off 139
cooperation 43, 95; insistence on 73; lack of 2; teaching 117
cooperative games, using 87
Coping with Kids courses 121, 122, 171
coping strategies, developing 69
corporal punishment 123; *see also* abuse
correction, positive 151–2
counselling: one-to-one 87; peer 119, 154; services 66, 85–7, 90, 99, 122; techniques 113; *see also* support
courage 38, 57
courtesy 31
criminal offences 32, 55–6, 131, 166; *see also* police
crisis support groups 56, 98
criticism 44, 72
cultural differences, and discipline 7, 8, 27–8, 52, 93, 103
culture, school 28
curriculum 105, 107, 108–12; accessing 90; appropriateness 5, 12, 76–7, 133; balance 76, 77, 133, 167; coherence 77; context 77; development 38, 60; and discipline 76; effective 60, 76; focused work 85, 87; knowledge 4; modular 110–12; national 10, 11, 51, 79; planning 38, 76–7; pressure 57; relevance 108; teams 56
cruelty, rejecting 125

deceit, rejecting 125
decision-making processes 2, 5, 25, 39–40, 71, 128; participation in 39, 129; *see also* consultation
decisiveness 55
defiance 4, 14, 61
delegation 55, 65, 74
demands: colleague 159; external 159; government 158; management 158; pupil 159; system 159; unrealistic 63
democracy, in schools *see* collaboration *and* consultation
demoralisation, teacher *see* morale
Department for Education 6, 9; Circulars, DfE (1994) 11–21, 33; *Pupil Behaviour and Discipline*, Circular 8/94 (DfE 1994b) 11–13; *Education of Children Being Looked After by Local Authorities*, Circular 13/94 (DfE 1994g) 33, 34;

Education of Sick Children, Circular 12/94 (DfE 1994f) 11; *Education of Children with Emotional and Behavioural Difficulties*, Circular 9/94 (DfE 1994c) 11, 13–18, 19, 58; *Exclusions from School*, Circular 10/94 (DfE 1994d) 11, 12, 18– 21; *Code of Practice* (DfE 1994a) 85, 89, 136, 152
Department for Education and Employment: *Excellence in Schools*, White Paper (1997a) 22, 25, 100; *Framework for the Organisation of Schools*, White Paper (1997b) 55
Department of Education and Science 61; *Better Schools*, White Paper (1985) 151
departmental teams 56
depression: pupil 13, 14; staff 64, 65
design, classroom 74–6
destructiveness 14, 62; preventing 96
detentions, imposing 22, 130, 131, 135, 138, 140, 165; *see also* sanctions
development: intellectual 58; moral 58, 127; personal 125, 146, 159; physical 58; professional 144–56, 169; school 144; self-confidence 50, 58, 73, 93, 95, 108, 114, 125, 126, 165, 166; self-esteem 2, 18, 30, 50, 58, 63, 73, 86, 93, 95, 97, 98, 102, 117, 125, 127, 134, 145, 165, 166; social 58, 80, 85, 87, 93, 99, 114, 126, 150; team 146; values 126–7
development plan, school 28, 37, 42, 45–6, 51, 168–70; training for 144, 156
dignity, treating with 58
disaffected pupils 83; *see also* problem pupils
discipline: assertive 22, 25, 36, 89, 100–3, 106, 133, 136, 154; and culture 7, 8, 27–8, 52, 93, 103; and curriculum 76; definition 1, 2; DfE Circular 8/94(1994b) 11–13; diversity and 7, 8, 27– 8, 52, 93, 103; and ethos 29–31; evaluation 159, 160, 162; expectation of 72; external *see* control; inconsistent 123; internal *see* self-control; maintaining 4, 9, 60; managing 1–3, 5–6, 10, 11, 14, 28, 37–49, 56–7, 59, 78, 93, 166; policy 2, 5, 10, 22, 58, 69, 72, 89, 125–43, 154, 156; problems 77; taught 126; training and 60, 61, 70, 145, 148, 149, 159
Discipline in Schools, Report of the Committee of Enquiry see Elton Report
discrimination 58; *see also* racial *and* sexual harassment
discussion *see* consultation
dishonesty, rejecting 125
dismissals, staff 79
dismissing the class 74
displays 74, 130, 160
disruptiveness 1, 2, 3, 5, 14, 56, 59; increasing 6, 8; managing 61; mechanisms for dealing with 60, 61, 108, 109, 139, 152; reducing 97, 103; types of 4, 61, 62, 152 ; *see also* intervention *and* sanctions
distance learning 146
distraction 152
distress 86
disturbed pupils 79; feelings of 88
diversion 152
diversity, amongst schools 25, 51
Docking, J.W. 5, 61
drama therapy 87
dress codes 12, 49, 138, 167, 175
drinking, excessive, as stress symptom 64
Drucker, P.F. 46
drug problems 32, 107
Dunham, J. 62, 71
duty teacher system 140
dysfunction, social 7, 8, 14

Earley, P. 150
Education Acts: (1944) 81;(1980) 55;(1981) 81; (1986) 55; (1993) 9, 11, 52, 81, 89; (1996) 81;(1997) 22, 52, 78, 81, 131
education of children in care, DfE Circular (1994) 11
Education of Children with Emotional and Behavioural Difficulties, The Circular 9/94 (DfE 1994c) 13–18
education of children not at school: DfE Circular (1994) 11; DfE (1997a:7) 22–3; management 37–9
Education Officers 84–7
education: plan, individual *see* individual education plan; policy 25
Education Reform Act (ERA, DES 1988) 6, 9, 10, 50, 51, 78
education of sick children, DfE Circular (1994) 11
Education (School Government) Regulations 21

education, theory 157
education welfare officers (EWOs) 6, 56, 79, 80–3, 85, 98, 99, 113, 114, 115; referrals 83
educational psychology service 6, 17, 19, 52, 56, 79, 85, 89–90, 98, 99, 124
effectiveness: curricular 60, 76; learning 9; management 5, 37, 44; organisation 74; promoting 37; teaching 9, 12, 148; training for 145
Elton Committee of Enquiry 9, 10, 62, 100
Elton Report (DES 1989) 9, 10, 11, 62, 79, 84, 88, 108
emergencies 32, 80
emotional and behavioural difficulties (EBD) 6, 14, 79, 166, 175; combined approach 86; definition 13, 14; DfE Circular 9/94 (1994c) 11, 13–18, 19, 58; education plan 87; evaluation 86, 91; expectations 15; expertise 84, 85; funding 106; identification 13, 15, 19; improvements 86, 91; isolation of 87; observation 16, 18, 86, 87; partnerships 85; pattern identification 86; psychology and 89; recording 17–18; review meetings 86, 92; stage 1 15–16, 18; stage 2 16–17, 18; stage 3 17, 18; support 16–18, 30, 58, 84–8, 90, 166; teams 84–7, 94, 113; understanding 86; watching brief 86; *see also* special educational needs
emotional problems, staff 5; *see also* stress
empathy 66, 86; developing 99
encouragement, giving 72
ending lessons 74
energy loss: families 88; staff 63, 64, 65; *see also* stress
enjoyment, of learning 88
enthusiasm 55; staff 64
environment, school 5, 7, 9, 12, 31–2, 63, 74–6, 107, 160, 165, 167; classroom 74–6, 131; creating 60; improving 35, 74
equal opportunities 27, 58, 146, 165
ethos, school 5, 7, 9, 11, 12, 24, 29, 30, 31, 126, 127; creating 37, 74; and discipline 29–31; empathetic 66; improving 95; and organisation 29; positive 30, 133; process 30; *see also* identity
evaluation 38, 80, 128, 141–3; classroom 73; communication 160; of discipline 159, 160, 162; EBD children 86, 91; pastoral management 57; self 63, 64, 70, 157–66; and training 145
Everard, K.B. 37, 43
examinations success 105
Excellence in Schools, White Paper (DfEE 1997a: 66–8) 22, 25, 100
excluded pupils, educating *see* alternative provision
exclusion 2, 59, 78, 82, 84, 87, 131, 135, 138; Bristol Primary Exclusion Project (BPEP) 97–100; conditions of 20, 21, 22; DfE Circular 10/94(1994d) 11, 12, 18–21; educating *see* alternative provision; prevention of 6, 11, 18, 21, 58, 72, 87, 97, 98, 100, 166; problems of 98, 166; rates 52, 55, 106, 129; reasons for 55, 56, 135, 136; responsibility for 55; review 22–3; warning of 19; *see also* sanctions
Exclusion from School, Circular 10/94 (DfE 1994d) 18–21
expectation 2, 15, 30, 52, 107, 115, 127, 137, 148, 167; and discipline 72; EBD children 15; examining 65; raising 106, 152; shared 106; of teachers 68, 128; variables 3, 71
experience: lack of 70; passing on 56
experimentation 128
expert advice 153–4
extinction, as alternative strategy 73
extra-curricular activities 107

facilities, for staff 63
faculty teams 56
failure 27
fairness 13, 58, 71, 72, 73, 130, 135, 165
family: breakdown 33; environment 14
Family Connections programme 122–4, 171
Family Nurturing Network 122, 123
feelings: of control 92, 164; of depression 13, 14, 64, 65; of disturbed pupils 88; expression 67–8, 95; of frustration 2, 90; of futility 65; of guilt 67; understanding 71, 91
Fidler, B. 39
fighting 58, 79, 80, 109, 135; *see also* aggressive behaviour
finishing lessons 74
firmness 9, 10, 31, 52, 102, 135, 165

first aid 80
flash points, recognising 117
flexibility, response 50, 67, 70, 111
folk-wisdom 157
Fontana, D. 52, 69, 70, 73, 76
force, reasonable, use of 22
forgetfulness, staff 65; *see also* stress
foundation schools 26
Framework for the Organisation of Schools, White Paper (DfEE 1997b) 55
friendship: groups support work 87; skills, teaching 117; *see also* interpersonal skills
frustration, feelings of 2, 90; *see also* stress
futility, feelings of 65; *see also* stress

Galloway, D. 61, 88
Gaunt, D. 150, 153
gentleness 97
Glover, D. 145
goals 40, 44, 137, 146; defining 43, 45; setting 38, 52, 71; short-term 111; teaching 148; *see also* vision
good practice 13, 105–24
government policy 9–23
governors 55–6; advising 79; role 10, 12, 22
Graham, J. 88
grant maintained schools 26
Grants for Education Support and Training (GEST) 153, 154
group work 85–7
grudges, bearing by teachers 71
guidance, parental 10
guilt, feelings 67
Gulbenkian Foundation 122

habits, irritating 70
Haigh, G. 163
Hall, V. 47, 142
Hargreaves, D.H. 29, 69
Hart, S. 129
headteachers 5, 6; management style 9, 30; role 10, 12, 22; training 144, 145; *see also* leadership
health, teacher 5
helpfulness 125
Henderson, J. 57
hindering other pupils 62
hobbies, teachers 164
Holmes, G. 53, 57
home: environment 14; improving behaviour at 99
home-school: agreements 12, 13, 167; communication 10, 25, 29, 108, 130; contracts 105, 107, 115–16, 165; liaison 85, 87, 99; links 5, 9, 22, 26, 32, 33, 65, 78, 79, 81; partnerships 154, 165; *see also* parental involvement
homework 167, 176
honesty, valuing 125
Hoyle, E. 103
humbleness 97
humiliation 130
humour, use of 31

ideas storming 94
identity: pupil 71, 86, 88, 126; school 7, 43; staff 63; team 44
ignoring, tactical 152
illness *see* education of sick children
impairment: physical 14, 89; sensory 14, 16
impertinence *see* answering back *and* cheekiness
imposition 116
in-class support 85
in-house training 146
In-service training (INSET) 4, 9, 29, 34, 42, 52, 79, 85, 99, 113, 129, 144, 145, 146, 151, 155, 156, 163; national standards 144; planning 156; presentation 154–6*; see also* training
inattention *see* attention difficulties
individual education plan (IEP) 87, 90–92, 115, 140–1, 154; *see also* action planning *and* home-school contracts
induction programmes 149–51; *see also* training
information: availability 49; gathering 86, 117; importance 52; sharing 49; on training 145; *see also* knowledge
Ingvarson, L. 156
innovation *see* change
insecurity *see* security
insolence *see* cheekiness
inspection, school 79, 85
integration, support staff 94
integrity, importance of 38, 53, 57
intellectual development 58
interpersonal *see* social; *see also* communication *and* relationships
interruption 14, 61, 62; avoiding 76; *see also* shouting

intervention: early 116–18, 136; procedures 99, 105, 115, 148
intimidation 94; *see also* aggressive behaviour
Investors in People programme 158
irrationality, of disruptive pupils 2, 8, 162
irritability 64; *see also* stress
Isaac, J. 158
isolation: EBD pupils 88; as punishment 59, 131, 139, 140, *see also* sanctions; teacher 4, 6, 7, 25, 41, 52, 61, 69, 156

job: exchange 146; rotation 147
Johnson, B. 128
Jones, N. 5, 30, 128, 129
Joyce, B. 103
judgmentalism 72
juvenile crime *see* criminal offences

keeping fit, teachers 164
Kemmis, S. 157, 158
Key Stage teams 56
Kinder, K.150
kindness 31
knowledge: common-sense 157; contextual 157; curricular 4; folk-wisdom 157; professional 157; skills 157; teacher 61, 70, 158 ; *see also* information
Kyriacou, C. 66

labelling, negative 3, 70, 113
language, bad *see* swearing
leadership: effective 5, 10, 11, 38, 50, 55; non-confrontational 55, 57; positive 128; school 51–4; situational 44; *see also* headteachers
league tables 51
learning: accelerated 108; action 146; difficulties 14, 16, 88, 89; distance 146; effectiveness 9; enjoyment of 88; implementation 38; meaningful 76; obligations 126; psychology of 88; styles 60, 74, 107, 108, 154; support assistants 87
legislation 9–23
lessons, ending 74
letters to parents 108, 130
Levačić, R. 145
Lifeskills Associates 64
limits *see* boundaries
listening: active 154; paired 94; skills 49, 55, 70, 71–2, 95; teaching 117
literacy 25
Lloyd-Smith, M. 131
Local Education Authority (LEA) 4; guidelines 105; representatives 55; role 12, 23; support 6, 23, 78, 79, 128, 154
Local Management of Schools (LMS) 10, 51, 78, 79
Lowe, J. 128
loyalty, divided 72
lunchtime: behaviour 107; clubs 87, 117, 154; observation 87; supervisors 79–80, 85, 87, 94, 154, 171

McCormack, R. 158
Maines, B. 100, 103, 104, 112, 129
management: behaviour 80, 85, 99, 105–8, 121, 152, 171; of change 37, 38, 46–8, 156; classroom 5, 9, 60–77, 85; of discipline 1–3, 5–6, 10, 11, 14, 28, 37–49, 56–7, 59, 78, 93, 166; education 37–9; effective 5, 37, 44; emphasis on 42; and ethos 29, 30; external agencies 41, 51; guidelines 108; learning 38; local (LMS) 10, 51, 78, 79; middle 56; open 54–5, 93; preventative 52; of pupils 42, 70–74; resources 37, 38, 92; roles 57; school 5; senior 50–59, 108; of stress 63–7; structure 38, 40–42, 43, 50; style 9, 30, 39, 40, 41, 55; teaching 38; teams 43–5; time 65, 69
Managing Partnership in Teacher Training and Development 148
marking, keeping up with 73
Martin, S.C. 101
mediation 90, 93–6; peer 93–6, 154, 171
Mediation UK Education Network (1996) 93
meetings 49, 54, 65; with parents 59; school council 121; structuring 54
mental illness 13, 17; parental 123
mentoring 149–51; *see also* training
merit marks 130, 136, 139; *see also* reward certificates
Merrett, F. 128, 129
midday supervision *see* lunchtime supervisors
mission *see* goals
Misspent Youth: Young People and Crime, Report 55
modular curriculum 110–12
monitoring 30, 79, 80, 92, 107, 141–3; academic 108, 175, 176; classroom 71,

73, 116, 148; pastoral management 57; progress 91; self- 63, 64; stress 166
moral development 58, 127; *see also* values
morale 129; factors affecting 62–3; improving 34, 55; low 7; *see also* self-esteem
MORI survey 144
Morris, G. 43
Mortimore, P. 5, 119
Moss, G. 102
motivation: improving 9, 39, 102, 108, 111, 121; lacking 14
moving around the school 160
moving on, teachers 161–2, 164; *see also* redundancy
music therapy 87

National Children's Bureau 27
National Commission on Education, *Success Against the Odds* (1996) 28
national curriculum *see* curriculum
National Foundation for Education Research (NFER) 150
National Policy Board for Educational Administration (NPBEA) 146
National Professional Qualification for Headship (NPQH) 144
needs: identifying 148; pupil 1, 2, 6, 41, 51, 52, 53, 88, 89, 91, 93; school 25, 41; teacher 1, 2, 40, 91
negative: labelling 3, 70, 113; reinforcers 72, 73, 74, *see also* sanctions
negotiation 58, 90, 91, 116
networking 44, 49, 66, 145
no-blame approach 103–4, 112, 113, 117, 154
noisiness 62, 152, 160; *see also* shouting
non-attendance *see* attendance
non-confrontational leadership 55, 57
non-directive counselling 86
norming 44
numeracy 25

objectives *see* goals
objectivity, developing 67, 69
obligations, learning 126
observation: classroom 87; EBD children 15, 16, 18, 86, 87; lunchtime 87
off-site work 86, 87
OFSTED reports 145, 154
Oldroyd, D. 47, 142
on task behaviour 103, 138
one-to-one: counselling 87; work 86
open management 54–5, 93
openness 44
operant conditioning *see* reward systems
optimum stress level 64
orderly behaviour 4, 30, 136–8
organisation: and behaviour 29; effective 74; and ethos 29; *Framework for the Organisation of Schools*, White Paper (DfEE 1997b) 55; structure 7, 24, 25; training 148
Ormston, M. 149
out-of-seat behaviour 62
Outreach 96–7, 171

panic attacks, staff 65; *see also* stress
paperwork *see* administration
parent-teacher associations 10
parental: choice 51; governors 55; guidance 10; guidelines 108; involvement 32–4, 35, 59, 97, 128, 131, 161; responsibility 10, 12; role 12, 19; skills 121–4; support 65, 87, 115, 121; *see also* home-school contracts
'parking' disruptive pupils 108, 109; *see also* sanctions
pastoral: care 57, 96, 97, 141; teams 56; under-emphasis on 57; workers 97
peer: counselling 119, 154; mediation 93–6, 154, 171; pressure 73; relationships 175; role 7, 12, 19; support 54, 68, 69, 105, 118–19
pensions 62
people-centred culture 56
Perfect, M. 55
performance, school 79
performing, team 44
permissiveness 124
persistence 38
personality: inadequate 104; teacher 4, 114
personnel services 79
philosophy *see* ethos
physical: development 58; difficulties 14, 16, 89 14, 89
picking on *see* singling out
placements 79: breakdown of 85
planning: action 9, 45, 66, 86, 89, 90–2, 99, 154; behaviour 56, 78, 105–8; curriculum 38, 76–7; development, school 28, 37, 42, 45–6, 51, 168–70; individual education plan (IEP) 87,

90–2, 115, 141, 154; INSET 156; strategic 45, 67, 73
play therapy 87
playground: skills, teaching 99; support 87
polarisation 27
police: involving 19, 104; liaison 32; *see also* criminal offences
policy: discipline 2, 5, 10, 22, 30, 58, 69, 72, 89, 125–43, 154, 156; education 25; making 38; school 6, 12, 22, 125–43
polite behaviour *see* courtesy
positive: attitudes (pupils) 134, 137, (staff) 30, 102, 103, 166; correction 151, 152; ethos 30, 133; feedback *see* reward; leadership 128; regard, unconditional 86, 97; reinforcers 72, 73, 74, 133; response systems 93
power: struggles, avoiding 117, 153; wielding 67, 71; *see also* control
practical work 74
praise 15, 22, 30, 44, 72, 102, 103, 123, 130, 139, 160; *see also* reward
Pre-School Teacher Counselling service 122
preparation, lesson 73
pressure: curriculum 57; peer 73; response to 58; time 5, 65
preventative: management 52; support 90
prevention, discipline problems 151–2
Priest, R. 152
prioritisation 65
privacy 86
privileges, withholding 130, 135; *see also* sanctions
problem pupils 53, 83; provision for 78
problems: dealing with 74; identifying 91; solving 117; understanding 91
procrastination *see* argumentativeness
professional: development 25, 42, 51, 55, 56, 62, 128, 144–56, 169; knowledge 157; qualifications *see* training
progress: assessment 45; monitoring 91
promises 73
promotion, staff 62
property, respecting 125
Prosser, H. 27
protection, child 80–82
psychology, of learning 88; *see also* educational psychology service
public commendations 130; *see also* reward
public relations 49
punctuality 62, 73, 138, 167, 175
punishment *see* negative reinforcers *and* sanctions
Pupil Behaviour and Discipline, Circular 8/94 (DfE 1994b) 11–13
pupils 58; council 119–21; needs 1, 2, 6, 41, 51, 52, 53, 88, 90, 91, 93, 148; respecting 58, 60; responsible 5, 10, 11, 12, 71, 135, 152; self-esteem 2, 14, 30, 52, 59, 165; -teacher relationships 2, 106
pushing 109

qualifications *see* training
questions, using 74
quiet room, as sanction *see* isolation

racial harassment 12, 32, 132–3
Ralph, S. 65, 66
reactions, appropriate 99
receptiveness 72
record-keeping systems 91
redundancy 62; *see also* moving on
referral 135; *see also* sanctions
reflection, self 71
reform *see* Education Reform Act
refusal, pupil 152
Reid, K. 71
reinforcement *see* reward systems
relationships 1, 51; building 18, 69, 96, 99, 166; difficulties 14, 83; home-school 5, 9, 22, 26, 32, 33, 65, 78, 79, 81; peer 175; pupil-practitioner 2, 106; restoring 153; staff 65; training for 145
relaxation techniques 66; *see also* stress management
remedial teaching 77
Renshaw, J. 55
repair and build 152
reporting 59
resentment 14
resignation *see* moving on
resistance 4, 61
resolving: conflict 65, 68, 80, 85, 87, 94, 123; learning difficulties 16
resources: allocation 25; improved 25; management 37, 38, 92; provision 38; shortages 63, 65; training 145
respect 2; mutual 71, 148, 165, 167; promoting 11, 12, 34, 35, 86, 125, 126, 127, 134, 136, 152; for profession 62; of property 125; for pupils 58, 60; rights 125, 137–8; self- 136

response: flexibility of 50, 67, 70, 111; positive 93; proactive 102; teacher 9, 71
responsibility: allocation 41, 51; collective 5, 9; developing 121, 125, 126, 137, 138; for exclusion 55; governors 12; parental 10, 12; personal 94, 125, 138, 139; pupil 5, 10, 11, 12, 71, 135, 152; school 12, 25, 44, 60; self- 3; sense of 34; teachers 29, 108, 160
reward: certificates 138; of learning 88; success 117; systems 5, 12, 72–4, 101, 107, 108, 116, 126, 129–31, 133, 137, 138–9, 160, 165; *see also* praise
rights: child 122; respecting 125, 137–8
ringleaders 130
Robinson, G. 99, 100, 103, 104, 112, 121, 129
Rogers, W.A. 5, 55, 61, 62, 63, 67, 68, 69, 71
role models: middle managers as 56; teachers as 30
role, school 8, 12
roles: clarity 57; identification 50, 51, 60; vocational 150
routines, setting 71
rowdiness *see* noisiness
rules, school 29, 52, 126, 129–31; breaking 56, 62; clear 101, 130; minimising 129; understanding 58
Rutter, M. 5, 51, 61, 119

safety 9, 32, 58, 60, 68, 93, 105, 107, 136, 148, 154
salary 62
sanctions 5, 12, 13, 22, 72–4, 101, 102, 104, 108, 116, 126, 129–31, 135–7, 139, 160, 165; appropriate 13, 19, 72, 73, 130, 135; avoiding 113; Buddy system 139; detentions 22, 130, 131, 135, 138, 140, 165; isolation 59, 131, 139, 140; parking 108, 109; referral 135; severity 152; types 135; withdrawal from classroom 17, 19, 90, 135; *see also* exclusion *and* negative reinforcers
Sarason, S.A. 72
scapegoating 19, 130
Schmidt, W.H. 40
School Attainment Tests (SATs) 98
School Attendance: Policy and Practice on Categories of Absence (DfE 1994h) 132
school council 119–21
school plans *see* action planning
Schools Outreach 96–7, 171
security 9, 32, 33, 58, 60, 72, 93, 105, 136, 154; lack of 71; staff 43, 53, 63, 68
self-confidence 1, 2, 59; developing 50, 58, 73, 93, 95, 108, 114, 125, 126, 165, 166; lacking 5; staff 44, 60, 64, 105, 165
self-control 2, 5, 12, 70, 106, 118, 121, 126
self-discipline *see* self-control
self-esteem 1; developing 2, 18, 30, 50, 58, 63, 73, 86, 93, 95, 97, 98, 102, 117, 125, 127, 134, 145, 165, 166; low 86, 88, 98, 99, 101, 106, 118; lunchtime supervisors 94; pupil 2, 14, 30, 52, 59, 165; teacher 5, 30, 52, 53, 61, 62, 63, 67, 90, 150, 163; *see also* morale
self-evaluation 63, 64, 70, 157–66
self-help groups 66
self-injury 14
self-monitoring 63–4
self-presentation 65
self-respect 136
Senge, P.M. 159
sensitivity; outreach workers 97; teacher 31, 71
sensory impairment 14, 16, 89
severity, sanction 152
sexual harassment 12, 132–3; *see also* equal opportunities
shaping 73
sharing 99, 117; information 49
Shaw, M. 149
shouting 61, 73; *see also* interruption
Showers, B. 103
singling out 71
situational leadership 44
Skelton, M. 45
skills: knowledge 157; teaching 4, 61
SMART objectives 45
smoking 107
social dysfunction 7, 8, 14
social services, involving 13, 19, 78, 98, 99
social skills: developing 58, 80, 85, 87, 93, 99, 114, 126, 150; problems with 89; teaching 99, 117
social workers 98, 99
society, and schools 7, 8, 27–8, 52, 93, 103
special educational needs 14, 52, 82; assessment 10, 13, 89, 133; Code of Practice (1994a) 6, 15, 16, 19, 21, 85, 89, 136, 148, 152; coordinator

(SENCO) 6, 15; identification 15, 19, 133; observation 15, 16; provision 81, 84; register 140, 141; training 87, 144; *see also* EBD
specialist units 87
speech characteristics, teacher 70, 73
Spinks, J. M. 38
stability 33; professional 62, 128
staff: alertness 64, 73; appearance 4, 70; attitudes 40; career development 25, 42, 51, 55, 56, 62, 128, 144–56, 169, *see also* training; emotional problems 5; facilities 63; governors 55; needs 1, 2, 40, 91; personality of 69, 70, 75; role 12; security 43, 53, 63, 68; self-confidence 44, 60, 64, 105, 165; self-esteem 5, 30, 52, 53, 61, 62, 63, 67, 89, 150, 163; sensitivity 31, 71; stress symptoms 64–5; support 4, 5, 9, 12, 30, 31, 41, 43, 52, 53, 55, 107, 137
Stance, D. 128
standards: behavioural 6, 133; maintaining 52, 167; raising 22, 25, 34, 106, 168; responsibility for 25
statementing 58, 84, 85, 89, 90, 175; *see also* EBD
status, professional 65
stereotyping 68
stigma, of stress 66–7
stimulation 77; lacking 123
storming 44
strategies: 'fine tuning' 56; generating 91; implementation 56; negotiating 91; planning 45, 67, 73; successful 53
strengths, building on 116
stress, emotional 14, 57, 60; admitting to 66; alleviating 5, 53, 61, 63, 66, 69, 70; causes 65; of change 65, 66; consequences 64; and control 64, 66; of indiscipline 60, 61–3, 128, 151, 164; levels 64, 65; management 63–7; monitoring 166; multiple, and behaviour 61; optimum level 64; overcoming 64; perception of 70; response to 67, 70; stigma of 66, 67; support for 61, 63, 69; symptoms of 64–5; withdrawal from 99, 117
structure: implementation 56; inappropriate 57; management 38, 40–2, 43, 50; meetings 54; organisational 7, 24, 25; provision of 5, 6; time 117
students *see* pupils
styles: learning 60, 74, 107, 108, 154; management 9, 30, 39, 40, 41, 55; teaching 60, 74, 107, 108, 154
subject teams 56
substance abuse 56
success: celebrating 157, 164, 166; code for 106–7; educational 88; examinations 105; noting 139; strategies for 53; *Success Against the Odds,* National Commission on Education (1996) 28
summarising 74
supervision: breaktime 105; lunchtime 79–80, 85, 87, 94, 154, 171
supply teachers, and behaviour 10
support: academic 99; agencies 78–92, 98, 165; awareness of 6, 78; for change 47; classroom 87; consultancy 10, 56; coordination of 23; counselling 66, 85, 87, 90, 99; EBD pupils 16–18, 30, 58, 84–7, 90, 166; expert 153–4; funding 58; groups 56, 87, 98; in-class 85; lacking 57, 63, 65; learning assistants 87, 90; LEA 6, 23, 78, 79, 128, 154; networks 66; parental 65, 87, 115, 121; peer 54, 68, 69, 105, 118–19; playground 87; preventative 90; professional 60, 68–9; psychological 88; pupil 8; reluctance to seek 60, 61; and stress reduction 61, 63, 69; services 4, 5, 10, 12, 23; systems 53, 60; teacher 4, 5, 9, 12, 30, 31, 41, 43, 52, 53, 55, 107, 137; teachers 79; *see also* mentoring
swearing 14, 109, 138

'take-up-time' 152
talking out of turn *see* interruption
Tannenbaum, R. 40
target books 116, 130, 172–6
target setting 79, 91, 92, 117, 148
Tattum, D. 30
Teacher Training Agency 55, 144
teachers *see* staff
teaching: good practice 13, 105–24; quality 22; remedial 77; skills 4, 61; social skills 99, 117; styles 60, 74, 107, 108, 154
teams 39, 43–5, 54, 154; approach 69; curriculum 56; departmental 56; development 146; EBD 84–7, 94, 113; faculty 56; formation 43; key-stage 56; management 43–5; multi-disciplinary

154; pastoral 56; performance 44; pride in 44; subject 56; yeargroup 56
tenacity 114
testing boundaries 9
theft 56
theory 158
therapy: art 87; drama 87; music 87; play 87
threatening: behaviour 14; pupils 72
time: circle 154; keeping 62, 73, 138, 167, 175; management 65, 69; pressure 5, 65; scale 91; structure 117
timetables, and behaviour 105, 108–12, 176
tiredness, staff 63, 64; *see also* stress
tolerance 134
training, teacher 4, 9, 25; agencies 147; for change 146; for development planning 144, 156; for effectiveness 145; and evaluation 145; grants *see* GEST; headteacher 144–5; in-house 146; information 145; initial 147–8; lunchtime supervisors 154, 171; in managing discipline 60, 61, 70, 145, 148, 149, 159; organisational 148; for relationships 145; resources 145; seeking out 158; skills 61; special educational needs 87, 144; *see also* induction programmes *and* INSET *and* mentoring *and* professional development
triggers, behavioural 117
truancy *see* attendance
trust 71, 102, 155
truth telling 125
Tuckman, B.W. 43
turn-taking 99, 117
turnover, staff 97

unconditional positive regard 86, 97
underachievement 118, 119
understanding: EBD 86; failure of 90; feelings 71, 91; of others 134; problems 91; rules 58; shared 1, 5, 25, 44; teacher 61
unhappiness 86
uniform *see* dress codes
United Nations *Convention on the Rights of the Child* (1989) 122
University of Sheffield 62

values 1, 7, 24, 25, 28, 40, 58, 127; developing 126, 127; middle-class 28; school 125, 128; shared 44, 50, 146, 157, 162
valuing, community members 30, 60
vandalism 32
verbal: abuse 55, 61, 62, 135, 140; warning 59, 101, 135
violence, domestic 32, 123; *see also* aggressive behaviour
vision 28, 29, 40, 42, 45; statements 29; *see also* goals
visualisation 94
vocational roles 150
voice, use of 70, 73
voluntary aided schools 26

Wagner, P. 3
Walker, L. 3, 27
Wallace, M. 43
Wardle, C. 106, 107
warmth 31
warning: of exclusion 19; verbal 59, 101, 135
Watkins, C. 3
Wedge, P. 27
welfare: benefits 82, 83; staff 79
Welton, J. 148
Whitfield, R.C. 67
whole school policies 11, 85, 90, 98, 102, 115, 126, 128–9
wholeness, personal 96
Willower, D.J. 103
withdrawal: from classroom 17, 19, 90, 135, *see also* sanctions; from stressful activities 99, 117
withdrawn behaviour 13
work: avoidance 62; classroom 86; focused 85, 87; group 85–7; off-site 86, 87; one-to-one 86; practical 74
working conditions 51, 74, 75

yeargroup teams 56
youth service, involvement 78, 79